REMNANTS OF A LIFE ON PAPER

REMNANTS OF
A LIFE ON PAPER

A MOTHER AND DAUGHTER'S
STRUGGLE WITH BORDERLINE
PERSONALITY DISORDER

By

Bea Tusiani

Pamela Ann Tusiani

Paula Tusiani-Eng

BAROQUE PRESS · NEW YORK

2013

SECOND EDITION MAY, 2014

All artwork by Pamela Tusiani
Cover photos by China Jorrin
Photo on page 304 by Sheryl Freedland

ISBN: 978-0-9855718-2-5
www.remnantsofalife.com

*"The meaning of life is that you have a role
to play in the future that you will never see."*

– Pamela's Loyola College class notes:
The Aeneid, Aeneas' trip to the underworld

INTRODUCTION

"There I stood, in a hole, deep in the ground. Did I dig it or just get in? Did I fall into it? Did someone else dig it and throw me in?"

These are some of the questions my daughter Pamela wrote about in her diaries while undergoing treatment for Borderline Personality Disorder (BPD), a psychiatric condition characterized by mood swings, unstable relationships and self-destructive behavior.

Pamela kept copious journals chronicling her thoughts and feelings. They detail her struggle with a chaotic personality dominated by fears that could not be controlled, despite daily therapy sessions and countless cocktails of medications. To regain feeling in a body wracked by emotional distress, she resorted to cutting and burning, drinking, drug abuse and indiscriminate sex.

Through interior dialogues written on scraps of note-paper and yellow legal-pads, and in journals, Pamela questioned why she was acting this way. She didn't understand what triggered her impulsive behavior, and was keenly aware that something was wrong with the way her mind was working.

Pamela's diaries, as excerpted unedited in this book, tell one side of the story. They represent her innermost thoughts, in her own words. My side of the story was written in retrospect, to provide a counterpoint to my daughter's experience. It portrays a mother trying to figure out what happened to her seemingly normal little girl, a mother who became an active, yet reluctant, and many times clueless, participant throughout Pamela's ordeal.

After Pamela's breakdown, I struggled too with the fact that I had not recognized the signs of my daughter's illness sooner. My husband Mike, and I, were filled with guilt and frustration, as we tried to understand why our world was being turned upside-down.

While Pamela's disorder progressed, and the level of dysfunction deepened, we found ourselves increasingly relying on the advice of medical professionals. They encouraged us to distance ourselves from Pamela, and trust the slow-going therapeutic process. Not having any other options because Pamela's case was so complex, we trusted her care-givers, but lost our parental instincts in the process. This blind faith came back to haunt us, and the story is further complicated by healthcare issues, government agencies, and lawsuits.

Other than the names of immediate family members, most names in this book have been changed. This is primarily due to legal restrictions and because of the fragility of individuals who are mentally ill.

Though Pamela inspired this book's writing, and my determination saw it to fruition, it was my daughter Paula who had the vision to weave together all the disparate material.

It is our collective hope that by sharing our story we may represent and validate the experiences of untold numbers of families, who may not have the emotional or financial resources to fight for the rights of their loved ones.

The clarity and honesty of self-reflection evident in the diaries Pamela wrote during the years of her illness show a wisdom far beyond her years. Her writings give voice and shape to an elusive disorder that few understand.

This book is meant to enlighten. The hole Pamela wrote about is still there, but through the telling of valiant struggle, she has extended a hand to help others climb out.

Bea Tusiani

REMNANTS OF A LIFE ON PAPER

CHAPTER 1

Baltimore

BEATRICE TUSIANI, called as a witness, having been first duly sworn, was examined and testified as follows:

Q: *Good morning, Mrs. Tusiani. My name is Ed Davis. We are here today to take your deposition. I represent Road to Recovery in a lawsuit you and your husband have against them and others in connection with the death of your daughter, Pamela.*

A: *Yes.*

Q: *You were given an oath. That is the same oath you will be taking when you come to California to testify in the trial. Do you understand that?*

A: *Yes.*

Q: *Have you had any discussion with anyone, other than your attorney and your husband, in connection with preparation for the deposition you are here today for?*

A: *Yes. My children.*

Q: *Specifically which of your children did you speak to?*

A: *Paula Tusiani-Eng and Michael Tusiani.*

Q: *How old is Paula?*

A: *Twenty-nine years old. They are twins.*

Q: *You are married to Mr. Tusiani?*

A: *Yes.*

Q: *Have you been married to anyone else?*

A: *No.*

Q: *Has Mr. Tusiani been married to anyone else?*

A: *No.*

Q: *Have you been employed during Pamela's lifetime? Were you employed outside of the home?*

A: *I worked for a local newspaper for a couple of years – mornings, from nine until twelve, while she was in school.*

Q: *What sorts of activities did Pamela engage in when she was in grammar school?*

A: She played basketball, she played volleyball, she was on the class newspaper, she did some service with the elderly.

Q: During the time that Pamela was in grammar school, did you participate in any of her activities with her?

A: I was involved in many activities. I was on the parents' council. I was an art lady in her class. I was on the school committee to paint the lunchroom. I ran her class newspaper. I took her to all of her – both myself and my husband as best he could – to most of her sporting events. I prepared food for all of the special cultural days. I was very involved.

Q: What kind of student was Pamela in grammar school?

A: She was just above average. She wasn't an A student consistently, but I would say she was a B, B plus student.

Q: Did Pamela exhibit any behavioral problems in grammar school?

A: No. She wasn't a problem at all in school. She was always considered a bit shy and introspective. She wasn't terribly verbal. When she reached puberty, we found that we had to kind of pull things from her. But at that point, it wasn't inconsistent with the way my son was either, so we just felt that it was normal behavior.

Q: Did you observe anything during the time she was in grammar school that led you to believe she was more challenged than your other children in terms of her emotional stability?

A: At the time, no. Looking back, yes.

———————————

BEA

"Pamela! Pamela!" I call out from across the room, hoping the sound of my voice will rouse my 20-year-old daughter from her hotel bed. I've already been awake and dressed for an hour, waiting for her to get up. She usually takes awhile to get going in the morning, I'm used to that, but this time it's different. I don't know what frame of mind she'll be in when she wakes up.

I try to read the newspaper, hoping the events of the outside world will somehow distract me. But my eyes keep coming back to Pamela.

Will she be coherent? Will she remember where she is? I look from the headlines, to her body lying listlessly under the covers, to the digital clock on the nightstand.

It's already 9:30 in the morning. I can't let her sleep any longer. There's too much at stake. In one hour Pamela's fate will be determined by a psychologist at Johns Hopkins Medical Center. He will decide if she needs to be admitted to the psychiatric ward there.

It was only yesterday that I dropped everything in New York and drove down to Baltimore in response to Pamela's desperate pleas. I found her in her Loyola College dorm room, sobbing, while her suitemates went about their business. The social and academic pressures of college life seemed so energizing for them. But not for Pamela. She suffered, quietly, as the world hummed around her.

I decided to take her with me to a hotel, until we could figure out what to do next. I was hopeful that if I took her away from all the stress she'd been under she might recover and not need to be admitted to the hospital at all. But now, as I nervously glance around the only hotel room in Baltimore I could find close to the hospital on such short notice, I secretly fear the worst. The clock says 9:38. I need to do something immediately.

I walk over to Pamela and shake her. Then, remembering the stalling antics of my son who never wanted to get out of bed when he was a teenager, I decide to try a different approach. Throwing open the curtains, I firmly demand, "Pamela! Get up!" as hundreds of particles of light stream into the room, blinding her.

The sudden shock of it causes my beautiful 5'6", dark-haired, olive-skinned college junior to fall off the side of the bed. Lying on the floor, she appears dizzy and disoriented. When I bend down, her glazed-over eyes suddenly meet mine. She looks at me, as if to say something. But no words come out of her strained mouth. I stand back and sense something is terribly wrong.

"Pamela! What's the matter?" I ask, my voice cracking. I grab her shoulders, and try to jolt her into responding. "Speak to me." But she continues to sit on the floor, staring blankly into space. My daughter is losing her grip on reality, and I've never been so scared.

13

Seeing the clock once again out of the corner of my eye, I force myself to take action. I strip off her pajamas, prop my arms forcefully under hers, and drag her into the shower. As I soap her down with a washcloth, she leans limply against the tile and doesn't resist. It's as if she's a baby again, and I am giving her a bath. My mind races as I towel down her naked body. She stumbles away from me, unclothed, and slowly slips sideways onto the couch.

I feel desperate, but try with all my might to hide it. I rummage through a hodge-podge of clothes in her duffle bag, and pull some things out for her to wear. Somehow, I manage to fasten her bra and button her jeans. A queasiness sets into my stomach as I feel how much against the natural order of things it is for a mother to be dressing her teenage daughter in sexy, bright purple underwear.

I finally collapse onto the couch myself, exhausted. All of a sudden, Pamela startles me by springing up. It is as if a switch has clicked. As she becomes aware of her surroundings, some energy returns to her lagging limbs.

I watch her move somewhat unsteadily about the hotel room. First, she makes the bed, then she cleans her hairbrush. I am momentarily hopeful that we will be able to make it out the door in a few minutes when, in the midst of gathering up my jacket and purse, I stop in my tracks.

Pamela has taken a napkin from the food tray and is wiping it across the top of the coffee table. She strokes the table with the napkin in repetitive motions that reflect some deep, compulsive instinct. It is bizarre behavior, as if her mind has become separated from her body. The calm, persistent circular movement of that napkin, over and over again, in round circles, framed by dust motes reflected in the sun, makes her seem like an alien. Who is this person? Could this be the daughter I gave birth to and raised for 20 years?

Suddenly, the phone rings, as if on cue. It's my husband Mike in New York. "I have good news, Bea. I was able to get Pamela an appointment to see a leading psychiatrist in New York City on Friday and" – he stops in mid-sentence when he realizes I am not responding.

"Mike, Pamela's shaking, doing crazy things, and she is not answering me when I talk. I don't know if she can wait until Friday," I say with increasing panic in my voice. Then, all the scrambled thoughts running through my mind over the past hour finally burst forth: "I think she's having a nervous breakdown."

"Don't say that," Mike responds angrily. He's in denial, as I would be, if I weren't actually seeing Pamela lose her mind.

Mike's a fixer. Problems are his specialty, not only in the world of gas and shipping in which he works, but also among family, friends and even friends of friends. Most every person we know has gone to him at one time or another for advice or intervention of some kind, and he always comes through.

As much as I know that there is nothing he wants more than to help Pamela, bringing her back to New York is just not an option right now.

"Look, Mike, I'm already late for an appointment with Pamela's psychologist. She's shaking, she can't stand or speak clearly, her mind is unable to focus. Let me at least have him evaluate her, and see what he says. Maybe he can advise us whether to have her treated in Baltimore, or New York."

"Okay, okay," Mike says. "Just promise to call me as soon as you have any news. Be strong."

I hang up the phone and a rich jolt of adrenaline pumps me up enough to get Pamela out of the hotel and into the car. When we arrive at the psychologist's office, she is trembling and shaking like a battery-operated doll with a broken switch.

"There's clearly been a dramatic deterioration from yesterday to to-day," the doctor says, after I describe her bizarre behavior. He slowly sits Pamela at a table, gives her a pen, and asks her to write her name. She takes the pen from him but cannot make sense of what to do with it.

Her hand is shaking so much the pen makes tapping noises on the table. I'm numb.

Writing is Pamela's hidden talent. It frees her from insecurities and allows her to escape. Her professors in the honors English Literature program at Loyola have frequently commented on the maturity and depth of her college essays. One even called her a future novelist. But now, as I witness her once fertile mind shut down by a pen that cannot write, it occurs to me that I'm losing her.

The doctor reaches over his desk and gently takes hold of Pamela's quivering hand. The tapping stops, and the room falls silent. With his other hand, he dials the hospital, finds a bed on the psych unit, and instructs me to take Pamela directly there. It's March 20, 1998.

Outside, my own hands turn to jelly as I fumble in my purse for quarters to call Mike. Finding a public telephone, I sit Pamela on a bench, and pick up the receiver.

"They're admitting her today," I whisper, my hand covering my mouth.

"Stay calm, Bea, you need to stay calm. I'll cancel the appointment in New York and call Johns Hopkins. I'll be down there in a few hours… hang in."

My heart pounds and my throat turns dry as I watch my depressed 20-year-old daughter from the tiny window of a heavy steel door in the psychiatric ward. She stares back at me longingly. Through the cloudy glass, I see two nurses take hold of her elbows, prompting her gently to move away. As the weight of her body slowly gives in, she makes one last effort to look back at me. In a split second, her big, brown, sad eyes lock into mine. The powerful connection makes me feel as if she is a little child again, saying, "Mommy, rescue me!"

Only then do I cry.

In a flash, Pamela is 3 years old and has gotten separated from me in the supermarket. After running up and down the aisles, I see an elderly woman leading her back to me. But what is seared in my memory is the petrified look on my little girl's face. It says, "How could you abandon me?" Words like these never came out of Pamela's mouth – her eyes always did the talking.

Then, she is ten, looking out her bedroom window at the neighbor's children playing in the snow. "Why are you just watching? Why don't you go out and join them?" I encourage her. She shrugs and says nothing, but the pained look on her face in the awkward silence, speaks volumes. The simple act of going outside to play with friends, who readily accept her as part of the neighborhood group, overwhelms her.

These odd looks that I remember so well – brief moments of communication between us, signaling unusual fear of abandonment and isolation – are what I know about Pamela that the nurses walking her down the hall behind the big steel door don't.

As her shrinking image fades, the reality sinks in. My poor Pamela has had a complete mental collapse. She's been admitted to the psychiatric ward of a hospital in another state. Can this really be happening? How on earth am I going to explain this to people she knows or people I know, when I don't even understand it myself?

I turn to the elevator and press the up button. It's the wrong direction. I have no sense of where I'm headed, and no control of what will happen next. I have to wait for Mike to talk to the doctors. Maybe he can fix it.

PAMELA

March 22, 1998

This is the second full day I have been on Meyer 4, at Johns Hopkins University Hospital in Baltimore, Maryland. So far, it's hard to describe the way I feel, everything I do is in slow motion, it seems weird. I walk differently and take a long time to do things. I keep thinking and thinking, it won't stop – so many thoughts are racing through my head. I'm confused, can't remember. I find myself drawn to my bed and cry for no reason at all. I really don't think that any medicine will work for what the doctors are calling a major depression. I don't remember ever feeling "normal" or happy so how will I know when I'm better? It's never going to happen. I think that this is the way I am. Maybe I just have to accept it.

I don't know if I belong here on the psychiatric floor, but the doctors seem to think that I do. I am so worried about getting better because then I will have to face the world all over again. I don't want to go outside or read or eat or go back to school, all I do is cry and I have no good reason to, except that my life is worthless and my instincts tell me I will never be happy. I suffer a lot, but I cause still more suffering for others.

Why does life have to be so hard? I have so many goals that I will never achieve. I am scared because I don't see my role in the world.

I don't know what to do, think or feel. There is such darkness and sad-

ness, it's almost possible to see it. John Milton explained it better in "Dark-
ness Illumine."

Nothing is worse than this disease, which is supposedly curable. I hate
myself, and my brain.

BEA

The phone rings and wakes me from a deep sleep. I jump up and see it's 9 a.m. For a split second I think I'm back home, but the digital clock reminds me I'm still staying at a hotel in Baltimore, this one on the Wharf, just minutes away from the hospital where my daughter remains under 24-hour watch.

I pick up the receiver worrying that it's more bad news about Pamela, but it's only Mike calling from his office in New York. He had been in Baltimore, but we had decided it would be best if he returned to New York to manage matters from there while also keeping an eye on his work.

"I'm glad you finally heard the phone," he says. He gets frustrated when I take my hearing aids out at night and he can't reach me. We both chuckle before realizing we have nothing to laugh about. "Hang on," I say as I put him on hold to search for my aids. Little does he know, my sleeping late had nothing to do with hearing. The truth is, I was up half the night thinking about Pamela's medications.

Trying to keep up with all of the prescriptions is like studying a foreign language. Pamela entered the hospital on a single anti-depressant, Nortriptyline. Now tranquilizers, a mood stabilizer, anti-psychotic and anti-seizure medications have been added to the mix. Each is having different side-effects, and it's hard to keep track of them all.

I ask the doctors why suddenly her blood pressure and heart rate have dropped and why she's anemic. They tell me they're aware of it, not to worry. But I am a mother, and my daughter's in the hospital, how can I not worry?

I take a deep breath, and listen to what my husband has to say.

"I just got off the phone with Pamela's college advisor," Mike says. "They're giving her two options. She can either take a short leave of absence for a couple of weeks and make up her schoolwork at the end of the semester or take an incomplete for her courses. What do you think, Bea?"

What can I think? I want my daughter to get better and resume her normal life, but so far that's not happening. Everything depends on when the antidepressants will kick in.

"One doctor assures me Pamela's 'affective mood disorder' – whatever that means – can be under control in as little as two weeks," I say, trying to sound hopeful.

But truthfully, school is becoming less important to me by the moment. All I care about now is Pamela's health.

"Do you think you can hold the school off for another two weeks?" I ask Mike.

"I'll try," he says. "But the lady in the Bursar's Office seems to be only interested in percentage of refunds, escrow towards tuition and course credits."

"You've got to be kidding."

"It's a business, Bea. In the end, she has a boss and it's all about money. They don't care about Pamela the way we do. In fact, I'm very concerned about how her transcripts and insurance records might cause problems down the road when she goes to look for a job."

Ever the practical one, Mike is always thinking ahead. I'm worried about just getting my daughter through today.

"How can we protect her from that?" I ask, not really expecting a solution.

"We won't leave a paper trail with the insurance companies: we'll pay for everything in cash," he says.

PAMELA

March 26, 1998
Today was a better day. I just took my medications (all 7 of them!) and was more talkative and involved with activities and attended a group on anti-depressant medications, which was very informative. I know I am on a long and difficult road to recovery but at least I am on that road.

19

I know I have to talk to my friends and family but don't know what to say. My concentration is beginning to improve but my memory is still very bad. I can't remember characters from my favorite novels or even what those novels are.

March 27, 1998

I had an anxiety attack this morning, which was very frightening.

All of a sudden, I got very hot and started shaking all over. My parents came and I was very nervous, I am calmer now, but I hope I can cope with talking to Teddy, whom I miss, but it's hard to deal with him at this time. I get irritated very easily.

March 29, 1998

I think I am gaining weight, I feel very fat. I still feel like I could be faking this illness. Is it possible?

March 30, 1998

I'm having a very hard day, with headaches and so much confusion about my medications. There are too many doctors and I'm afraid to trust them. Will I get better? Please God help me and everyone else here. I love Mom and Dad and Michael and Paula and my friends Teddy and Cathy too. I want to be a happy and different person but I am so miserable. I am in your hands now. Please help me try my hardest to get better.

BEA

Balancing a plastic bag filled with Pamela's favorite – a chocolate-chip muffin – in it in one hand, and a cup of hot coffee in the other, I step off the elevator and press the buzzer on the steel door that seals off Meyer 4 from the world outside.

A guard inspects my purse and the muffin bag for "sharps." Sharps, I quickly learn, are objects like nail files or pins that patients can use to hurt themselves.

Then the guard points to the muffin bag.

"Sorry Ma'am, plastic bags are not allowed," he says.

"Why?" I ask innocently, not understanding the problem.

"Patients can put them over their heads to commit suicide," he replies.

I shudder as I hand over the plastic bag, frightened that my daughter is exposed to people who would go to such extremes. Thank God she's not like them.

Cradling the muffin in a paper napkin while trying not to spill my coffee, I head down the brightly lit hall to Pamela's room and find her curled up in bed, sleeping. The sheets are crumpled and she's hugging a large stuffed animal.

I settle into a chair. Looking up at her sparse surroundings – a bed, a closet, a bathroom, and a window that faces a parking lot – I wonder how my baby girl wound up in this unlikely place.

The first inkling Mike and I had that something was wrong, was one day during the summer of 1996 after Pamela's freshman year at Loyola. The three of us were sitting outside, on the deck of our high-ranch home in Manhasset, Long Island, when she turned to us and said, "I need to tell you something and I don't want you to be upset."

I looked at Mike, he looked at me. We shifted uneasily in our chairs.

"What is it?" I said.

"Why would we be upset?" asked Mike.

"I think I'm depressed," Pamela said very softly, her eyes avoiding ours.

"What makes you think that?" I asked nervously, having gone through a brief period of depression once myself.

"Nothing makes me happy," she said. "I cry a lot for no reason."

The three of us talked for hours, in somber voices, until the dark drove us in. Together, we tried to identify the possible cause of Pamela's unhappiness. Could it be school? A boyfriend? Being so far from home?

"Are you upset we're moving?" I asked, with trepidation, fearing that our decision to move from Manhasset to New York City in a couple of months could have triggered this.

Mike and I had been discussing making this move for a long time. Our twins, Michael and Paula, Pamela's older siblings by four years, had already moved out on their own, and Mike was tired of his 20-year commute to the city, which took more than two hours out of each day.

Moving to the city would give us a better quality of life, we thought, as we anticipated becoming empty-nesters. In all likelihood, our children would be looking for jobs and apartments in the city, and we would already be there, living close to them.

Of course, a momentous decision like this would never have been made without discussing it with Pamela, since she was still living at home. Although she said the city was a good idea, her being depressed now made me wonder.

As if she could read my mind, Pamela looked straight at me and shook her head sideways. "No, I'm okay with it," she insisted.

I was somewhat relieved, but the heaviness in the air remained.

"How do you feel about seeing a friend of mine who does talk therapy?" I gently suggested. "She's a psychiatric social worker and might be able to help you."

Pamela shrugged, and using a body language we'd all become used to, said "Whatever you think is fine with me."

Her first appointment worked out well and she continued to attend sessions with this therapist twice a week throughout that summer.

Then in August, right before she was to return to campus, my own world was abruptly turned upside down. A routine breast exam revealed a lump that tested positive for Stage II Breast Cancer. It floored me. Cancer – a dirty word that ran through my genes. My mother died of colon cancer and my sister of pancreatic cancer – both when they were 55. I had just turned 50 and thought it was inevitable that I too would fall victim to the family curse in five years.

I was useless, but Mike quickly put all of our moving plans on fast-track as my surgery and treatment were scheduled at New York City hospitals. Decorating and furnishing our new apartment served as diversions from thoughts of surgery, stitches, drains and chemotherapy.

Although I focused on taking aggressive measures to ensure my own survival, in the back of my mind there was a nagging fear that Pamela would sink under the pressure of this sudden turmoil in her life.

To my surprise, she came to me right before leaving for her second year at Loyola and said, "Mom, take care of yourself, don't worry about me. I'm a mature woman, and I'll be fine."

Our roles had reversed. For the first time I could remember, my baby daughter was trying to be strong for me. It was as if my illness had given her courage.

A hundred-pound weight was lifted off my shoulders when Pamela kissed me goodbye and headed back to college smiling. That whole sophomore year, she seemed to fall comfortably back into good routines.

It was a great relief, since that year was tough for me. Following the mastectomy, I not only endured an exhausting six months of chemotherapy but Tram-flap reconstructive surgery that left a gaping hole across my mid-section and a breast as flat as a fried egg. A new plastic surgeon told me I'd need additional surgeries to fix both. But before I scheduled any more operations Mike insisted we take a break and go on vacation.

We were in France when Pamela began to get headaches. She called from Baltimore, where she was taking summer classes and working in the college library.

"Mom," she uttered in a voice I could barely hear over the bad connection.

"Pamela, what's wrong?" I asked, worried. "And speak up. I can't hear you!"

"My head is killing me, I can't take it anymore," she wailed into the phone. She told me she'd been having unrelenting headaches all week.

"Did you try Excedrin?"

"It doesn't help. Nothing does. I can't go to work and I have a paper due, I just can't deal with it." I could feel her throwing herself at my mercy.

"Where's Teddy? Is he with you?" I ask, inquiring about her boyfriend who also had a campus job over the summer.

"He's right here. He told me to call you," she said.

Even with Teddy at her side, she sounded utterly helpless, and being an ocean away, so was I.

My instinct was to fly home, but Mike got on the phone and managed to calm the two of us down by assuring us he would find a better solution. After he hung up, he made some calls and set up an appointment for Pamela to see a neurologist in Baltimore the very next day.

We called her back to tell her about it, and she seemed relieved.

When I returned to the States a few days later, I drove down to Maryland to accompany Pamela to her follow-up appointment with that doctor.

"All her tests are normal," the neurologist said, "but she's suffering from homesickness, and doesn't really know where she belongs: Manhasset, New York or Baltimore." I felt suddenly paralyzed.

Could our move from Manhasset a year ago be blowing up in our faces? Had Mike and I misread Pamela's signals? Had we been too selfish in moving to the city and putting my own health needs first, especially knowing she was going through a rough patch? I wanted to stop everything, reverse the clock and return to our neat little suburban life.

Before we left the neurologist's office, he gave Pamela a prescription for Nortriptyline, a mild anti-depressant that also relieves headaches. When we later went to the pharmacy to fill it, we made a surprising discovery.

"Look, Mom, 'Pamelor' is the brand name for Nortriptyline," Pamela pointed out. She was a firm believer in paranormal messages.

"It mirrors my name. I think this is a sign!"

I secretly prayed she was right.

Pamela began her junior year on this new medication and the fall semester that followed was uneventful. But shortly after Christmas, Teddy noticed that she had become unusually angry and reclusive. He encouraged her to seek counseling on campus. What followed were weekly therapy sessions at the Loyola counseling center. We thought, between the therapy and the medication, Pamela's problems were under control.

But when she came home for spring break, she clung to me like a toddler. For ten days, while her friends partied on Florida beaches, she stayed in our New York City apartment and watched videos. She isolated herself, not wanting to initiate conversation or make plans. When she did venture out, it was close to my side.

I tried my best to be a source of amusement.

"Let's go shopping," I'd suggest, thinking that a trip to Urban Outfitters would instantly make her feel better. Or, if that didn't work, I'd scour the newspaper for things to do.

While Pamela seemed momentarily happy on these outings, as soon as we returned home, she'd go into her bedroom and close the door. No matter what I did with her – shopping, movies, cooking, the nail salon – nothing seemed to lift her mood for more than a few hours.

It was the first time I felt uneasy about my daughter's attachment to me. It seemed unnatural. She was relying on me to be a constant companion, to satisfy her social and emotional needs. Something about this didn't seem normal.

By the end of spring break, I was so exhausted that, I must admit, I was somewhat relieved when she returned to school. Little did I know that less than three weeks later Pamela would be a patient at Johns Hopkins University Medical Center.

———————————

"Mrs. Tusiani?"

The voice sounds far away, but it isn't. I open my eyes, and see Pamela's nurse standing a few feet from me. Her colorful scrubs with smiley faces floating all over them seem too cheerful for a psychiatric ward.

"Hello." I smile faintly. "Pamela's having terrible headaches. Do you think you can give her something?"

"Well, I'll have to call her doctor. He has to give an order for anything stronger than Tylenol," Nurse Betty replies matter-of-factly.

This is her routine, I am sure, but it is not mine.

"Who is her doctor, right now?" I ask.

"I'll have to check her chart," she says.

In a teaching hospital residents and interns rotate on and off each unit once a month, and the revolving door of medical personnel is frustrating.

"Look, my daughter is suffering, and she's in pain. All of these different meds are having negative effects on her body. Is there anything more that can be done?"

"I'll call the doctor right after I take her blood pressure," Betty says, walking over to the bed. Pamela opens her eyes and extends her arm outside the blanket.

"Your Mom tells me you're having headaches," the nurse says.

Pamela gives me a quizzical look. I'm beginning to feel set up. I don't want her to think I'm talking about her behind her back. I'm only communicating her needs because she's too drugged up to do it herself.

"Yeah, I was trying to sleep it off, "Pamela says rolling her eyes. Betty, of course, catches the awkward moment between mother and child.

"I'll let the doctor know, and we'll see what we can do," she says, and she and all her smiley faces push the blood pressure cart out of the room.

PAMELA

March 31, 1998

People are doing things behind my back, I know it.

April 2, 1998

This is so difficult. I can act happy, but never really feel happy inside. I believe I have chronic depression because I've always been sad and the medicine will not change that. How am I going to go on with my life? How am I going to be the person I have always dreamed I would be if I could? That isn't me!

God, please help everyone on Meyer 4 and all the others in the world conquer their depression. I am very scared about the future.

BEA

I glance at the clock in Pamela's hospital room: 7:00 p.m. Thank God, a shift change will soon occur. We've been watching TV to pass the time, but truthfully, it is just background noise to fill the void in conversation between us.

It never used to be this way. Pamela and I always talked at length without hesitation, like girlfriends staying up all night at a slumber party, sharing secrets and gossip.

But after just over a week at Johns Hopkins, I know that anything I say can only temporarily distract her. So I've decided not to force myself to talk tonight. As we sit together quietly, the door opens, and a doctor I don't recognize walks in.

"Hello I'm Dr. Martin. I'm on duty tonight." Here we go again, another hotshot resident just a few years older than Pamela offering more ideas to confuse us further.

"How are things today, Pamela?" he asks as he looks over her chart, which is becoming thicker by the hour.

"I don't really feel like I'm ever going to get better," she responds flatly. "Everyone I meet in group talks about relapse, and drugs not working. I'm afraid I'll be stuck in this hospital forever."

"Electro-Convulsive Therapy (ECT) is the quickest way you can find relief," he says matter-of-factly.

The tremors in Pamela's legs double when she hears this. My back arches. I can't believe he is suggesting shock therapy so soon. It seems such an extreme measure for a 20-year-old who has just been diagnosed with depression.

"Isn't ECT used as a treatment of last resort?" I blurt out. "My daughter has only been here ten days, and we're still waiting for the Nortriptyline to work. The other doctors never suggested this."

He backs away from me – the lioness mother protecting her cub. As soon as he leaves the room, I turn to Pamela, and give her a big hug.

"I promise you," I say, "we're going to find the right medication." She buries her head on my shoulder and cries.

PAMELA

April 3, 1998

Today I sat with the head honcho of Psychiatry, Dr. McKee (or something) and about 40 residents who asked me questions about my depression. They seemed very interested in knowing why I wasn't suicidal. I told them because I felt God put me on this earth for a reason. I felt better talking about my illness with them. They may be able to learn from me.

God, I pray for everyone, especially Ben, that he doesn't hurt himself. He told me he killed his friend in a drinking and driving accident and now I know why he's so intent on killing himself. I will never kill myself, but sometimes, almost most times, I wish I were dead because the pain is so strong and I need some relief from this suffering. Everybody should have

relief from this kind of anguish. Why do we suffer? I have to find the the-
ology paper I wrote on "God and Suffering."

I hope I am a good person. Help me be one please.

Last night was my junior prom and I missed it sitting here in a psychi-
atric ward. I just can't believe it!

BEA

On my way up to Meyer 4, I bump into the social worker in charge
of Pamela's unit.

"Would you mind coming into my office for a few minutes?" she asks.

"Of course," I say, but her tone of voice makes me wary.

I look down the hall to see if Pamela is waiting for me. She isn't, so I
scurry into the social worker's tiny office and shut the door behind me.

"Is there a problem?" I ask.

"Mrs. Tusiani, you have been coming here twice a day for over a
week and it's important for your daughter's recovery to distance yourself from her," she says coldly. "She needs her own space. The best thing
you can do for your daughter right now is to go back to New York."

"Go back to New York? You want me to leave Pamela in a hospital
five hours away, when she's not in her right mind?" I ask. How could
she make such a suggestion?

"You're impeding Pamela's recovery if you're here all the time. It's
counterproductive."

Counterproductive? Isn't this what a mother is supposed to do, stay
by her sick child's bedside? The more she talks, the more I can feel my
blood boiling. She's got me pegged as a meddling mother, and I'm a
hair's breath from knocking her off her lofty chair.

"You wouldn't ask me to leave if Pamela had cancer," I say, the
wounds from my own ordeal fresh in my mind.

She remains silent.

"From the time this first started, I promised Pamela I would never
abandon her. Did you ever think she might need me to manage her care,
to ask questions about medication because she's not able to do it herself? It would torture me to be far from my child while she's having a

nervous breakdown, any mother would feel that way," I say as a parting shot to the perfectly framed family photo on her desk.

"Please think about it, Mrs. Tusiani. It will be best for Pamela."

My head is reeling. My leaving is best for Pamela? Am I preventing her recovery? I walk out of the social worker's office more confused than ever.

I'm angry at the suggestion that I need to leave, and guilty at the same time because I know I need a break, too. The stress of worrying about Pamela and being judged by people like this social worker, who can't possibly know me or my relationship with my daughter, is really getting to me. I'm frightened that, if this goes on much longer, I may wind up in the bed right next to my child.

I find a pay phone and call Mike, thinking he will comfort me. To my great surprise, he agrees with the social worker.

"Bea, I know you want to stay with Pamela," he pleads. "I want to stay with her too, but we agreed I should stay in New York. I'm worried about you, Michael and Paula are worried about you. You've been down there nearly two weeks. You need a break. I don't want you to lose your sanity. I already have a daughter in the hospital, I don't need a wife there too."

But how am I ever going to explain this to Pamela? She will resent me. I know it.

After hanging up the phone, I go and find her in the common dining room where she is finishing a late breakfast. She looks very tired, her shoulders curve inward like an old lady's.

I try engaging her in a game of Scrabble, but she can't get past the three little squares that spell the word "DIE." When should I tell her, I wonder, as we aimlessly move letters across the game board. Do I tell her now?

PAMELA

April 5, 1998

Thank you, God, for bringing Ben back alive and well from his suicide attempt. I love everyone, especially Teddy. I hope we can be in love forever and, of course, get married. I would help him with his schoolwork so he can get into law school which is his dream. He is my true love. I hate to see him hurting because of me. I must write a book about suffering but I don't understand it yet.

I hope Mom and Dad aren't offended when I am mean. I have so much anger and feel so bad they have to be hurt by this. It's so hard not to dwell on your disease when you're in a hospital and everyone is always asking how you feel. I want to be cheerful but I can't imagine it. Even though, I know I can get through this and I will! (I'm in good spirits now, but that may change shortly). God please bless everyone on Meyer 4, help us all get better and able to deal with the pain that comes with depression. And bless you, too.

BEA

I open the door of our eighth floor apartment on the upper east side of Manhattan and drop my bags on the floor. I don't even have my coat off before our golden cocker spaniel races toward me.

"Lulu!" I call out, hugging her and feeling her beautiful, soft fur. Lulu is Pamela's dog. She reminds me of what I left behind.

What I left behind was a daughter in tears.

Mike, Paula and Michael had come down to Baltimore to visit with Pamela before my departure.

"We love you so much Pamela," I said before leaving.

"I will do everything in my power to get you the best medical care I can," Mike assured her. But Pamela walked away from us, and stood next to Teddy, as if to communicate: you are abandoning me, he is not.

I follow Lulu's wagging tail into the kitchen. By the phone I see a list. Mike has recorded the names of people who have called in the past two weeks, expressing concern for Pamela and asking for me. It's two pages long.

I dread facing all the questions from family and friends that so far I've been avoiding. It's human nature for people to be curious about Pamela's breakdown, but it's equally human to want to protect my child from gossip and pity. To avoid what I just don't want to face at the moment, I put the answering machine on and retreat to the comfort of my very own bed.

Two days later, it's midnight when the phone rings. I nudge Mike to wake up because I know it can only be Pamela, or bad news about her, at this hour.

"Mom," she whimpers.

My chest tightens. I silently press the speaker so Mike can hear.

"Calm down, Pamela, tell me what's wrong."

"I had such a bad day. There's so much I can't do. I'm too scared to go outside to walk around the hospital grounds, I can't concentrate on reading a magazine and I'm afraid my friends won't realize what's affecting me is a chemical imbalance in my brain. I'm so confused."

"Daddy and I will be coming down this weekend," I console her. "If you're not feeling good now, it's important you go to the nurse's station and tell them."

"Okay, Mom. I will."

"Maybe you can get a day pass to leave the hospital on Saturday so we can go to the mall," I say, and add, "Your brother and sister plan to come down too," trying to give her something to look forward to.

We hang up. Pamela might feel better, but I feel worse. I turn to Mike and find him shaking his head.

"I can't take much more of this," I say.

I know Mike has been spending several hours every day consulting and visiting with psychologists and psychiatrists to research the illness and get advice about treatment options, but I'm quickly losing my resolve.

"Remember what Dr. Edwin said," he says. "'Turn off the volume and watch the video.' It's not what Pamela says, but what she does that indicates she's on the road to recovery."

"But I can't see her, so how can I tell?"

"We have to look at the big picture," Mike says. "Two weeks ago, she couldn't take a shower or hold a pen, now she's styling her hair and writing in her journal. She is making progress."

"That might sound like progress to you, but she was supposed to be in the hospital a few days, and it's already two weeks and there's no end in sight. This could go on forever."

"Let me talk to the doctors next weekend and we'll reevaluate where we stand," he says. "If they tell us this will take longer than they originally anticipated, we may just have to bring her back home to New York."

PAMELA

April 12, 1998

Support group was very interesting tonight. There is a new patient who is a psychiatrist! I couldn't believe it, but I suppose anyone can get depressed. I cried while one woman, Jane, told us how she has really tried everything and nothing has helped her. Everyone with this disease is suffering a great deal. I am trying to make it out, but need strength and courage. I really want to be well, to get excited, to love myself, to love living, to want to go outside and enjoy life. These are my hopes and wishes but I can't stop cursing myself. I can't stop criticizing myself. I can't stop thinking about how I wound up in such a deep, dark hole.

BEA

Pamela and I are smiling, as we walk down the halls of Meyer 4, trying to conceal our overstuffed shopping bags from the patients who weren't lucky enough to go out on a pass.

It's been good for both of us to escape the hospital setting and do something so frivolous and familiar. If there's anything Pamela and I share genetically, it's our love of shopping. Unlike my older daughter, Pamela is a fashion maven, who has a keen sense of what is trendy.

While she heads to her room to savor her stash, a nurse whisks me aside to fill out some paperwork.

"Mrs. Tusiani, can you give me an idea of how much you think Pamela has improved since she first came here?" she asks with a clipboard in hand. "Would you say 25%, 50%, or 75%?"

Thinking of Dr. Edwin's advice, I tell her what I have observed when I shut off the volume and watched the video.

"Well, I noticed today that Pamela's activity level has greatly improved. She finished an entire burger at Chilis. She gassed up the car at the self-service station and paid for it with a credit card, all by herself, and I thought that was a big accomplishment. Plus, I'm thrilled that her legs have stopped shaking." I think for a moment. "I would give her a 75% on activity and 30% for mood, since she still seems down."

"Thank you, Mrs. Tusiani. It sounds like you had a good day."

32

I tell Pamela that I am going to the hotel to meet her father, and we'll be back after dinner.

When we come in, she doesn't even say hello.

"Why did you tell them I'm getting better?" she says accusingly to me. "I'm not better and you should not be telling anyone I am."

I'm taken aback. I've rarely seen Pamela so angry at me.

"When the nurse asked me about our day, I thought it was a good one. You seemed to have fun shopping, and that's what I told her."

"Well, you don't know what's in my head. Just because I went shopping, I am not better!" She suddenly turns to her father, and lets off more steam.

"All these doctors don't know what they're doing," Pamela tells him. "Dad, please do not call them anymore, it's a wasted effort. They're not making any difference, and I'm not getting any better."

"Pamela, I know it's frustrating," Mike responds. "What do you want me to do?"

"All I want is relief, Dad. How can I get that?"

"If I could move mountains for you, Pamela, you know I would," Mike says, just as frustrated.

Heading back to New York, our heads are spinning. After two and a half weeks, we've hit a brick wall.

"One thing Pamela has always had is good instincts," Mike observes. "I'm on the phone with her doctors every day, and no one seems to have a handle on exactly what her diagnosis is. Maybe she's right."

I agree. We look at each other and sense that the time has come for us to step in and determine when Pamela can be released.

She is not feeling hopeful about her recovery, and the longer she stays in the hospital, the more she's being brought down by other people, many of whom are treatment-resistant and relapsing. Pamela knows depression is more difficult to treat the longer it lasts, and she's beginning to lose confidence. Plus, the pressure on us, running back and forth every weekend, trying to communicate with a myriad of medical professionals between New York and Baltimore, is starting to take a toll on the whole family.

The next morning, the first thing Mike does is phone Pamela from his office and patch me into the conference call.

"Mom and I thought about what you said yesterday. Maybe the best way for you to get relief is to come home. How do you feel about continuing your treatment in New York where you could be closer to us and we could be closer to your doctors?"

She takes a few seconds to think about it.

"Dad, I'd rather be in New York with you than stuck here where nothing is happening," she says.

"You know that means you'll have to leave Teddy, and all your friends at Loyola. Are you prepared to do that?" he asks.

This question takes longer for her to answer.

"I don't want to leave Teddy or my school or my friends." She starts to cry. "But what choice do I have?"

Mike tells her "Don't worry I'll take care of getting you discharged and finding a doctor in New York. Mom will come down and pick you up."

We wonder if we're doing the right thing, but feel a certain degree of confidence because Johns Hopkins highly recommended Dr. Parker, who trained at Johns Hopkins, for Pamela's continued treatment on an outpatient basis in New York.

I remain in the background while Pamela says her goodbyes to the hospital staff and patients. Many hugs, kisses and tears later, she finally separates from the psychiatric ward that exists behind the locked door of Meyer 4.

I call Mike from a payphone in the lobby, to let him know we're on our way. He says, "Bea, I have bad news about Pamela's new psychiatrist in the city. Her office called and said she had an unexpected trip and will be away for a week. Pamela won't be able to see her until after then. I can't believe Johns Hopkins didn't do a better job of coordinating this," he says, sounding annoyed.

"Oh, God, Mike. How are we going to take care of her all by ourselves? It's impossible."

In an instant, I go from being happy about Pamela's release, to being completely terrified.

My head is pounding. I'm thinking about the eight different medications my daughter has to take. How am I ever going to keep them straight?

I don't know how Pamela will be able to get through the next week without therapy, without groups, without someone checking her blood-pressure and Nortriptyline levels. Did we do the right thing releasing her from the hospital into our care?

Hanging up with Mike, I put a brave face on, turn toward Pamela and hustle her into the car for what feels like the longest ride of my life.

CHAPTER 2

New York

MR. DAVIS TO MRS. BEATRICE TUSIANI (WITNESS)

Q: *How would you characterize your husband's relationship with his daughter during the grammar school years?*

A: *He was a very busy man, but he happened to be at everything that was important. He went to most of her volleyball games. He was very often called upon to be the assistant coach or timekeeper. We went to all the functions at night that she was involved in, playing the clarinet in the orchestra.*

We had family dinners around the table. We ate as much as we could together on the weekends. He would barbeque and the whole five of us would sit down and have what Daddy made. We have a summer home out in East Hampton. He and Pamela swam a lot together and, you know, dove into the pool. That's what my recollection is.

Q: *How many hours a week did he end up devoting to his professional time. Was he working sixty, fifty, or forty hours a week?*

A: *He's a very successful man. And to get as successful as he is, he had to devote time to business.*

Every family event that was meaningful in terms of my family, his brother, birthdays, functions, my husband was there.

Q: *I understand that. I'm trying to get a sense of the number of hours that he has spent. Before 1997 and Pamela's problems began to surface, on average how many hours per week did he work?*

A: *It varied because his schedule is so erratic. He travels.*

Q: *I'm talking about the time he was away. On average how many hours a week was he away from the family setting?*

A: *It's hard for me to calculate that. You would have to ask him.*

PAMELA

April 13, 1998

Today I left Meyer 4 and am now in my bed in our New York City apartment where I've spent the last few hours crying. I'm so scared to be home. I love my family so much but am frightened of the world that engulfs me. My mother is such a beautiful person and my father is trying so hard to be there for me but it's hard to talk to anyone. I feel like a baby. I told them I'd rather be back on Meyer 4 than here. I don't know why. I don't think I can handle life. The walls are crushing my mind. My anxiety is way up there tonight and I'm afraid I won't be able to sleep and if I do fall asleep, I'm afraid to wake up. Can I really face tomorrow? Like a baby, I'm unsure how and where to crawl.

One minute I'm up, the next I'm down. I can't control my moods. I don't want to go on, but that is not an option. I know there is some purpose to my existence, it's just, right now, I can't conceive of what that is.

April 16, 1998

This morning started out good. Mom and I went to get my blood drawn, we looked at New York Sports Club which I thought was too crowded and intimidating with a lot of half-naked women walking around, then to a craft studio where I painted a frog to give Teddy. But as soon as we came home my mood seemed to change rapidly.

I can't stop thinking about this wasted summer and an internship at a men's fashion magazine I never got to take. School, friends, parents, everything is making me crumble. And I don't know what to do. I have no desires, no goals, no hope. As time passes, I don't think I have any chance of being normal. I feel trapped but I also don't want my freedom.

April 17, 1998

Today is hell. There is no other way to explain it. I feel like I am being tortured for eternity. I wish I could be all right but it isn't in my control. I stayed in bed all day and thought about ways to end my life. I don't know what death is like, but I am anxious to escape from where I am now.

I smashed picture frames, took a piece of glass and shredded pictures of myself, then broke a foot-long plastic vase from my trip to Cancun and punched at a ceramic elephant I made in the hospital until it broke apart. I cut myself too, with the glass. I wanted to rip myself apart, but instead, called my mom to come into my room.

BEA

I'm in the kitchen washing dishes when I suddenly hear a crash. I momentarily pause, wondering, could Pamela have dropped something? Trying not to let my mind run away from itself, I go back to the pots and pans. Then, a split second later, she cries out for me. Instantly, I know something bad has happened.

Shaking the suds off my wet hands I run down the hallway and fling her door open. What I find terrifies me. Pamela is sitting on the bed with her arms extended. In one hand she's holding a sliver of broken glass, and the other hand is covered with blood dripping from a deep gash in her forearm.

I quickly glance around the room to make sense of what happened and see smashed picture frames and shards of ceramic pottery scattered about.

"Oh my God, Pamela. What on earth did you do?" I ask with a mix of fear and exasperation. She doesn't say a word.

Instead, a beatific smile spreads across her face. It's eerie . . . she's oddly calm and at peace . . . almost saintly, like the picture of Padre Pio that sits on her bookcase with the stigmata on his blood-stained hands. An unlikely contrast, an old man and a young girl, generations apart, both with blood on their hands: one self-inflicted, the other from mysteries beyond our understanding.

Silently, I pray to the old saint.

Even though I basically gave up on Jesus Christ when I begged Him to spare my mother and sister from early deaths, I now find myself side-stepping around Him for my daughter and petitioning the familiar saints who perform miracles.

That's what is needed right now, I think, as I lead my daughter in her trance-like state to the sink where I wash her wound and wrap clean towels around it. I tell her I'm going to call her father and she nods her head, knowing full well that Daddy is the one savior we can rely on.

PAMELA

April 18, 1998 (a few hours later)
Will this ever end? I am driving my parents crazy.
We went to the movies tonight, which seemed to distract me, but I'm
back in my bed again feeling as awful as I did before. Where do I go from
here?

BEA

I'm exhausted. Taking care of Pamela is becoming a 24-hour mar-
athon. Her cutting is so out of control. Yesterday she "accidentally"
nicked her arm with a knife in the kitchen, and this morning, she
slashed herself with a safety razor in the shower. Keeping her from
harming herself has become the focus of my every waking moment.

Sitting at my desk with a cup of coffee, in the farthest corner of our
apartment – where I can find a few minutes of solitude while Pamela is
at the dentist – I glance up at the calendar. Could it be we've only been
back in New York six days? It feels like an eternity.

Whatever progress Pamela made in Baltimore has completely dissipated in the week it is taking for her to see Dr. Parker. Why did Mike
and I agree to bring her home from Johns Hopkins without a psychiatrist in place, who could see her right away? We had no clue how far
we would be in over our heads – dealing with spiking mood swings and
self-mutilation. There is still one more day before a professional sees
her and it can't come soon enough, she's cratering by the minute, and
so are we.

The phone rings. It's our family dentist.

"Bea, I don't want to upset you, but I noticed scratches on Pamela's
wrists. Do you know about them?"

I suck in my breath and explain what Pamela has been going
through. To this point, I've been trying to keep everything under wraps
to protect her. But hearing someone else suggest my daughter is slitting
her wrists makes me realize this is a tidal wave that can't be kept at bay.

Hanging up the phone, I spin into frenetic action, opening drawers in
every room, looking for things Pamela could cut with – scissors, screw-

39

drivers, letter openers and knives – and throw them in a box that gets heavier as I carry it from kitchen to den to one bathroom then the next.

Everything looks dangerous to me. I get a second box, then a third and fill them with paper clips, nail files, a stapler, a potato peeler – it's an impossible task. Where do I hide it all?

Walking past Pamela's room, I catch two large windows from the corner of my eye. I go in and open the blinds and look at the street below. It's eight floors down. Would she ever think of jumping? I check the locks to make sure they're secure. How did I go from being a concerned mother to a paranoid prison guard overnight?

———————————

It's midnight when the phone rings in my bedroom. I hold my breath. Pamela is calling from the intercom in the very next room.

"Mom, I can't take it anymore, I'm thinking of taking pills," she says.

Blood rushes from my head to my legs as I scramble out of bed.

"Hang on Pamela, I'll be right there," I say, while nudging Mike.

"Pamela's threatening to take pills, you've got to go through the medicine cabinets and confiscate any bottle you find."

"What? Oh Christ," he says, springing immediately into action.

I, meanwhile, slip into bed with Pamela and sleep right by her side throughout the night so I can see and feel her every move.

Thank God, Dr. Parker will finally be able to see her tomorrow.

PAMELA

April 20, 1998

The doctor put me on Ritalin today to give me more energy and concentration. It's supposed to work in about 48 hours. She's worried about my blood pressure because it's low and I get dizzy when I stand up. If the Nortrip doesn't work then we can try another drug with a last resort being Electro Convulsive Therapy. I am not even at a therapeutic level yet, it will take 4-6 weeks. I would be better off in the hospital except, I guess that won't change anything.

I hate to be awake, sleep, dream, think, look at myself in the mirror, go outside. God, help me love these things again. I'll do whatever it takes to get better, even if it takes the entire summer.

April 21, 1998

I didn't want to get out of bed this morning – Mom made me, and we drove out to East Hampton. I feel very weak and my leg won't stop shaking. Paula sent me home-baked cookies but I don't want to call her. I feel like such a bad person. I don't even want to call Teddy tonight because it's so hard to have a conversation.

This is the worst disease in the world yet a part of me doesn't want to get better because I can't face all the responsibilities that lay ahead.

Everything is closing in on me. I'm the little child sitting in the middle of an empty room with four white walls moving toward me. Crying, I hug my knees and rock back and forth. I want the walls to move back but I don't want to be out of the room. It doesn't make sense.

BEA

We walk side by side, Pamela and I, along Madison Avenue, not to shop, as we might have done a year ago, but en route to the Columbia Presbyterian Day Program for group counseling. It's only ten blocks away, but Pamela is afraid to go alone and once again, I feel like she's 3 instead of 20, and I'm taking her to nursery school.

I'm worried sick because in the eighteen days she's been released from the hospital I don't see any progress. Dr. Parker must sense that too because she has decided to wean her off Nortriptyline and start a new antidepressant.

"Once the Effexor kicks in, Pamela will be happier than she's been in years," Dr. Parker assures us.

PAMELA

April 23, 1998

I went to the Columbia-Presbyterian Day Program today and was very agitated, I don't know what's wrong with me. I'm very confused. I don't even know what my diagnosis is. So many doctors, so many opinions. Am I chronically depressed or is this just an isolated episode of major depression?

I found a notebook today that I wrote in when I was 13, dated 1991. There were poems and other things that seemed familiar. I was very nega-

tive and aware that something was wrong with me. I hated myself then and asked what the point of life was. I don't want to feel this way about myself.

God, bless everyone. I love you Aunt Rosemarie and Jeannie, since you both died I think about you all the time. I hope you are at peace.

April 26, 1998

I have been sick with a stomach-ache for two days. Supposedly, it's due to the new drug. My head pounds and pulses excessively. I hope group goes well tomorrow. I don't know what I'll talk about. Michael came over tonight but I had a hard time talking to him. The pain and sadness is difficult to understand if you're not going through it.

May 3, 1998

Yesterday I was in a very bad mood. My parents made me go out for a drive to the Island for lunch, but I was extremely distressed and couldn't eat. When we got home I ran to bed and thought for a long time about how mean I was to my parents. I decided to hurt myself ... went to the bathroom and cut myself 15 or 20 times with two razors and a scissor until I was bruised and bleeding enough that I felt good.

I wound up being admitted to Beth Israel Hospital. I just couldn't stay there though, it wasn't like Meyer 4.

BEA

"I hate this fucking city," Pamela says the minute she steps in the front door. I can hardly believe the nasty tone in her voice. We're the ones that should be angry after the roller-coaster ride she just put us through!

Returning from a weekend drive to Long Island, Pamela's not in the house more than ten minutes when we find her bleeding. How the heck did she find sharps? Mike throws the gauntlet down, knowing we can't care for Pamela in such a wild state, and immediately calls Dr. Parker. She's busy on this Saturday night, but arranges for Pamela to be admitted to the psych ward at Beth Israel Hospital.

Mike and Michael drive her downtown. Four hours later, Pamela calls, begging to be released because the bizarre behavior of the psychotics and schizophrenics is upsetting her.

What can we do? As if on auto-pilot, Mike and Michael retrace their steps and bring her back. Now, she's complaining? I've had just about enough.

"Pamela, if you don't stop this crazy cutting you'll wind up right back at Beth Israel. And if there is a next time, don't count on us to rescue you!"

"I'm sorry Mom," she whimpers, "I won't do it again."

I'm not so sure. Pamela's cutting has become a way to "show" her emotional pain when she's upset. It usually takes place when someone says something she can't cope with. Instead of expressing herself verbally, she cuts. While it provides relief for what she's feeling inside, those of us around her are held hostage to what we say.

It takes only two days for Pamela to break her promise. Walking past her room, I catch her trying to scratch her wrists with a hair barrette. Instinctively, I grab it from her and recoil when she starts biting into her own flesh. It's like she's possessed by demons.

"I want to kill myself," she screams.

Horrified, I yell for Mike.

"Please take me back to Meyer 4," she begs when he walks in.

I point to the bite marks on her arm. His eyes widen.

"Take it easy, Pamela," Mike says trying to soothe her. "Everything's going to be okay. We have to think this out. Going back to Baltimore is very far away, and it may not be the best solution for you right now."

She begins to wail. He tries to reason with her.

"Look, Pamela, don't you remember you thought the doctors in Baltimore weren't paying attention to you . . . they weren't helping you? You lost faith in them, and we understood that. That's why we brought you home. I promise, tomorrow morning I'll make some calls, and find the right place for you here in New York."

PAMELA

May 5, 1998
I was admitted to Lenox Hill Hospital yesterday. Although it's a lot better than Beth Israel, I feel the staff doesn't care. I bite my wrists right in

front of them and they don't notice. I can't wash my face or use deodorant without supervision. I suppose this is because I have been hurting myself. I feel like I need to hurt myself – I feel better when I'm in pain.

I'm very scared for tomorrow when I'm scheduled for my first ECT treatment. I will have a seizure for 20 seconds. I'm afraid that I will get sick or have a headache afterward. I want my Mom to be there but she can't. Do I really need this? Am I really depressed? Am I making it all up?

A very nice nurse told me to write down why I'm getting ECT as I may not remember tomorrow. I am getting ECT so I can be happy. I'm getting it so I won't hurt myself or want to die.

BEA

I can't believe I'm signing a consent form for Pamela to have ECT. Just five weeks ago, I swore to a resident at Johns Hopkins it was such an extreme measure. Now I'm praying it saves my daughter's life.

PAMELA

May 6, 1998

I was very scared for the ECT. I remember crying and the doctor holding my hand, then I was in recovery and when my doctors came to me I didn't know who they were. It's frightening being out of whack – my memory is jumbled a bit and I have a constant headache.

BEA

The phone is already ringing when I get back to the apartment. I lunge for it, clumsily dropping the mail to the floor. I think it must be Mike, with an update on Pamela's first ECT treatment, but to my surprise, it's her.

"Mom, I'm looking for something to hurt myself with," she says.

My heart drops. I guess the ECT didn't work.

"Pamela," I say forcefully, "I want you to go directly to the nurses' station. They're the ones who are supposed to keep you safe, tell them how you feel. Are you going to do that?"

She says yes, but I'm not sure I believe her, so I call to tip them off. They tell me they can give Pamela an Ativan to calm her down.

I take a Valium and make an appointment to see a therapist myself.

PAMELA

May 7, 1998

I felt very suicidal today. If I had access to a knife I would have slit my wrists. I am going to ask to speak with a priest.

May 8, 1998

The treatment went very well because I did not have a headache, but a nurse walked in on me while I was stabbing my wrist with an earring. I was put in the quiet room. And then let out when I thought I could handle myself, but was put back in again because I was banging my head against the wall. Now I have to have an aide with me at all times which is good for my safety, I suppose.

God bless my parents, brother, sister, Teddy and everyone. I love them all. I love you God and have faith you'll help me through this, even though I can't remember what the priest I talked to today said.

BEA

I have a menacing premonition that something terrible has happened when Mike and I arrive at Uris 8 and don't see Pamela's usual blanket-draped figure leaning against the wall waiting for us.

"She's probably resting," Mike assures me.

But I sense otherwise. As we walk down the hall, I peer into the padded isolation room – and sure enough, Pamela is sitting on the floor, on a bare mattress, staring back at us like a baby from its crib.

"This isn't the script we foresaw for Pamela when we first started to treat her," the kind psychologist from Johns Hopkins tells Mike, when he frantically reaches out to her doctors. If they can't be sure of Pamela's diagnosis, how can we?

PAMELA

May 13, 1998

For the first time I feel uplifted. The 4th ECT must have done something. I hope my mind isn't tricking me. I'm going home tomorrow for a few hours on a pass. If all goes well, the doctor will arrange for me to have the rest of my treatments as an outpatient.

46

BEA

A flower Pamela draws after her fourth ECT is spectacularly bright and jubilant, compared to the wilted, gray one she sketched a week before.

Could the ECT be working? Or is the Effexor finally kicking in? Whatever it is, I feel a glimmer of hope – her round-the-clock nurses have been discontinued and she's making eye contact, her speech is quicker and her posture, straighter.

PAMELA

May 15, 1998

The doctors don't know what to do with me. I had ECT then cut myself on the wrist with a plastic knife. Someone caught me and I got put back in the quiet room. I can hardly remember anything. God, I need help. I want to be well but nothing seems to be working. My parents are freaking out and I feel so badly that I have to put them through this. I know I need help.

If not, I'm really going to give up. I want to be happy and enjoy life. I want to get married, have kids and a good job. I am losing hope though and don't know what to do. I want to live.

BEA

"The people on Uris 8 are delusional," Pamela tells us. "They hear voices. If I stay here much longer that will happen to me." Mike and I are sitting across from her in the day room. It's hard to know how to respond, when she's up one minute and down the next.

"I've heard patients talk about other really nice facilities like Silver Hill and Four Winds where you can get treated in more of a campus setting," she says. "Maybe that's where I should go."

I look at Mike, his eyes get big. I can tell he doesn't want me to encourage her.

Picking up on this, Pamela pushes herself away from the table and goes to get a drink. As soon as she's far enough away, I say to him, "Maybe we should be looking into these other places."

"Bea, we can't start giving into everything Pamela wants," he says.

47

"She's totally impulsive and look where that landed her. I don't object to any type of care, whatever the cost or location. I want the best for her, but it should be recommended by the doctors, not manipulated by Pamela."

"Don't you feel her desperation?" I counter. "She's been in three hospitals already. She's looking for answers and so am I, and you should be too."

Mike and I are starting to split into two camps – emotional vs. practical. I'm reacting to Pamela's neediness and trying to satisfy her momentary whims, and he's more focused on the doctors and seeing the bigger picture.

It's beginning to cause a strain between us. At night, when we're not in the midst of a crisis with Pamela, we retreat to separate places in the apartment. I brood in our bedroom and he reverts to the den.

I've never seen Mike so riddled with nerves. He's even talking about taking a leave of absence from work – an oil and gas brokerage firm he's headed for twenty-five years and is passionate about. I can't believe he's even considering it.

PAMELA

May 18, 1998

I had my 6th ECT treatment today and nothing is better. A medical student grilled me for over an hour to find out if my father was abusive to me, which really pissed me off.

BEA

"What's the matter with the young girl?" a man in a wheelchair asks, beckoning me over with his shaky index finger.

Pamela and I are sitting on orange plastic chairs, waiting for her next ECT treatment as an outpatient at Beth Israel Hospital.

I pretend not to hear, but he repeats the question louder. If I don't get up, I'm afraid he'll make a scene and I'm trying to keep Pamela calm. With supreme effort, I rise from my daughter's side, move over to the man, and bend close to his unshaven face.

"She's depressed," I whisper. It's obvious everyone in the room is suffering from the same.

48

"But she's so young," he continues, looking up at me with a rheumy stare. I nod and return to my seat.

Like everyone else in the crowded room anticipating shock treatment, we wait for the doctor to emerge from behind the massive, reinforced, door.

Pamela's left leg shakes when another person's name is called because that means there will be at least another half hour of waiting. She's anxious, anticipating the assault of electric currents running through her body.

The man in the wheelchair beckons me again. "Do you know who I am?" he asks, then goes on to identify himself as a former television newscaster. Immediately, I recognize the familiar face behind the stubble. He confides, in a soft voice so the orderlies won't hear, that he doesn't like the way the hospital is treating him. He feels trapped in the system. I touch his hand in a comforting gesture – pained to see this former powerhouse reporter reduced to a bundle of misfired nerves – and guiltily walk back to my seat.

"Why are you crying?" a nurse asks me, after Pamela's name is finally called and she gets up from her seat. I mumble something into my tissue and move closer to the heavy door to keep my eye on my child.

It's left ajar, and I can see her slide onto what looks like an operating table. Within seconds, a group of jovial young doctors enter the room. They are laughing and it doesn't sit right with me.

"Why are all those doctors with my daughter?" I ask the nurse.

"They're interns," she says, matter-of-factly. "It's their first time observing ECT."

Suddenly I feel nauseous. It makes me sick to think I'm out here crying for my daughter, and they're inside in a happy mood.

A short time later, when the interns come out, they look grim. What did they witness in that room that wiped the smiles off their faces? I guess it's not so funny after all.

PAMELA

May 20-22, 1998

This morning was my 8th ECT treatment. I'm just so sick of hospitals (psychiatric wards, in general).

Now that I'm home, there's something strange happening to me. I keep getting this weird flashback but can't remember what it is. It's really scaring me. I'm so confused and have no appetite.

May 23, 1998

Teddy came to visit from Philadelphia. We bought a fish tank today and later this week I'll buy goldfish to put in it. Am having a hard time adjusting to being out of the hospital. I am so scared of what's ahead. Teddy must be so bored because I don't want to do anything. I feel so bad for him.

BEA

I take Teddy aside.

"Do you notice any changes in Pamela?" I ask. Of all the people in Pamela's circle, he would know best, since they've been dating for over a year.

I've always kept a healthy distance from Teddy because I never thought he and Pamela would wind up in a serious relationship. But after so many months of chaos, I value his faithfulness, and feel the urge to connect to him on a personal level.

"Before any of this happened, Pamela was a lot of fun to be around," Teddy says. "She joked and laughed."

The words bounce off me. I never would have described my daughter that way. Of my three children, Pamela was the quiet, moody one who preferred to stay alone in her room, rather than play.

While the twins would engage in conversation at dinner, telling about their days' adventures, Pamela usually ate in silence. She was at the table, but the talk always seemed to take place around her.

Could she portray herself as strong and funny to her boyfriend, but weak and shy to us? Does she have two sides to her personality?

I never thought about this possibility before, but it does seem surreal that Teddy, who is the person closest to Pamela, paints a totally different portrait of her than the one I know – and I've raised her for more than twenty years.

"So, you wouldn't say Pamela is shy?" I ask Teddy. A part of me wants his validation after everything we have been through.

"Not with me," he says looking me straight in the eye. "Right now, she's struggling with being at home because she feels controlled."

My stomach sinks.

"Teddy, I'm controlling because she's out of control. Everything I do is to keep her safe, to keep her alive."

He shrugs, not knowing what else to say.

PAMELA

May 24, 1998

My mind keeps racing – non-stop thoughts up and down and around my head. Why do I have to go through this? Why do I have this disease? It's horrible. I can't take it. I don't understand it.

I almost broke something today. Even worse, I opened up my wounds which caused my parents to panic. Now I can't do anything out of sight of my mother, I am even sleeping with her.

I am so in love with Teddy. I regret ever going out with Hank. I think he is haunting me.

BEA

Sitting in the living room, Pamela is very agitated, her legs are trembling and she's gulping deep breaths.

"Pamela what's wrong?" Mike asks.

"Dad, I did something very bad," she says.

Mike and I look at each other. What is it now?

"Remember Zach, who I used to work with in the mail room at your office during my summer breaks?" she asks.

"Yeah, he left and took another job downtown. Why?"

"Well," she says, with her whole body starting to spasm, "he used to sell me pot."

"What? You took drugs? Zach sold them to you? In my office?"

She nods, but says nothing more.

"Pamela, how could you?" I jump in. "Why would you take drugs? And buy them in Daddy's office? Don't you realize how hurtful that is?"

Mike, whose instincts about people are usually spot-on, gets up and starts pacing the floor. "I never liked that son of a bitch. I'd like to find him and kick his ass."

I'm frightened. Now Mike knows.

Pamela told me she experimented with a mushroom once, when she was a sophomore in college. She called me in hysterics, saying her roommate gave it to her, and then left her alone. It was such a horrifying experience, she swore she'd never do it again.

I was so angry I told Pamela if she ever did take drugs again, I'd go straight to her father. I thought that ended it.

Now I feel like a traitor. By protecting my daughter, I betrayed my husband. He's totally unprepared for this. Mike grew up in a poor Bronx neighborhood, with some junkies he considered lost and big losers. Now he sees his daughter as one of them. I'm afraid it's going to destroy him.

He looks defeated, lying on the living room couch with the back of his right hand pressed against his forehead and doesn't say another word.

Pamela's eyes widen. She seems suddenly concerned about her father.

PAMELA

May 27, 1998

I did something stupid today: I cut up my wrist with a plastic razor. It felt good while I was doing it – I was in control. Am sleeping in my mother's bed with her tonight.

The day program was crowded with many people and it was very depressing because almost everyone talked about their suicidal thoughts and they joked about the "charcoal shakes" they get in the emergency room after suicide attempts. I guess that doesn't offer me much hope.

Tomorrow I go for my first bi-lateral ECT. I hope I can trust Dr. Parker with my life. God be with me, and all the mentally disadvantaged.

My 10th ECT went better today because they used a different anesthesia and I wasn't nauseous.

I am upset because I can't do anything to occupy my time, like watch TV or read, because I can't concentrate. All I keep doing is thinking about how miserable I am and that's not good.

My fish, Theresa, died and I had Dad flush her down the bowl before he took off for Greece and Italy. Please keep Dad safe, God, I love him so much.

BEA

Mike's away, and I'm on full-time duty. He was reluctant to make this business trip, but felt he had to while things were relatively stable at home. It's probably a good break for the two of us because we've been bickering lately. The other day Pamela even mentioned, she's seeing a psychiatrist because of it, and that, of course makes us feel awful.

Our relationship as a couple works. We're both very verbal, and often voice our grievances to unload resentment and clear the air. But now, because of Pamela's fragility, we find ourselves muzzled.

Everyone has a breaking point. Mike had his when Pamela revealed her drug use, and now I find mine when Pamela and I are on the subway coming home from Dr. Parker's office.

"What I need is more free time," she tells me.

"Free time?" What is that?" I yell, startling the other passengers.

She needs free time? I'm the one who has no free time, watching her every second of every day. I go with her to the doctor, to the day program, for ECT, to the ceramics shop. My whole world revolves around Pamela and her ever changing needs.

On the walk home, I'm thinking I have to find a way to get free time for both of us, so we can distance ourselves from each other and maintain our individuality.

Suddenly, I remember how well Pamela reacted to the private duty nurses who watched her in the hospital. I ask Mike if we should get one, and he agrees it would be a good idea. I make some calls to healthcare agencies and hire a companion for a few hours a day. I can't believe I'm doing this without Mike – he's the one who usually makes these kinds of arrangements – but he's not here, and I'm desperate.

When I find the courage to tell Pamela about this new development, I'm dumbfounded when she says, "Thanks, Mom," throws her arms around me in a bear-hug, and gives me a kiss.

After two days with a private duty aide, however, Pamela says, "I feel like a rich kid who has her own servant."

"She's not your servant," I say. "You're sick, and the aide is trying to keep you safe."

When I cry to my therapist about this, she tells me this is no time to be heroic, and starts me on Zoloft.

PAMELA

June 2, 1998

I am frustrated. I feel bad for my Mom, but she hired a nurse to stay with me so she can do her own stuff.

Help me get through tomorrow's treatment without getting sick.

BEA

After her twelfth and last ECT, Pamela tells Dr. Parker she wants to visit Teddy in Philadelphia over the weekend. The doctor says, "Go," and that causes yet another upset in our household.

It's easy for Dr. Parker to encourage Pamela to visit her boyfriend in Philadelphia. When the session ends, she ushers Pamela out the door and moves on to her next patient without comment, leaving Mike and me to worry about what could go wrong. Will Pamela become disoriented by all the chaos at Penn Station? What will she do if she can't sleep at night? What if she forgets to take her pills? Teddy has no idea about the kind of emotional baggage Pamela drags along with her.

Mike and I are deeply disturbed by the dual messages Pamela is giving us – on the one hand she's totally helpless, on the other she wants to be independent and make her own decisions. Does Dr. Parker realize this?

Just the way Pamela portrays herself as funny and strong to Teddy, I am wondering if she puts on a different face for the doctors too. They must view her as more capable than she really is because she's smart. Why else would Dr. Parker support her impulsive desire to travel alone to Philadelphia while she's on so much medication in her current mental state?

Sooner or later Pamela is going to have to live with her choices. But we're paying the medical bills. Shouldn't we have a say in deciding what she can and cannot do?

Mike calls Dr. Parker and arranges to speak with her privately. She reinforces that Pamela should be allowed to make her own decisions. He's not exactly sure the doctor is right, but accepts her advice.

PAMELA

June 7, 1998

Just got to the 30th Street train station in Philadelphia. I'm going to miss Teddy so much. I had a good time with him this weekend. Last night was his graduation party. I still don't feel any better. I cut my wrist yesterday with a scissor. I'm scared about going to a new psychologist tomorrow. I am so ugly and I'm such a loser. What's wrong with me?

BEA

"Why isn't Pamela getting better?" I ask Dr. Reese, Pamela's new talk therapist, during a private session Mike and I are attending. Mike arranged for Pamela to see a psychologist in addition to a psychiatrist because Dr. Parker is not available to see her as often as she needs.

"The doctors in Baltimore said it would take two weeks for her to snap out of this depression," I continue, "and it's already been two and a half months with no progress." I know I shouldn't pin this new doctor to the wall, because she barely knows Pamela, but my frustration is starting to get the best of me.

"Surely this must be difficult for both of you," Dr. Reese says, trying to defuse the tension. "I've only met with Pamela twice, but from what I can tell, it seems many of her symptoms fall into the category of personality disorders."

Mike and I look at each other questioningly.

I pick up my pen and prepare to write down what she says.

"Specifically what I'm thinking of in Pamela's case is Borderline Personality Disorder – BPD. It's somewhat complicated. Inwardly, this type of person is socially shy, tends to see most situations as black or white, good or bad, and is afraid of acting alone or being abandoned. Outwardly, they often engage in impulsive and self-destructive behaviors like cutting, eating disorders, sexual promiscuity, and substance abuse. Does any of this seem to resonate with you?"

I stop writing and stare at what I've scribbled. My mind and hand disconnect as I slowly absorb each characteristic of this disorder – a socially shy person, afraid to be alone, acts impulsively – it doesn't just resonate, it sets off an explosion of emotions for me.

"Dr. Reese, you've just described Pamela perfectly. Don't you think so?" I ask, turning to Mike.

He says, "That might explain why the antidepressants and ECT aren't working."

"Borderlines walk a fine line between being psychotic and normal," the doctor explains. "That's why they're called borderline. If this is indeed what Pamela has, she will need years of intensive therapy to deconstruct her personality and rebuild it."

"But what can we do about it now? Is there a medicine she can take?" asks Mike.

"Sometimes other psychiatric illnesses like bi-polar, or depression can overlap with, and mask, personality disorders, and medication can be effectively used in those cases. But there's nothing that's prescribed specifically for personality disorders."

Mike and I are relieved because for the first time, a diagnosis makes sense. But we're also worried about Pamela's reaction when she finds out medication won't help her.

PAMELA

June 9, 1998

Horrible, horrible day! I feel like I'm going to explode. Screamed, and cried hysterically today and wanted to die. Think of death all the time. More than anything, I want to be happy and live forever, but doubt I ever will.

Dr. Reese says I have to wait and this depression will pass. It is so hard, waiting.

Please help me, God. I love you so much, like my parents. I am putting them through so much pain. My father cries a lot, which is so devastating to me, and my mother doesn't know how to deal with me.

Tomorrow I start another day program – Manhattan Psych Systems – which I hope will help me in some way.

June 16, 1998

My dad and I had a long talk tonight. I expressed a lot of my feelings and so did he. He told me how much he is trying to help me by talking to experts every day and is positive I will get better. He asked what I would have liked better from him as a father while I was growing up. I told him I would have liked to be closer to him and to have known him better. He was so sincere when he expressed how much he loves me. He said that he's in this with me and will fight until I'm better. I love my father so much. I just wish I knew it earlier.

BEA

I am thumbing through titles in the Psychology section at Barnes and Noble on Lexington Avenue. Pamela stands behind me, disinterested.

I never used to frequent this section of the bookstore, but now I know exactly where it is. In fact I have become a regular.

This collection of books has become my lifeline to educate myself about psychological lingo, drugs, and treatment options, so I can hold intelligent conversations with Pamela's doctors and stay on top of her care.

"Look, Pamela, a book on Borderline Personality Disorder. This is what Dr. Reese thinks you might have. Let's see what is says." We find a bench and sit down. I start to read excerpts describing symptoms of BPD.

"It doesn't sound like me," she interrupts. But the more I read, the more I recognize her in its pages.

Ever since our conversation with Dr. Reese, Mike and I reach out for other opinions about Pamela's having BPD.

One is from Dr. Winters, a psychiatrist affiliated with Lenox Hill. He concurs that Pamela is suffering from a Personality Disorder.

"Pamela's case," he tells Mike and me, "is like a bridge that's collapsed from too much pressure. The depression has to be fixed before her personality can be rebuilt, and that may take up to ten years."

I shudder. How can we tell Pamela it will take ten years for her to get better?

PAMELA

June 23, 1998

Something traumatic happened yesterday and right now I'm in a hospital bed in Lenox Hill again. I started crying hysterically and shaking uncontrollably at home last night. Medicine calmed me down and I fell asleep but I woke up at 3 a.m. with an urge to cut so I went to the kitchen and picked out a big knife. As I held it, my father walked in.

June 24, 1998

I met with Dr. Winters today for an hour. He seems to know what he's doing but I'm still very confused about my disorder. I have moments when I cry a lot and there are other times when I just feel numb. I'm glad I'm here.

June 26, 1998

I thought I heard voices today. Two people were talking and I was responding, but when I turned around, no one was there. It was probably a dream since I'm sleeping a lot. It's a combination of drowsiness and wanting to isolate myself. My soul needs mending.

I wish I knew what was wrong with me. The doctor doesn't even know my diagnosis, which scares me. I am sick and need to be helped and treated correctly.

Am very happy to be starting Prozac today – please God, let this be the drug that works! I am glad that I got to go on a community walk because we went to church, which made me feel closer to You. I started feeling down when my parents visited because I feel like a burden to them – although I keep telling myself I'm not.

My problems right now have to do with eating. I'm gaining weight since I've been here and feel hungry all the time.

BEA

Just as I'm walking out the door to visit Pamela, the phone rings.

"Mom, when are you going to be here?" she asks. I sense, from the low tone of her voice that something is up.

"I'm ready to walk out the door, is everything okay?"

"I fainted this morning. My blood pressure was low," she says.

"Oh my God! Did you get hurt?"

"No, I'm okay, but I'm starving. Can you pick up a turkey burger for me on the way over?"

"Of course." The Italian-mother in me is glad to oblige as food in our family has always been the salve that heals all wounds.

Pamela is waiting in her usual spot when I arrive. I hand her the turkey burger and we walk to the day room to find an empty table. I'm happy to see her gobble up the burger with gusto. Then she excuses herself to use the bathroom.

When she returns, there's a twinkle in her eye.

"I just stuck a toothbrush down my throat to vomit my lunch up," she says matter-of-factly.

Something tells me she knew all along she would do this, and it leaves me feeling like I've been manipulated into being an accessory to her self-destructive behavior.

"Why are you telling me this?" I sputter, pointing angrily to the nursing station. "Go tell them what you just did!" She shamefully drops her eyes to the ground, and walks sluggishly down the hall.

PAMELA

July 7, 1998

A psychologist came by to do some tests to evaluate my personality. I got upset because there were a few vocabulary words that I couldn't define. I feel very stupid because there are many things I don't know, like the seven continents – it was too much to handle.

I had a dream about Hank this afternoon and it really disturbed me. I am so glad it was only a dream. I miss Teddy and want to hug him so badly.

July 9, 1998

Met with Dr. Parker today about my plans to go home. It seems there is a pattern: every time I get discharged and go home, things get bad again.

BEA

"You have to back off, she's too dependent on you," says the Resident on Uris 8, as if I could snap my fingers and make it happen. I look back at the diminutive woman in the white coat, incredulous.

"Why are you pinning Pamela's recovery on me? Do you actually believe I want a 20-year-old tied to my apron strings?" I say, not even pretending to hide my annoyance.

How dare this young upstart judge me and my relationship with my daughter. Does she even realize that Pamela cuts herself, and throws up to get my attention? Does she understand how hard it is for me to separate, knowing that each time I do, her self-destructive actions only get worse?

"Look," the Resident says, responding to my bitter outburst, "Pamela needs to fall on her face before she learns to walk. She might get angry and she might hurt herself, but she won't kill herself. This will be a long process," she says, "you have to go and live your lives normally."

She may go home to live a "normal" life, but I sure as hell can't. Normal does not exist for me or my family anymore.

PAMELA

July 14, 1998

*(note: 2 months till I am 21 and legal!)

I want to leave this place! The hospital is really getting to me but just spoke with the social worker and I won't be out until I have a day-treatment program in place. I have to choose between Columbia Presbyterian and Psych Systems of Gracie Square. I think I am ready and will do well this time. I have a feeling inside that I am getting better.

July 20, 1998

I went to Dr. Parker's office but couldn't go alone on a day pass as planned because the medications are causing me to feel faint and be sick to my stomach. Dr. P said she would do things differently if she was in charge of my meds. She doesn't like that I'm in the day program either. After ten minutes, I felt so dizzy and nauseous, I had to lie down.

When I got back to the hospital, I ran right to bed and fell asleep. What the hell is happening to me??

I don't like Dr. Winters! He said I'm overweight!

BEA

After visiting hours end at the hospital, Mike and I invite the twins over for a family meeting.

Although we speak to Michael and Paula about Pamela on the phone daily, the kids are busy with their careers and social lives. Michael works in sports management, and his job takes him on the road ten days a month. Paula just returned from a year-long assignment as a community organizer in Las Vegas. Both are in serious relationships, and they spend all their time either working or with their significant others.

As much as Mike and I don't want to burden them with every detail of Pamela's illness, and have tried to protect them from the worst of it, we now realize that we need to have a plan in place if she is going to be released from the hospital for the third time, and succeed at living at home.

As soon as I begin pouring the coffee and passing around the cookies, Mike begins.

"If Pamela is released to our care at home, it's critical that we work together as a family – and your mother and I need your help. This is too much for us alone – to create activities to keep Pamela busy. So far, only a day program and her therapist are scheduled, but she will need more activities than that. Otherwise, we all know, she tends to crater."

Paula, our good-hearted child, who doesn't know how to say no, and often takes on too much, immediately volunteers. "I'm thinking of joining a gym," she says. "Pamela could join too, and we could go together. Maybe it'll help her feel better."

"That's a great idea," I say, but add a gentle dose of realism. "Are you sure you'll have time to make this commitment, with your graduate school classes starting soon?"

"Well, I can't go every day, but I think twice a week is realistic."

"Okay, what else can we do?" Mike tries to keep the conversation moving where it needs to go.

"I'll take Pamela to ceramics after the day program, since her pottery seems to make her calm," I offer.

Then Michael, who has a much better sense of his limitations than the rest of us, chimes in.

"Look, I'm so busy at work, all I can promise is to visit Pam on the weekend when I'm not traveling. But I've got to tell you, Dad, I think Pamela's whole problem is that she's too drugged up. These doctors have her on so many medications," he says, his voice rising uncharacteristically. "It's like she's one big experiment. She shakes, she can't sleep, she can't remember things. It is not right. Sometimes I think these doctors don't know what they're doing."

Mike and I are momentarily speechless at Michael's outburst. This is the first time we've heard our son express such deep concern over his sister's care, and it really shakes us up.

"Believe me, I'm talking to Pamela's psychologist and psychiatrist every day," Mike says, equally frustrated. "I'm mad too, because they keep contradicting themselves and changing medications, but this is not something that's going to go away overnight."

I take out the book I bought on BPD, give it to Michael and Paula.

"This is what the doctors say Pamela has. Read about it so you understand it could take ten years for her to get better."

"Ten years?" Michael says, "I don't think Pamela will make it ten years like this. She's going crazy, and we have to find someone who will help her now."

"He's right," Paula says. "We have to find a way to keep her from harming herself."

"Look, the most important thing we can do for your sister is stick together, communicate openly and help whenever we can," Mike says.

"We're trying our best, believe me, we're trying our best," I say. And even though I know we are trying our best, I can hear the lack of confidence in my own voice.

PAMELA

July 21, 1998

Went to the day program today and thought it was very good. I think I might call a few friends tonight. I think I am up to it. Today is the first day that I'm considering the idea that Prozac is working.

My moods are so inconsistent. I'm very confused about my discharge plans and what I should do this weekend. I can't be alone without any structure. Teddy is taking an LSAT on Saturday and I'm scared to go to his house because of it. I think I should stay home, but that might be bad also. Maybe I should just stay in the hospital. I hope I can make the right decision for myself.

July 23, 1998

I am home. Dr. Parker thinks I should go back to Loyola. I am so confused because it's almost August. She showed me a letter from my Latin teacher and he said I would have gotten the Latin award last semester. That made me happy.

Had a strange dream – I don't like dreaming, it freaks me out. God, please get Hank out of my mind, it's driving me nuts!

I miss Teddy, he's sad and depressed. I hope I didn't cause it.

BEA

It is almost midnight. I walk into the kitchen to get a drink of water and find Pamela standing in front of the open refrigerator.

"Is everything okay?" I ask, surprised to see her up. I checked on her a few minutes ago and thought she was sound asleep.

"I'm having terrible dreams – and I'm so scared."

"Why? What are they about?"

"People from the past. I see faces, but I don't remember everything. It's confusing. I think my memory is all screwed up from the ECT."

Not wanting to play psychiatrist, I respond, "Maybe you should tell Dr. Reese about it tomorrow."

Pamela sighs, "Maybe," and closes the refrigerator door.

PAMELA

July 26, 1998

I couldn't sleep last night and became very agitated. The solution came with an urge to hurt myself. I wanted to feel the pain of putting a knife against my skin and pushing it down. I made two small slits on my fore-arm that did not bleed but did scar today. Then I used a scissor from the knife holder in the kitchen and just cut a piece of skin off my arm, it was so easy to get the blood. Am I still sick? I tried twice to write some poetry but felt uninspired. I want to be able to express myself in writing.

Something bothering me is the terrible dream I had last night of being raped over and over again and no one believed me. I hate dreaming.

August 2, 1998

Paula got engaged! I am so happy for her. She asked me to be her maid-of-honor!

She drove me down to Philly for the weekend. Teddy and I went to a Phillies game, the zoo and out to dinner where I ate BBQ pizza with chicken and chocolate-chip cannoli for dessert. I loved seeing Teddy and forgot how good it feels to be in his arms. I know he is my one and only true love and hope we have a wonderful future together.

There is something bothering me besides school and my future – it seems as though my brain is screwed up from the ECT. I can't remember anything. When Teddy was talking to me, my mind would wander off and I couldn't concentrate on what he was saying. How can I go back to school if I can't remember what I study anymore?

August 4, 1998

I just came from Dr. Parker's office. I really don't think I am getting therapy – Dr. Reese did a better job at that. Dr. Parker talks too much about her own life and goes into so many digressions, I feel I'm not getting any help from her. She even told me how her landlord walked in on her when she was naked once when she lived in Baltimore. Maybe I'm over-reacting but something is wrong here.

BEA

We take Pamela out to East Hampton for the weekend – she roller-blades on the tennis court and does some laps in the pool – she seems happy, but all that changes on the ride home.

I ask Mike to pull over near a farm-stand so I can buy some fresh vegetables. When I return to the car, I find Pamela doubled over in the backseat, her face streaked with tears.

"What's wrong?" I ask. Her mouth opens wide, but nothing comes out.

"I told Pamela I agree with Dr. Parker, that she should go back to Loyola, and she became hysterical," says Mike, without turning around.

"Can't you see you're just putting more pressure on her?" I snap, before jumping in the back seat next to Pamela. Her body is shaking and I try to comfort her on the long ride home while Mike stays silent.

When we get home, he pulls me aside and apologizes for bringing up Loyola.

"I didn't mean anything bad by it, Bea, I was just trying to keep the conversation going," he says sullenly. "I don't know what to say to her anymore, it's like tip-toeing through a mine field."

PAMELA

I shook the whole way home from East Hampton. Everything felt over-whelming. When I got home I went through Mom's bathroom to find my razor, went into my room and began to slice up both my arms. They hurt tremendously. Dad got very upset. I have no real reason why I did it other than I feel very suicidal today.

God, help me get through this. I don't want to give up on being happy. Bless my parents for dealing with me.

BEA

"It's all my fault," Mike says angrily after cleaning Pamela's wounds and wrapping her arms in towels. "Could this be because of what I said in the car about going back to Loyola? I can't take it anymore. I've had it with this cutting, I'm calling Dr. Reese and Dr. Parker right now."

I feel so bad for Mike. He is doing so much that Pamela does not see or appreciate – on the phones with doctors and hospital staff every day – this bloodletting over his remark only makes him feel worse.

Plus, he's under tremendous pressure dealing with another emergency situation involving his 94-year-old mother. She fell, hit her head and had to undergo a craniotomy to remove a blood clot on her brain. So Mike is not only dealing with Pamela's daily crises at home, but he is also managing his mother's care. He always takes care of everyone so effortlessly, but who takes care of him?

I make an effort to comfort him by rubbing his shoulders as he dials Dr. Parker's number. His neck tenses when she answers the phone.

"Hello, Dr. Parker? This is Mike Tusiani. We need to talk…"

PAMELA

Saw Dr. Reese today, she said I needed a year to heal. I am so confused. Dr. Parker said I should go back to school.

BEA

"I think I'd like to enroll at Fordham University's Lincoln Center Campus," Pamela says to Mike. He's momentarily uplifted she is making a step in the right direction. But when he takes her across town for an application, she becomes jittery, and he finds himself caught, once again, in the seesaw of her emotions.

"You don't have to go through with this," he tells her.

But Pamela somehow gathers the courage to make an appointment with the Dean and, after an interview with him, she is thrilled to be accepted.

When she asks her father to help her fill out the University's health information form, his main dilemma is how to acknowledge her mental illness and at the same time, protect her from being rejected because of it.

PAMELA

August 12, 1998

That terrible dream came back of me getting raped several times. I talked about it in group today. I don't know if I've been raped. I'm not sure. I don't think I did, maybe I'm scared about being raped.

I'm so tired. Am going to register for one course: History of Ancient Greece and Rome. I hope I'll be able to do it.

All this talk of Paula's wedding is getting to me but I don't know why. I guess I'm just a confused person. The world is turning and I'm not.

BEA

Paula and her fiancé Roger, Pamela and I sit in the living room in a celebratory mood. We have just returned from a surprise engagement party that one of Paula's cousins held for her, and we are all in high spirits.

"Let's open your gifts," I suggest. Most of my time has been consumed with Pamela, and I want to experience these precious moments of joy with Paula.

As soon as Paula unwraps her first present, Pamela makes it a point to walk out of the room. She leaves us all stunned.

"Did I do something wrong?" Paula asks. "Maybe we shouldn't open the gifts now?" I know she is concerned, as I am, that Pamela is upset and might cut herself.

Clearly, this recent shift of the family's attention to Paula because of the wedding is difficult for Pamela. Paula has always been the agreeable, outgoing child, whose character is as strong as her father's. Pamela found that frustrating because she couldn't relate to her sister's upbeat personality and accomplishments. So it's not surprising that the joy Paula is experiencing surrounding her wedding is a reminder to Pamela of her own unhappiness – and that makes her even more depressed.

I'm split in two. Which child do I focus on? The one who's happy, or the one who's sad? I take a deep breath and try to make the right decision.

"Don't worry, go ahead, Paula, open the gifts." I say, not wanting to ruin the day for her. "I'll check on Pamela in a while."

For that night, at least, there is no further drama.

Pamela sleeps late the next morning, and then smashes yet another object in her room and cuts her arms. She just can't take it anymore.

Something has set her off. Was it all the wedding talk? The pressure of going back to school? Bad dreams?

Her doctor advises me to give her two Ativans, but the frenzy continues. She paces around the apartment like a caged animal on the prowl, stopping for brief moments at the windows and in front of the knife drawer. Mike and I are scared, we don't know what she is going to do from one moment to the next.

Mike calls the doctors to seek advice, because we're fast running out of solutions.

Dr. Winters tells us to bring her back to Lenox Hill for a 48-hour calming down period. The nurses on Uris 8 are stunned to see Pamela on the unit again, and she is just as embarrassed to be there.

"I just want to get better," she tells them, meekly.

PAMELA

August 22, 1998

I wrote the past few days on loose paper because I'm back in Lenox Hill Hospital. Teddy is very upset because he doesn't understand why I want to die – actually, why I feel my life isn't worth living. I didn't know what to say to him . . . don't know what to say to myself.

DREAMS

Dreams fill my days and nights,
I fall from buildings.
I am teased by bullies
I am scared and angry.
How can I stop them from taking charge of me?
I might be happy one morning,
But how can I continue to be, when dark nightmares
Burn flames inside my head?

BEA

"I can't wait that long!" Pamela screams when a doctor on the ward tells her it will take at least one to two years for recovery. She wails and bangs her head against my chest in hysterical convulsions as we sit on her hospital bed.

"Dad, you have to help me, you have to get me out of here, and find a place that can make me better. I want to live." Mike is beside himself, feeling the depth of her anguish, and yet he does not know what options are available for her outside of the hospital.

"I promise I'll talk to Dr. Winters. We'll figure this thing out," he says, putting his big bear arms around both of us. It feels like we are back in Baltimore, when he promised the same thing, but this time the answer is not to go home. We don't know what the answer will be.

Desperate for a solution, Mike confers with Dr. Winters and the staff. Exactly five months and five hospitalizations after Pamela's initial breakdown, the recommendation is for treatment in a residential facility called Austen Riggs, in Stockbridge, Massachusetts. Long-term treatment in an institutional setting is better care than we can give her at home. Such a young girl should not keep getting bounced in and out of psych wards, they tell us.

Mike works hard to find out about Austen Riggs. Apparently, it's well known in the psychiatric field, and has a good reputation for treating people with BPD. I am thrilled to hear this. Finally, the medical professionals will start to focus on dismantling and rebuilding Pamela's personality. I am convinced that treating Pamela's BPD is the key to her recovery, but no doctor, so far, seems to take it seriously.

Mike tries every contact he has to get Pamela admitted to Riggs. He finally speaks to the right person, but there won't be an opening for another two weeks.

"Go back to work!" Pamela snaps at him, when she hears the disappointing news. Her nasty tone stings. She is used to having her father move mountains. But she doesn't understand that we're dealing with an admission process that's akin to getting into Harvard.

While our daughter feels trapped, languishing in a hospital room, Mike and I are on pins and needles, wondering if they will even admit her at all.

"Can I come home on an 8-hour pass tomorrow?" Pamela is calling from a pay phone. "It's so boring here." I hesitate. What are Mike and I going to do to occupy Pamela for that length of time?

Her voice sounds strong and confident, just enough to convince me that she can handle herself. Against my better judgment, I believe her, and give in.

When she walks into the apartment, her mood quickly shifts. Strong once again morphs into weak. She mopes around aimlessly, her big sad eyes staring at Mike and me like a lost puppy. As we try to lift her spirits, the phone rings.

"Mrs. Tusiani?"

"This is she."

"I'm Dr. Jordan from the admissions office at Austen Riggs." I flap my hands to get Mike and Pamela's attention, and put the doctor on speaker phone.

"We had an unexpected cancellation, and an interview slot has opened up for nine o'clock tomorrow morning. Can you be here?" I am not sure. I am blind-sided. Massachusetts is two and a half hours away. We don't even know what is involved in getting Pamela discharged from Lenox Hill. I look at Mike and Pamela, and they give me the thumbs up.

"Yes, we'll be there," I blurt out, watching Pamela jump up and down, getting caught up in the excitement of the moment.

"We suggest Pamela bring her belongings in case she is admitted," Dr. Jordan says. Mike picks up the receiver, and takes it from there, while Pamela and I go to her room and begin stuffing duffle bags full of her clothes.

PAMELA

August 25, 1998

Today I found out that I'm going to Austen Riggs tomorrow at 6 a.m.! I had to say good-bye to Michael, Paula and Uncle Joseph. It was very hard. I cried a lot. I am really scared. Please help me, God. Be with me tomorrow. Bless everyone. I love my family.

CHAPTER 3

Stockbridge

MR. DAVIS TO MR. MICHAEL D. TUSIANI (WITNESS):

Q: *Mr. Tusiani, we are here in your office, this company is your current employer.*

A: *Yes.*

Q: *Are you a partner?*

A: *I am the sole owner.*

Q: *I don't need to know a lot about the finances of the company. This seems very self-serving and a little bit redundant. You were never expecting Pamela to provide any financial support to you at any time in your life, would you agree?*

A: *Agree.*

Q: *During the grammar school period, approximately what was your average hourly work-week like?*

A: *Including travel, I would say twelve to fifteen hours a day.*

Q: *I would like to know what percentage of your time was spent out of town, whether you want to tell me how many times a month, how many times a year, whatever makes the most sense to you on average; do you remember this time frame?*

A: *Thirty percent.*

Q: *Can you characterize for me what your relationship with your daughter was like during her grammar school years?*

A: *Daddy's little girl, very, very positive.*

Q: *Your wife mentioned some extra-curricular activities that she was involved in in grammar school. How were you involved in those activities?*

A: *Well, I would describe it as minimal, more as an observer rather than participant.*

Q: *Your wife made a point of indicating that you were very intent on being present for important events and for weekend activities; is that a fair assessment?*

A: Whenever I was in town and there was an event, I made it my business to be there.

Q: Did you ever have any indication from Pamela that she thought that you were not spending enough time with her during her life in grammar school?

A: At that time?

Q: Yes, at that time.

A: At that time, I was not aware of it.

Q: Did Pamela have in your estimation a happy childhood during her grammar school years?

A: I think so. I think she was a happy kid.

Q: Do you have any sense looking back now as to when her emotional or psychiatric problems began in your estimation?

A: I would say from my perspective it was during her college years.

BEA

"It can't be far now," I say to Mike, fixated on the countryside outside the car window, when we pass a sign that says "to Stockbridge." The Berkshires are new territory for us, they're further west than we've ever been in Massachusetts. We've been driving mostly in the dark, but as the sun rises, several quaint New England towns appear, dappled with clapboard houses and white bell-towered churches.

The sleepy setting becomes more idyllic as early morning activity builds, with shopkeepers opening their doors to locals stopping in for newspapers and their first cups of coffee. It's a peaceful contrast to the manic bustle of the big city, and certainly seems like a calm and welcoming environment for Pamela, who is sleeping in the back seat.

"We're here," says Mike as we make a left off Route 7A onto Main Street. "Pamela, wake up. It must be that big white house on the right."

"This is Riggs?" she asks, as she groggily moves forward to get a better view.

"How can that be Austen Riggs?" I ask, expecting a long-term psychiatric facility to look more like Creedmore – a massive concrete building with barred windows and locked gates that I used to pass along the Grand Central Parkway in Queens. Even when I was a child, my father never failed to point out, "That's where the nuts live," when we drove by it. I used to think that was funny, but not anymore.

My worst fear is to leave my daughter in an institution like that.

So, it's an enormous relief and surprise to see the "Riggs" sign on a big, sprawling boarding house, nestled among sturdy old trees on a wide expanse of lawn. We're all struck by how unassuming it is, blending in nicely among other houses along Main Street.

Mike pulls into the driveway and turns off the engine. Pamela remains glued to her seat.

I try to be encouraging, "This looks like a lovely place to spend some time," I say. "It's like an old inn." But her frozen expression and jittery legs say it all.

Here we go again. Just a few hours ago, she was squealing with delight to make this change, and now her fears of separation and abandonment are causing her to regress.

Mike opens the passenger door and gently extends his hand to help her out of the car. Thankfully, she takes it.

Within minutes of entering the front door, we are being led on a tour of the facility's three main buildings, The Inn, The Elms and Lavan Hall. We peek into the cafeteria, meeting rooms, greenhouse and art workshop.

Immediately upon our return, Pamela is whisked into an interview with the admissions officer, Dr. Jordan. Mike and I, meanwhile, take seats in the entrance hall waiting room. Its atmosphere is rather austere, with high ceilings and sparse furnishings – so different from the warmth I felt outside.

At first, I am grateful to relax after the long car ride. But after an hour of watching patients and doctors walk in and out of various rooms and no sign of Pamela, I start to panic.

"What if she's not accepted?" I ask Mike.

He whispers back, "I can't understand why the admissions officer is making us sit here, leaving us on pins and needles for so long."

74

Another fifteen minutes pass before Dr. Jordan appears.

"Pamela's been admitted to Riggs," he says matter-of-factly.

Instantly, I breathe a sigh of relief.

Mike stands up, with a broad smile on his face, and grips the doctor's hand. "We just want the best for our daughter so she can get better," he says. The two of us are so thrilled, it's as if Pamela has been accepted to college all over again. But we have little time to savor the moment before Dr. Jordan's tone becomes businesslike.

"Pamela is going through intake now," he says crisply. "You two will need to go downstairs and meet with the social worker assigned to her, Dr. Spellman. He will take your family histories and explain how our facility works. We operate in an open setting."

"What does that mean, open setting?" I ask, familiar up to this point only with hospitals and day programs.

"We offer intensive therapy, support groups and a wide variety of social activities, but patients have to take the initiative to participate in them. They are expected to be responsible for their own actions and are pretty much on their own. There are no locks."

A red flag goes up.

"What happens if Pamela cuts herself? Will anyone check up on her?" I ask, my mind flashing back to the many trips we've taken to the emergency room over the last six months.

"She's an adult and we'll treat her like one," Dr. Jordan says. "There's a 24-hour nursing station and on-call medical assistance for Pamela to reach out to in a crisis. But she has to seek them out herself."

"Is Pamela aware of this?" Mike asks.

"I explained it all in the admission interview, and she signed the contract," the doctor says.

"But, can a person in Pamela's state be responsible for making such an agreement?" Mike asks.

"Yes," he responds, staring directly into Mike's eyes.

"Good, if you say so, I'm glad she understands," Mike says.

"One more thing," says Dr. Jordan, as he leads us toward his office door, "after you finish with Dr. Spellman, you'll need to stop into the Bursar's office to pay for Pamela's first month's stay."

Walking down the hall, Mike pulls me toward him and whispers in my ear, "That's going to be $20,000, without the cost of medications or extras."

My eyes widen in disbelief. I never even thought to ask about how much it would cost.

PAMELA

August 27, 1998

My first full-day here. Lonely, frightened, uncomfortable, nervous. I had a physical, met with my social worker and had a therapy session, which was very good. I'm feeling lost on another planet.

BEA

Back in New York, I sleep well for the first time in months.

The next day I tell Mike, "It's strange, I feel guilty saying it, but I'm actually relieved that Pamela's not here."

He looks at me, stunned. "I feel the same way."

PAMELA

August 30, 1998

Had a pretty good weekend, went to the movies both Friday and Saturday nights. I also went shopping at some thrift shops and bought a teddy bear, which is cozy to sleep with.

I also went to church, which was good for me.

Teddy called and said something that upset me. Actually, it was about our future and my place in it. I don't see myself anywhere, my mind is going crazy. I cut myself all over my left arm. I did go to the nurse to get some meds to calm me down, which she gave me. I am sorry for doing it but can't help my impulses.

BEA

These past few days Mike and I have been undergoing a slow decompression. He's back at the office, concentrating on his work, and

I'm trying to make sense of what I should be doing. It feels good, and strange at the same time, to be separated from my sick child . . . sort of like playing hooky from my responsibilities as a mother.

Still, the phone rings at least three times a day, and I always catch my breath at the sound of Pamela's voice. Mostly, she's just checking in, but this time, I can hardly make out what she's saying.

"They're giving me Klonopin," she whispers into the receiver.

"Speak up, Pam, I can't hear you," I say, raising the volume.

"The nurses took my razor away because I cut myself pretty badly," she says.

"Oh, no! What happened?" I ask with trepidation.

"I was upset over something Teddy said," she explains.

"Well, I'm glad you went to the nurse," I say, trying to reinforce a positive behavior. "That's what they're there for, to help you."

But this isn't the response she wants and she quickly changes the subject.

"Are you and Dad coming up next weekend for Labor Day?"

I'm caught off guard and feel cornered. If we go, we're doomed because we'd be repeating a pattern of running every time she asks us to, and if we don't go, there's a good chance Pamela's self-destructive behavior might escalate.

"Pamela, we already agreed to wait two weeks and come up on your twenty-first birthday, remember?" I ask, wondering if she has a hidden agenda.

"But, Mommmmm," she whines in a child-like voice. "This place is going to empty out for the holiday, and I don't have any friends here yet."

"Let me discuss it with Daddy and I'll call you back tonight," I say buying valuable time. There's something inside me that fears saying "no" to Pamela. I'm too afraid she'll hurt herself.

Even though I know it's wrong, I still try to convince Mike that we should drive up to Stockbridge.

"What else do we have to do this weekend?" I ask. "We can go for a quick day-trip – to give Pamela something to look forward to."

"It doesn't matter that we have nothing else to do, Bea, we just can't keep giving in. Pamela is too far away for us to run back and forth on a whim. The doctors tell us she needs to learn to manage herself – even if it means having setbacks. Let's stick to our original plan to celebrate her twenty-first birthday with her, and I'll see if someone else can visit her this weekend."

Thank God for my husband – he always has a solution.

PAMELA

September 3, 1998

Don't know exactly how to put my feelings into words. My father is not a bad person. I love him, but his lack of attention toward me drew me to loser guys.

God please help me to stop harming myself. I don't know why I do it, I really don't.

September 9, 1998

When I was two or three years old, I was the happiest little girl. I loved to play and sing and dance. I remember being so outgoing. This is what I want . . . I want to be three again. I was so cute and everyone loved me. It was a wonderful feeling to have everyone's attention and love. I was able to wear cute, little adorable dresses. I can look at pictures of myself at that age for a very long time. They bring me joy and sadness because I can never be that little ballerina again. I feel as though my life – at least my happy life – is completely over with.

BEA

"Cheers!" Mike, Pamela and I clink plastic flute glasses filled with Bellinis – a champagne drink that Pamela sipped once from my glass, and absolutely swore she'd have when she turned 21. I brought the fixings from home to make her milestone birthday memorable, in a rite-of-passage sort of way, even though I'm sure she'd rather be partying with her friends.

Instead she's stuck celebrating with her parents in the small room of a hotel across the street from Austen Riggs.

"Happy Birthday," we sing as she opens presents, swats balloons and bounces on the bed in our daintily-decorated room. For a split second, she could be six years old again, jumping up and down with her new Cabbage Patch doll. Her joy is infectious, and Mike and I share in the happiness of the moment.

But the mood suddenly shifts when we go downstairs for dinner in the Red Lion Inn's spacious dining room.

"Can I have a glass of red wine?" Pamela asks.

"A glass of wine?" I repeat.

"Oh, just to get a buzz on? I'm legal now," she says, coyly.

Mike and I exchange glances. "Get a buzz on?" What kid talks to her parents like that? Does she expect us to sit here and watch her get loaded? Mike and I drink wine socially, but never to get drunk, and we certainly have never partied with our children.

"You'd better not," Mike says, shaking his finger at Pamela. "You're on medication."

He's right. What was I thinking giving Pamela a Bellini? She's on Depakote, Prozac, Buspar, Klonipin, Trazodone and Zyprexa. I only wanted to make her twenty-first birthday special, but I never imagined she could have a drinking problem on top of everything else.

"Don't be so naïve. There's temptation to 'use' all around me in this place," Pamela says. "Drugs used to make me feel good."

"Well, do you feel good now?" Mike asks, rather disgustedly. "Look where it's gotten you." Pamela has hit a nerve. She knows her father has zero-tolerance for alcohol or drug users. I sense his mounting anger and step in.

"What do you mean, there's all this temptation to use?" I ask. "Are you telling me Riggs residents take street drugs?" Here I am thinking her experimental use of drugs is in the past . . . maybe it's not.

"It's an open setting, anyone can do anything they want here," she says, to both of us, rolling her eyes.

I'm worried we'll lose her.

Mike sadly thinks we already have.

PAMELA

September 16, 1998

I'm upset with myself for sleeping the afternoons away. I'm so lazy and I'm such an idiot. God, why did You put me on this earth? How can I change? I want to do things I can be proud of. I should exercise like my Latin professor told me to seven months ago. I can't even remember his name. At 21, I'm supposedly an adult. I oppose that suggestion.

BEA

In a four-way early morning conference call between Dr. Spellman, Mike, Pamela, and me, the sergeant-like social worker puts me on the hot-seat.

"You have to stop treating Pamela like a baby," he chastises me.

"Exactly how do I do that?" I ask.

"Well, you told Pamela how well she handled herself during our last conference call . . .you shouldn't praise her for what she should be, which is an adult."

"All of our kids look to my wife for approval," says Mike. "She's the center of the family and tends to be critical of things. She doesn't mean it – she just has the need to point out what she likes, and expects others to follow her lead. If they don't, her disappointment is obvious."

Pamela is noticeably quiet.

I'm shattered to be attacked in such a way by both Dr. Spellman and my husband. "I'm just trying to do my best as a mother," I say feeling more defeated than ever.

"There's a book called *Codependent No More*," says Dr. Spellman. "It explains how to put healthy boundaries between you and Pamela. I strongly recommend you read it.

"Are you suggesting I'm as dependent on Pamela as she is on me?" There is a long pause.

As soon as I hang up the phone, I run to the bookstore.

PAMELA

For the first time in about a week, I felt motivated. I had a nice time walking through town and sitting on the front porch. I am excited because Teddy is coming to visit me this weekend.

In therapy today, I got something out. I am too dependent on other people. I need to find my own voice, have my own opinions. I need to be able to take care of myself and to defend myself. I want that kind of personality. What is my problem? I am such an ass!

BEA

Mike, Paula, Michael and I have been traveling to Riggs every three to four weeks for family therapy session led by Dr. Spellman and Pamela's new talk-therapist, Dr. Frasier. It's no easy task for Mike with his heavy workload, Michael with his travel schedule and Paula with graduate school classes, to drive to Massachusetts for these 8:30 a.m. meetings. But we all decided to make it a priority.

These family meetings are supposed to encourage open communication among the five of us, and support Pamela in her recovery.

In reality, they're like boxing matches, with the therapists waiting to pounce on the first person who opens his mouth. Mike and I have become the easiest targets. Like punching bags, we're accused of being too controlling, projecting our feelings onto Pamela and victimizing her with our expectations. We're not numb to these punches – every jab hurts.

For the most part, Pamela remains silent and lets us duke it out on our own. When she does speak up, her comments are thick with resentment.

"Why did you hang a 'Do Not Enter' sign on your office door when I was little?" Pamela asks me during one of these sessions. "It made me feel like you were too busy for me and I had to go away."

Caught off-guard by her version of this memory, I think long and hard before responding.

"Well, I didn't do that all the time," I say. Turning to the doctors, I explain that I worked at home as a free-lance journalist for a local newspaper. Then I turn back to Pamela.

81

"I only put the sign up maybe one or two hours a week, when I was interviewing someone important on the phone, and didn't want to be interrupted by one of you looking for the pencil sharpener, or Twinkies – and remember it's hard for me to hear."

What I don't say, and what Pamela failed to notice is that I worked from home, not at an office. It was the 1980s, and very few moms we knew had home offices then. At times, my family poked fun at me for putting up a sign, but the truth is, I was trying to be a professional while still being a stay-at-home mom.

Pamela backs off me and turns her attack on Mike.

"I can't believe you actually go to the store and pick out greeting cards to send me now that I'm sick, since you didn't pay much attention to me when I was growing up."

"I'm sorry you feel that way," her father says. "Don't you remember how many times I ran home from work to watch you play basketball and volleyball? What about the elephant collection I brought you from around the world and our weekend trips to the record store?"

"I was never the center of attention in our house, it was always Michael and Paula who got that," says Pamela, "and now that I'm getting it from both you and Mom, I don't want to lose it."

What troubles me, as she begins to express herself in family therapy, is that she feels she's been abandoned. She believes I abandoned her by putting a sign on my door, saying that I was working. She believes her father abandoned her by going to work. In actuality, she was no more abandoned than our other two children, who did not interpret our actions so negatively.

During a short break, Dr. Frasier pulls Mike and me aside.

"We've completed a psychological profile on Pamela, and it shows she's more angry than depressed. Our aim is to get her to talk about what makes her angry so she won't rely on 'cutting' as a coping mechanism."

"It's not easy . . . we aren't bad parents, and yet Pamela sees us that way," I say, trying to hold back tears. She remains stone-faced.

Upon reconvening, Dr. Spellman speaks.

"We think, Mrs. Tusiani, your hearing problem, which we've noticed during family meetings and conference calls, may be the cause of Pamela's not speaking up."

I can't believe what I AM hearing. I look at Pamela and her eyes dart sideways. "Just because I wear hearing aids and often ask people to repeat themselves, my daughter is afraid to talk?" I respond. Now I'm angry.

These therapists are pathetic! First, I baby my daughter too much. Then, I am fostering codependency. I abandoned Pamela by working at home, and now my hearing loss is rendering her mute. I guess they have to justify their salaries by conjuring up cockamamie theories, but this one crosses the line.

PAMELA

October 18, 1998

Hi! I'm at The Shop and I don't know how to get onto the Internet, so I will try to write something on the computer worth saving.

It is October 18, 1998 and I am in Stockbridge, Massachusetts, staying at Austen Riggs Center. I have been here for about two months and am very unsure about how I feel. I am depressed. I have actually had depression since I was a child. Now that I'm 21, I feel as though I should be on top of my life, but I'm actually at the bottom, trying to break free from all of the pressure keeping me down. All I do is sleep these days. I try to feel better on the outside but my insides are burning with anger and sadness. I want to cut and burn myself, but haven't done so in a very long time.

Why is my life so complicated? So harsh? So unbearable? So disheartening? I am really, really trapped. I feel as though I don't want to live. Where do I go from here? This isn't how I intended to be.

BEA

Pamela's anger continues to mount in our next conference call.

"Everyone in the family ignored me. I came home drunk and stoned every night during my last summer of high school, and no one knew it," she says.

My head spins.

"I thought that summer was the happiest of your life!" I say. "The phone rang off the hook – someone called for you every night. I believed you when you said you were going to a friend's house or to the pizzeria. I had no idea you were drinking and doing drugs."

When Michael was in high school, I was aware of the keg parties taking place around the neighborhood, and regularly snuck to his room to smell his breath after he'd fallen asleep. But it never occurred to me to do the same with Pamela – for some reason, I trusted her, just as I did Paula.

"I wanted to get caught," Pamela says in an unusually rebellious tone.

"Well, we did catch you that one summer after your junior year in high school. Remember that?" I ask.

In that instance, I heard the front door open late one night and I heard Pamela stumble up the stairs to her room. She was moaning. I knocked on her door for a full ten minutes.

"Pamela, are you okay? Open up," I said with increasing anxiety. The commotion woke everyone in the house.

She finally unlocked the door, then immediately rolled backwards onto her bedroom carpet. When Mike pulled her up, I noticed the open buttons on her pants.

Her gait was wobbly and she had a hard time focusing. Mike put her arm around his neck and walked her into the kitchen where all four of us started peppering her with questions.

"What did you drink?" I asked. She looked back at me in a daze.

"Did you take anything besides alcohol?" Mike asked.

I snapped at him, incredulous. "How can you even think that?"

To stem the escalating argument Mike and I were about to have across the table, Pamela found her voice.

"Zima," she slurred.

Mike and I looked at each other and hunched our shoulders. We had no clue what she was talking about. Paula, who was a Resident Assistant in college, explained that Zima was an alcoholic drink sold, like beer, over the counter.

Mike was heartbroken to see his baby girl in a drunken stupor. He plied Pamela with coffee, walked her through the house, and when she was sober enough to understand the consequence of her actions, grounded her for two weeks.

I learned what really happened that night, just before Pamela's nervous breakdown. We were staying at a hotel in Baltimore when she complained of having frightening flashbacks about that night.

"It wasn't Zima. I don't remember if someone gave me something, but I blacked out. When I came to, I was naked and felt as though I had been raped ... but I'm not sure. It's haunting me."

Surely this is the crux of Pamela's secret torment. She was sexually abused at a young age ... she should be angry ... but not at us. We didn't know. She didn't tell us. She didn't talk about it then and she won't talk about it now. But I blame myself for not questioning her further. I saw her pants were open.

PAMELA

October 22, 1998
The cuts made all over my neck and wrists are hurting ... throbbing with pain. I'm angry, but can't figure out why. It's confusing.

BEA

Immediately after the next conference call, Pamela calls back to say she tried hard to slit her wrist with a razor because she's not being taken seriously at Riggs.

In New York, we were the bad guys because she felt we were not paying attention to her 24/7. Now, in Stockbridge, the therapists are the targets of Pamela's unspoken anger.

"This alignment, pitting one against the other, seeing one as good and the other as bad, is called 'splitting'," Dr. Spellman explains. "It's parents vs. therapists, Mom vs. Dad, sister vs. brother, boyfriend vs. boyfriend, everyone is either black or white, there's no ability to see shades of gray. It's a typical trait of Borderlines."

I wonder how Pamela's brain can be wired to judge people that way?

85

It drives a concrete wedge between Mike and me.

Pamela thinks I'm the "good" parent for always being there, and Mike is the "bad" parent for working. Will she always look at him as "black" and me as "white", without seeing us as more than one-dimensional?

No matter what Mike does for Pamela – calling five times a day, sending cards, flowers, money – it's never enough. She always has a negative opinion of him despite his unconditional love.

She resents that he spends so much time on his business and travels, but that's because he's passionate about what he does. Ultimately, he's working hard for all of us. Pamela doesn't realize we wouldn't be able to afford the kind of care she's getting without it.

It's hard for me to watch him trying so hard to win her affection and love. I hope she can accept it, and see she's still Daddy's little girl.

PAMELA

November 9, 1998

To Teddy

Sitting on the green mountain
With the half-moon shining,
My lips are enlightened by your fervor.
That night, a rose left at my door
With a note . . .
Two years later, the rain hits my cheek
In shades of purple.
You walked long and hard for that flower,
And I will be here endlessly to find it at my doorstep.

Big problems! Teddy and I fought tonight over our relationship and we decided to talk again in two days. I called Hank and we were on the phone for about an hour. I miss him and I don't know why. I want him so badly, but at the same time I love Teddy. I am confused: I love Teddy and sexually want Hank who is really haunting me. God, what should I do?

86

Just before Thanksgiving, a friend and I drive up to Canyon Ranch Spa in Lenox, Massachusetts, for a three day stay. It's ten minutes from Riggs. I figure it would be a good opportunity to get away before the holidays and spend some time with Pamela. She seems down since her break-up with Teddy, and I'm hoping a few day passes to the spa will lift her mood.

After a few days together in such an idyllic setting, I easily fall into old habits, and give in when she asks to come back with me to New York for the weekend.

"Weekends at Riggs are so lonely," she says, with her big, sad eyes.

How can I say no? My daughter just broke up with her boyfriend of two years, and I suddenly feel bad for her. I know how much she cared for Teddy and relied on him for support.

But I'm nervous too, because Mike, Michael, Cathy (Michael's girl-friend) and I have been invited to a Redskins football game in Washington on Sunday. I tell her that we'll be away for the day and express my concern about her being alone in the apartment.

"Why don't you come along with us? It'll be fun," I say, morphing into cheerleader mode.

"You go ahead, Mom," she pleads. "I can meet up with some of my friends from the Columbia Day Program. I'll be okay. Don't worry."

I feel like a rag doll being pulled in opposite directions: nervous about leaving Pamela, yet mindful of her co-dependence on me, and her therapists' warning that I need to treat her like an adult, not a child.

Thankfully, Paula comes to the rescue. She reassures me she'll be in her apartment on the West side, studying, should Pamela need company while we're away.

After an exciting Redskins win, which gives me the opportunity to let off some steam and get to know Michael's new girlfriend, the four of us are in good humor as we head to our apartment by taxi.

"Don't get out," the doorman tells us. "I just drove your daughters to the emergency room at Lenox Hill."

"What on earth . . . .?" I scream.

"Pamela overdosed on pills," he says, with eyes downcast.

Our cabbie steps on the gas and makes a sharp left toward the hospital.

As we tumble through the emergency room door en masse, I immediately spot Paula, her face streaked with tears. Beside her, in bed, half draped in a hospital gown, is our precious and unconscious Pamela, her lips black from a "charcoal shake." We all start to bawl and wail.

"The 'friends' Pamela was supposed to meet from the Columbia Day Program turned out to be Hank," says Paula. "Pamela came back to the apartment drunk after seeing him, and overdosed. She called me, but I could barely understand her. She kept repeating, 'I did something stupid.'"

Paula had jumped in a cab, and when she got to the apartment, Pamela was lying on the floor in her bedroom, moaning. Paula picked up a bottle of tranquilizers on her nightstand and started shouting at her.

"Is this what you took? How many? Pamela! Do you remember how many?"

When Pamela didn't answer her, Paula called our doorman, who happened to have his car parked out front, and he drove them to the hospital.

It feels like we're in *The Twilight Zone*.

Pamela started going out with Hank during her senior year in high school, when he was already a college freshman. At the time, a friend of mine, who had a son who grew up with Pamela, told me she wouldn't let her son hang out with Hank, but she wouldn't say why. I thought that was strange, and I became suspicious.

One day while I was cleaning Pamela's room, I came across a letter Hank had written to her. In the letter Hank confided that he was suicidal, needed to talk to someone about it, and would be going to smoke pot at some local hangout on the weekend.

Trying to keep my wits about me, I waited for Pamela to come home from school to confront her about it.

"I found this letter from Hank. He's suicidal and using drugs? This is not the type of person who you should be dating."

She grabbed the letter out of my hand. "This is none of your business," she said. "Stay out of my room."

I was stunned at her boldness.

There was a moment of frozen stares between us.

"Mom, Hank is a good friend. I can help him stop the drugs," she said convincingly. "You have to trust me. I'll even go and ask Dr. Regan how to handle it."

With that, she marched out the back door and went to our next door neighbor, who was a psychologist, for advice.

I believed Pamela sincerely wanted to help Hank, but I was uneasy about the influence he was having on her. She had started listening to music by Rancid and Nine Inch Nails, talked about mosh pits at concerts and bought a pair of black combat boots. She even started burning sticks of incense in her room. I watched with fear, as a dark side of Pamela began to emerge that I hadn't known existed, and I naturally connected it to Hank.

What I know now is, Pamela's relationship with him flourished shortly after the Zima incident, the night, she recalls, she was sexually abused. Whatever happened that night – to her body, her psyche – was traumatic. She latched onto Hank like glue, changing her music, her friends, her style. Maybe he made her feel safe and protected after being abused? I'll never know. But what I do know is, my sweet, innocent daughter was not the same person after she met him.

That bad feeling resurfaces now, as Pamela lies unconscious in a hospital bed with three red hickeys on her neck.

When she eventually comes around and is able to talk, a psychiatrist is at her bedside, acting to protect her interests, while Pamela tries to explain why she overdosed.

"I love Hank, and know you don't," she tells all of us, "so if I can't have both of you at the same time, I might as well be dead."

"But you told me yourself, he uses drugs," I say, trying to remain calm.

"Taking drugs was my fault, not Hank's," she says defiantly. "I went looking for cocaine, crack, weed and ecstasy and blamed it on him. He broke up with me because he wanted to stop."

I can't believe what I am hearing. My daughter took crack and ecstasy? She lied to us, and played us for fools? As it turns out, we are.

Mike seems to be handling this better than me. He pulls me aside.

"The stakes are too high, Bea. She might try to overdose again. I know this is hard, I don't like it either, but there's no other way. We don't want to lose Pamela over this. Even though I'm against it, we have to accept Hank into our lives."

And without further discussion, we do.

Two days after being readmitted to Riggs, and despite our acceptance of Hank, Pamela's overdoses again, on Excedrin. This time, an ambulance rushes her to Berkshire Medical Center. It is her seventh hospitalization in nine months.

PAMELA

November 24, 1998

It's hard to believe what I did on a weekend pass. I am in a very difficult position now. I don't feel close to my family and they question my credibility.

I went to see Hank and feel psychologically in love with him. Is it love? I feel I need him. There is such a void inside of me, I can't live without it being filled. My parents aren't doing such a great job with it.

I want Hank to call me again tonight. I want to talk with him all night and dream about him. I want to make love to him . . . be held in his arms. Can I be on my own and be so in love at the same time?

BEA

All of us, including Uncle Joseph, drive up to Riggs to take Pamela out for Thanksgiving dinner. We decide, after two suicide attempts, it's safer for Pamela to be at Riggs, than home for the holiday.

After we return, we try calling her, but are unable to reach her. We keep dialing the payphone on her floor, and it rings incessantly. Eventually, someone picks up and tells us Pamela left on a bus for New York.

I am enraged. We were just there two days ago to celebrate Thanksgiving, and agreed it was best for her not to come home for the holiday weekend. Now, she's taken off, by herself, on a bus, in her mental state, with our money – on her way, Mike and I surmise, to see Hank. For what? Sex? Drugs? I can't tell anymore whether she's sick or bad. How can we stop her from ruining her life?

I go into Pamela's bedroom to search for Hank's phone number.

"We're very worried about Pamela, she's on medication," Mike tells Hank, in an uncharacteristically calm voice. "It's the busiest weekend of the year and she's off traveling from state to state right after two overdoses."

"Yes, Pamela was here, but she's already on her way back to the Port Authority Bus Terminal," Hank says.

Mike gives me the thumbs up. I close my eyes with relief. I know she's okay.

"We don't want her to think we're hunting her down or put you on the spot like this, but our main concern is her safety," says Mike, somewhat apologetically. For Pamela's sake, I'm sure he's holding back what he really wants to say.

"I'm concerned about her too and wish this wasn't happening," Hank answers. "We were young and did things that were stupid, but it's not like that anymore."

PAMELA

November 29, 1998

I went to see Hank this weekend. I felt I couldn't be here (Riggs) by myself. That is going to change! I am going to be independent!

I am so sorry Dad and Mom, please forgive me. I am so sorry God, please be with me and help me change.

> *Tanned by the perfect sun,*
> *Two imperfect souls*
> *Exchanged joy and laughter.*
>
> *His wide eyes look*
> *Up toward the pert,*
> *Sparkling yellow sunflower*
> *That she resembles . . .*
>
> *Petals open and she*
> *Jumps into his arms.*

Embraced . . .
As water splashes.

Surrounded by screaming
Sounds of celebration,
How powerful it seems
To be loved with gentle care
And never-ending peace.

BEA

It's a cold, brisk morning, just before Christmas. As I walk down Fifth Avenue, I see shops decorated with snowflakes and santas, but the yuletide atmosphere feels alien compared to the universe I'm living in. Everyone seems to be in the spirit of the season, bustling by with their shopping bags and dropping cards in the mailbox with a sense of merriment. I don't have the energy or desire to send cards this year, and shopping is the last thing on my mind.

This is a day when I should be happy. Paula and I are meeting at a bridal salon where she'll try on white satin wedding dresses with long trains and lacey veils, a moment I've always looked forward to.

I want to share Paula's exhilaration – it's wonderful to see her so happy and in love with Roger. But every time I look at her I think of Pamela, who is falling apart someplace else.

New crises are occurring in Massachusetts at a dizzying pace. This time it's not only cutting and drug abuse, but sex. Over the past two weeks, I find out from various sources that Pamela has slept with three different guys and a girl at Riggs.

Unable to control her sexual impulses and erratic behavior, she ends up twice in the emergency room where, on top of everything else, she is tested for HIV and pregnancy.

I'm momentarily distracted from this living hell as I walk through the doors of Saks Fifth Avenue.

"Hi, Mom," Paula says, as she grabs my arm and pecks my cheek. "Isn't this so exciting?"

PAMELA

December 14, 1998

There was once a girl who was scared of basically everything. Starting something new and different was something she cried and cried over. She never would go anywhere or anyplace by herself. She needed someone to accompany her so she wouldn't be so anxious and upset. Her mother was the person she trusted most and she is very dependent on her for most everything, even walking on the street. She is scared to walk down the street by herself but she forces herself to do it.

BEA

"Mom, put Dad on speaker phone," Michael says in a phone call a few days before Christmas. "I just spoke with Pamela.

This can't be good.

"You know Lenny's Bar, the seedy joint two blocks from Riggs?" he asks.

"Yeah," Mike says, "it's just past the Red Lion Inn, right?"

"Yes. . . . well Pamela went there the other night, bought herself mixed drinks and shots. Two guys offered her pot and she smoked it. Then they took her to a field. She blacked out and doesn't remember how she got back to Riggs. She thinks she was raped. The doctor gave her a morning-after pill and she'll be staying at the nurse's station until after the holidays."

"Pamela was raped? Is she okay?" I plead.

"Well, she sounds calm on the phone, but I'm sure she's scared. There's no way she asked for this, Mom. I believe she knows right from wrong, and she was clearly violated."

With mounting anger, he continues, "Dad, you're spending thousands of dollars a day, and they're supposed to keep Pamela safe. What are those doctors doing up there letting Pamela go to a bar and get raped?"

"That does it," Mike declares, feeding off of his son's frustration. "I'm calling Dr. Grayson to find out why this was allowed to happen." Dr. Grayson is the head of Riggs.

93

I'm equally frustrated. We've been brainwashed by the administrators at Riggs about how good an open facility is, because it allows mentally-ill patients to recover in a real-life setting. But they never tell you about the bad things that happen when someone, driven by impulsive behavior, has more freedom than she can handle.

I'm mad at my daughter for going off the premises to drink, but I'm even madder at the facility for giving us a false sense that Pamela would be safe there. And I'm beyond furious at the lowlifes who took advantage of a girl clearly out of her element and out of her right mind.

"We have to go up there," I say. "She must be in a state of shock."

"No," Michael says. "Pamela wants me to come and says I can bring Cathy but she doesn't want to see you and Dad."

I'm crushed. "Why?"

"She's afraid to face you."

Days pass and nothing more is said about the rape. When we try to bring it up at the next family meeting, Pamela doesn't want to talk about it. There is a long silence. I look at Mike, he looks at Pamela. She's looking out the window ignoring our advances, while Paula and Michael shift uncomfortably in their seats.

Considering all we've been through, it's hard to believe she's not communicating with us. We make sacrifices to travel to Riggs, many times a month, early in the day, to talk about her problems and support her therapy, but find ourselves stalled by her unwillingness to open up.

She sits among us like a statue, using her silence as a shield, and I don't recognize the daughter I once knew. Her refusal to talk has put her in control of these family sessions, and thereby in control of us, even though she's lost control of herself. She's gone. The only thing I'm sure of is, she's my flesh and blood.

CHAPTER 4

Stockbridge

Q: The records suggest that it was sometime during her high school years that your daughter began to drink alcohol; is that your understanding as well?

A: Yes.

Q: When did you become aware that your daughter was drinking alcohol?

A: There was one incident when she was in high school that she came back late one night and she looked like she had taken something. We put her at the kitchen table and we gave her coffee. We grounded her for two weeks and that was it.

   Subsequently when she was in therapy I found out that she did a lot of drinking and we were not aware of it during the time.

Q: Despite that fact you did consider yourself to be close to her, your daughter, during her grammar school and high school days?

A: Very close to her.

Q: Apparently she was able to conceal this drinking from you for a period of time?

A: Yes.

Q: Did you ever learn of anything in therapy about how it was she concealed her drinking from you in terms of when she would drink, how she would conceal it?

A: It came out in therapy that once, one summer when she was working in a children's camp, every night she said she was drinking with her friends. She never looked drunk to me. I never smelled liquor on her breath, so in effect, she concealed very well what she was doing.

Q: Would she have had access to alcohol at your home? I mean is there regularly alcohol at the home, like a bar?

A: We had a bar.

Q: Did you ever notice whether any alcohol was missing from the bar *that you weren't able to account for?*

A: I never did.

Q: Did your interaction with her in terms of amount of time you spent, did it decrease when she went to high school?

A: She went away to high school so she took a bus every day. But because she was in after-school activities I had to meet her and bring her to her games. However, because the other two children were away at college, Pamela and I wound up eating together and spending a lot of time the two of us.

Q: How would you describe the quality of your relationship, the closeness of your relationship with your daughter in high school as opposed to the way it was when she was in grammar school?

A: It was much closer in grammar school. Because in high school I would assume, like most kids, they are trying to assert their independence. And in her senior year she had the use of a family car, so she did more things on her own at that point.

PAMELA

February 14, 1999

From this day on, my life is going to change. I am ready to do some serious work on myself. I will not drink or drug anymore. I am not going to continue to be intimate with Jerry. He is struggling – I want to love him and hold him and kiss him, but I also have to think about our treatments and how they are in jeopardy.

It's hard not to have a Valentine today, but I will try with every bone in my body to get up and go snow-tubing tomorrow and help get myself together.

BEA

I'm looking on Mike's desk for a wedding invitation when a small white piece of paper catches my eye. In his neat, evenly scripted handwriting are contact numbers for The Retreat in Vermont and Sierra

Tucson, in Arizona. Both are drug and alcohol rehab facilities Dr. Spellman told us about as a result of the latest crisis.

Pamela was caught yesterday doing drugs with Jerry, a new patient from Boston who is depressed. She told us he was a nice fellow, and we hoped he might be a stabilizing influence on Pamela. But what our daughter failed to include is, Jerry's a crackhead. Both of them were found buying crack from a former Riggs patient.

The staff is meeting right now to determine whether they can remain at Riggs, or will be discharged and sent to rehab because of their stupidity.

Neither Depression nor Borderline Personality Disorder can be treated effectively while she's doing drugs – that has to be resolved first in rehab.

But, Arizona? It's so far away. It would be so hard for us to visit, meet with the doctors and stay connected to what's going on. Everything hinges on whether Pamela can attend regular AA meetings and remain drug-free.

Mike is on his way up to Riggs now for a meeting with the head honcho. I couldn't bear to go with him. Pamela's using crack – CRACK – and there's no way I can defend her anymore. She's throwing all the progress she's made down the drain and will have to live with the consequences, even if it means having to go to Arizona.

But can we live with the consequences?

PAMELA

February 18, 1999

I am allowed to continue my treatment here. Jerry just left this morning: God help him through his struggles. Dad is coming here later for a meeting with Dr. Grayson. I am nervous and don't want to cry anymore though I deserve to. I hope this community can be a loving and safe environment for me.

February 19, 1999

Today was a difficult day. I am really hesitant to trust myself, I don't know what honesty is because I can never tell if I'm being truthful. I know

97

I lied about smoking crack to my mother, but I don't know if I lie when I say I am going to reform. It's what I want but can I really make it happen?

February 26, 1999

I threw two dishes on the pottery wheel today, which makes me very happy. It feels good getting my hands wet with clay and making beautiful things with my own hands. It's amazing.

I've been sober for two weeks now, please God help me to be sober for the rest of my entire life, which will be long, hopefully. I want to live!

March 3, 1999

I am now in my double bed located on 70th Street in New York City and actually feel happy! Thank you God for everything . . . please help me with this relationship with Jerry, I don't want to hurt him but he has to stop calling me and telling me he loves me. I guess I want someone who is there for me, but not Jerry.

BEA

I smile. It feels like old times. Pamela is chasing our dog, Lulu, throughout the house. The routine is always the same. The two of them carouse wildly and drop to the floor. Then Pamela covers her face with her hands, and the dog nuzzles her way in to plant slobbering kisses all over her lips.

Pamela has changed in many ways, but – unlike the rest of us – her faithful companion hasn't noticed any of it. And Pamela seems to relish the dog's devoted attention. Perhaps it's the one constant in a world turned topsy-turvy.

I wish I could freeze this moment. Seeing Pamela happy makes me long for the child I knew so long ago. The Pamela who sang Karaoke in the shower; the Pamela who surprised us with mounds of fresh baked cookies; the Pamela who took cannonball leaps into the pool.

That same Pamela has been sober nearly three weeks now, and although I don't want to jinx any short-lived progress, I quietly savor the moment . . . which is soon interrupted.

"Mom, I'm thinking it's time for me to step down to The Elms," she informs me.

"Really?" I ask, guardedly, not knowing what's coming next.

For five months, Pamela has been housed in the main building at Riggs – The Inn – where all health-related and therapy services are located. When patients are ready for more independent living, they can apply for a spot in an adjacent group-home, The Elms.

How do I respond? I know she's seeking my approval.

While she has made some healthy adjustments since regularly attending AA meetings, I don't think it's wise for Pamela to rush into a new living arrangement without thinking it through. But, I also don't want to seem unsupportive, or have my words misinterpreted, so I do what the therapists tell me to do, and put the ball back in her court.

"Well, what does Dr. Frasier say about this?" I ask, empowered by *Codependent No More*.

"Uh . . . ," Pamela stalls. "I haven't asked her yet."

PAMELA

March 8, 1999

My mouth is hurting, I got my wisdom teeth pulled out three days ago. It was nice to be in New York with the family. I'm back at Riggs now and feel lonely. I really want a boyfriend – someone to fall in love with and who will hold me. I called Teddy and told him I missed him. It was probably a mistake. I must focus on myself.

March 10, 1999

Dr. Frasier is leaving on vacation. I had my last session with her this morning. God, help me get through the next week without her. She kind of feels like my best friend right now.

I had a dream last night that Hank came back to me and loved me. It felt really good but I think of it as a nightmare because I woke up and the dream ended.

March 24, 1999

I am very anxious to find out if I can move into The Elms. I'm approved but Laurie also wants Elms and she had her application in before me. I want to move there so badly, please God help me, there have been too many disappointments lately.

I wish my relationship with Mom and Dad gets better. I am so angry with them. I miss being in love . . . or lust. I want to be in love.

March 25, 1999

I am moving to The Elms. Thank You, God. But now I am nervous. I'm so confused because I am telling people that I am bi-sexual, even though I'm not sure myself. I am attracted to women but don't know if I want to be with them for a long time. I like men too. I hope I don't get a bad reputation. People might think I'm weird. Everyone is weird here.

BEA

No sooner have I pulled my car into the back parking lot at Riggs, than Pamela runs out to greet me. I am here because she has asked me to help her move from The Inn to The Elms. I can't say I'm as excited about it as she is. After all these months, I've learned that no environment will seem stable enough for Pamela. It's got me in a constant state of flux. But I want to be optimistic, so I have come prepared with packing boxes, ready to roll up my sleeves.

I follow my daughter up the rickety stairs. I haven't been in her bedroom for awhile, since we generally meet in the reception area on the first floor. I'm hoping it's not a mess. The last thing I'm in the mood for is having to clean up her leftover food and dirty underwear.

She opens the door, and my jaw drops. The walls are covered in an explosion of color. Dozens of drawings are taped haphazardly above the bed, on the closet doors, and around the mirror.

I walk around the perimeter of the room to take a closer look. I see a girl with a blank face, one with no eyes, a young woman wrapped in chains, and another crowned with thorns.

Blood is spouting from a spiked rose in one drawing, from a crucified body in another. There are sketches of young couples drinking, smoking and having erotic sex.

Reading what is written on them is even more disturbing.

"I am on empty, please fill (pump) me up . . . Rancid waste spewed all over myself . . . what is the easiest way to fuck myself?"

I flinch, realizing these jarring words and scathing images come from my daughter's hand. They depict what she can't say out loud. They're angry and dark and reflections of how she views herself. Maybe the therapy is unlocking what has for so long been buried deep down inside of her.

Still, these images are so profoundly painful, it hurts to look at them. Pamela is silently watching me.

"Do you like them?" she asks.

I gulp. "I had no idea you were so talented," I say. "I know you do pottery, but I didn't realize you could draw too. How did you learn?"

She shrugs. "I don't know, I just bought a pad and started to sketch."

I'm blown away by this burst of creativity that seemingly came out of nowhere. It's thrilling to know that Pamela has an outlet for expressing herself through the images she creates, and some of it seems frighteningly good. Maybe when she gets out of this place, she'll be a famous artist and look back at these days as part of her destiny.

PAMELA

March 30, 1999

I am going crazy. I want to kill someone and make love at the same time. I know that I'm struggling and I will be for the rest of my life. I can cry every second of every day if I let myself. I am so pissed at Jerry, I want to tell him off so badly. He is such an asshole! I want to fuck Hank so badly it hurts. I want someone to hold me and love me. Help me God, please.

April 7, 1999

I went to Barnes & Noble with Peg, Jaimie and Gil and looked at a lesbian book with pictures of female couples loving each other. So what happens now?

BEA

Dr. Frasier begins the family meeting with a topic that sends us all reeling. "I think we should begin by addressing the anxiety Pamela is feeling surrounding next weekend's shower."

Pamela's eyes pop. Paula squirms in her seat.

She let the cat out of the bag.

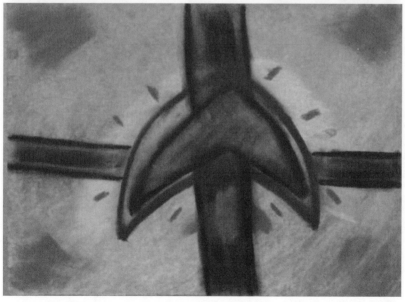

MY WORDS RESEMBLE LADY BUGS IN HEAT HOT, THRASHING, FIRING FUCKING LETTERS IN A STRAIGHT LINE MAKING INCOHERENT SENSE

"I don't know what you're talking about," I say, trying to salvage whatever surprise is left of the bridal shower I've been planning for Paula over the past few months. I am so angry I want to lash out at the woman, whose stupidity is beyond belief.

Where's her common sense. . . to blow the whistle on a surprise shower, that she learned about in a private therapy session, when the BRIDE is in the room?

You can hear a pin drop. Dr. Frasier and her cohort, Dr. Spellman, offer no apology, no human empathy for this insensitive blunder. Instead, they sit back and coldly observe the rest of our reactions, like we're a scientific experiment.

We're not lab rats that can be poked and prodded for research. We're a real family with real problems and feelings – all five of us. Sometimes, I wish these doctors would understand that. The point of family therapy is to encourage open communication but what just happened here is unethical.

Planning this shower has been a good diversion for me. Getting caught up in its details has helped me overcome the disappointment of cancelling my follow-up surgery because of Pamela's repeated crises. Plus, sending out invitations and hearing back from friends and family excited about the celebration, has provided a semblance of normalcy amid all the chaos in our lives.

I'm furious at Dr. Frasier but don't express it, because Pamela is already showing signs, through her jittery body language, of discomfort and self-recrimination. And none of it is her fault.

PAMELA

April 13, 1999

Dr. Frasier spilled the beans about Paula's surprise wedding shower at our family meeting. I feel awful, like I'm fucking up this whole wedding.

Last night I was so angry I wanted to cut but I painted my face with black eye-liner and mascara and spiked my hair and listened to Metallica songs. I looked evil.

Today I told my friend, Eve, that I want to be closer to her. I hope that was a good decision on my part. I don't think she's interested in getting that intimate with me – I don't know if I should be intimate with anyone other than myself right now.

BEA

Pamela is home for Paula's shower and a small part of me wishes she had stayed at Riggs. I know it's selfish, and I feel guilty about it, but just for a few hours, I want to be a normal "mother of the bride" without the burden of having to worry about Pamela.

The party is being held at my friend Ellen's house, in Manhasset. Ellen and I have been friends for twenty years, and she offered to host and help with some of the details. The whole planning process has been a welcome distraction for me, and I just want it to go well with Paula and her new in-laws.

Despite my mixed emotions, I have to give Pamela credit. After last week's family meeting ended in disaster, she could have let her anxiety get the best of her and gone off to cut, or drink, or do drugs. She could even have made an excuse not to come, but she's trying to do the right thing. Pamela loves her sister, and genuinely wants to be the maid-of-honor she's expected to be. That's progress isn't it?

PAMELA

April 22, 1999

Paula's shower was very hard. I spent most of the time in Ellen's bedroom.

I want to cry now. I've been hooking up with Joe and I don't even think he likes me. I'm such an asshole, I want to cut.

April 24, 1999

It's 12:25 a.m. Saturday night and I'm waiting for a 17-year-old boy to come out of his room and rescue me. I am going mad. My laundry is in the dryer.

I could have gone to a lesbian dance tonight but I chose not to because of the alcohol and drugs and sex that I would probably have a hard time resisting. Will this void inside me ever be filled?

> *All alone, in the deep, dark night, waiting for some hint of relief.*
> *I feel endless buckets of emotion.*
> *That is all I can do – feel, hurt, think, cry.*
> *I hate feeling. I hate longing.*
> *I hate lonely days and despise lonely nights.*
> *I can hear the sorrow dripping from my heart.*
> *I can feel anguish creeping through each muscle of my body.*
> *I can see the wind blowing me down and can touch the wrinkled skin on my burned arm.*
> *Bound by layers of dripping clay wrapped tightly around me,*
> *What do I do now?*

BEA

"They told me I'd only be at Riggs a month or two and already eight months have passed," Pamela tells Mike and me during a phone therapy session. She sounds frustrated.

"It's a process," Dr. Spellman interjects, "and you can't rush through it."

After we hang up, Pamela calls back to talk to us privately.

"I've been in The Elms two months and feel like I'm stuck. I can't stay here forever, I have to move on with my life," she says. "All my friends are graduating and I still have three semesters of college to finish."

Our ears perk up. It's great to hear Pamela talking about going back to school, but we're cautious.

"Do the doctors think you're ready for that?" Mike asks.

Pamela tries another angle to make her case.

"You always worry about what the doctors say. Don't you see what's going on? They don't want me to go back home. Riggs knows you have money and that's why they're keeping me here. They're using you Dad."

It's unusual to hear Pamela speak to her father so forcefully, especially since he's no pushover.

"You could be right. You always have good instincts when it comes to doctors," he says. "But you've made a lot of progress at Riggs. You're sober now and you're staying out of trouble, your meds seem to be stable too." He's thinking. "If you want to come home, and you feel that you're ready," he continues, "you have to come up with a plan that the doctors' support, and we will support it too."

PAMELA

April 28, 1999

I just got off the phone with Mom and Dad. They support my wishes to discharge in the upcoming months. I feel the need to break free from Riggs and experience life on my own, even though it's the scariest thing in the world.

They also support my plans to get an apartment and attend Fordham, going to therapy, etc.

I am really excited! I want to move on with my life. God, help me through this. I know my emotions go up and down. Please, give me the strength I need to prove to myself that I can do it and do it well.

BEA

Pamela is at her lowest weight ever. Clothes she once filled out nicely, now hang loosely on her tall frame. Her face seems tinier and you can wrap one hand's fingers around her upper arm. She attributes this to having to shop for and cook her own food at The Elms, but the rest of us are not convinced.

"She looks so thin, Ma," Michael tells me after a family meeting. "How can her body tolerate all those medications if she's losing weight?"

Paula has her say too. "If she keeps up like this, I'll have to return her bridesmaids' dress, again, for a smaller size. And her hair gets shorter and shorter every time I see her. What will she look like walking down the aisle?"

I commiserate with my children, but don't know what to do, other than raise their concerns at the next family meeting.

PAMELA

May 3, 1999

Dr. Frasier doesn't support my idea of discharging so early. I was really mad, but then Dana asked me to move in with her in her apartment, so I quickly changed my mind and am really excited about going into day-treatment. I know this plan is better. I really hope Dr. Frasier agrees.

BEA

Pamela is using Mike as a ping-pong ball. First she begs him to sublet an apartment in New York because she expects to be discharged. Then she asks him for rent money so she can move in with her friend Dana in Lenox, Massachusetts. He's so confused, he doesn't know what to think.

"Pamela can't go to New York yet," Dr. Spellman explains to Mike in a private phone call. "She has an eating disorder that needs watching. Starving is another way Pamela is using her body to express herself."

I sit down and cradle my head in my hands. Three months ago, it was drugs, now it's an eating disorder. When Pamela manages to control one self-abusive behavior another surfaces to take its place. It's so bizarre and upsetting. Is it her brain or her will that is making this happen?

Dr. Spellman recommends day treatment. Pamela can live off campus with her friend while she continues at Riggs as an outpatient.

PAMELA

I am in Dana's apartment. All my stuff is basically moved in. I love it here though I'm not approved for day-treatment yet. I don't see why not. Mom and Dad came to visit this afternoon for Mother's Day. God bless my great Mom and I love you Nanny with all my heart. God bless Cathy, Theresa, Deborah and everyone in need. Thank You for creating me. I can't believe I just said that! Do I really want to exist?

May 11, 1999

Had a really hard day. Team was tough on me. They think I should stay at The Elms to deal with living with others whom I feel uncomfortable with (John, Joe). I understand I have a big problem with friendships, relationships and intimacy. Team does not recommend I move to day-treatment but they approved it anyway.

BEA

I marvel at the way Pamela convinces her doctors she can do what they don't think she's capable of. They said she wasn't ready to move from The Inn to The Elms, but after speaking to her, they approved it. Then they tell Pamela she's not ready to go into day treatment, but she's managed to talk her way past that hurdle too. What mystifies me is, Pamela uses language so eloquently to make a case for herself before the doctors, and yet hardly speaks during family therapy. There are two sides to her personality, and I can't make sense of either one.

PAMELA

May 12, 1999

I bought $60 worth of groceries but probably won't eat much of it. I'm 118 pounds, so according to the scale I bought today, I lost 12 pounds. Do I care? Do I want to impress my family, or Lauren or Allie or Kristie?

I just don't want to eat. Maybe I'm punishing my body for all the crap I use it for – sex, drugs, exotic dancing. My body is a tool, like a screwdriver. . . . I screw people with it . . . I screw myself with it. Am I beautiful? Am I worth it to the world to be here? What are my motives?

May 14, 1999

I miss Cathy. I hope her graduation goes well for her tomorrow.

I suppose I would be graduating too, if things worked out as planned, but I'm learning more here than I could have ever learned at Loyola.

> Pretty as the Slow winds blow
> The days come and go.
> Raspberry smiles and scattered tears
> Divided on this turbulent highway.
> Smeared illusions and dusty fantasies
> Stand crooked up a spiny hill,
> Slanted and curved with fever.
> Bolts of lightening strike down hard.
> Angry rushing fire warps
> The internal destruction swimming through
> Infinite microscopic wires twisting in my mind.
> A hammer smashes harshly against my cranium,
> Cold, red blush fancies my raw skin.
> Chattering teeth, quivering hands.
> I want out!
> But freedom is simply a nightmare
> I wake up to every day.
> Invisible shackles embrace my feet.
> A vice tightens around my head.
> Silence envelopes me just as some new mother
> Holds her baby boy
> In the grape fields of a remote place
> Referred to as the "real world."
> I can see something small,
> It's wrinkled and tattered.
> It could take centuries to get to.
> Yet, some stranger said that it's
> Right across the street.

May 25, 1999

I eat less and less each day. Today I had 300 calories. I was weighed by the nurse tonight and was 114 pounds. My parents are really worried about me. I feel so horrible putting them through all of my symptoms.

What's going on with me? Will it ever stop? My life is a twisted circle of destruction.

BEA

I'm nervous about what I'll find as I drive up to see Pamela's new living arrangement. I'll be meeting Dana for the very first time, and for all I know, she could have blue hair or be a former heroin addict.

It seems the people Pamela befriends at Riggs look different from what we're used to. They have body piercings, tattoos and spiked hair – as if their tough exteriors hide their inner turmoil.

At first, it disturbed me. I didn't want my pretty daughter to be influenced by that group. I feared she might become one of them. In some ways, she already has, for in recent months she had her tongue pierced and dyed her hair a gothic black.

I'm starting to get used to it, the way a parent who drives her daughter to dorms in the West Village at New York University must be used to being surrounded by a strange cast of characters. After a year and a half of shuffling Pamela in and out of psychiatric facilities, very little surprises me anymore. I've come to understand it's not appearances that matter . . . and that has become the new normal for me.

Still, I can't help but wonder what Dana will be like, what her story is, what she's struggling with, and how it will become woven into our family's life.

These thoughts quickly dissipate when I pull into the two-level, chalet-like apartment complex and see a family of ducks skimming across a pond. Three small ducklings are following their mother, calmly, obediently, in search of food. They nuzzle their beaks under her wing, and I realize I'm witnessing a tender moment between a mother and her flock.

If only raising children were that simple. Fifteen years ago, Michael, Paula and Pamela followed me around the house, waiting to be fed, begging for my undivided attention. I miss those days, when life was not fraught with complicated issues like eating disorders and depression.

Just yesterday, I stayed up half the night preparing chicken cutlets with peppers, stuffed artichokes, pasta salad – all of Pamela's favorite dishes – in an effort to get her to eat. She's wasting away before my eyes, and I can't just let it happen.

I'm relieved when she throws open the door and a broad smile spreads across her face when she sees the food.

"Oooh, Mom, chicken cutlets. Thanks so much," she says as she lifts the lids off the plastic containers, checking their contents.

"Dana, look what my Mom brought us," Pamela says, motioning for her to come out of her bedroom.

The petite young woman with curly blonde hair, and no tattoos, dispels all the dark images I concocted about her in my mind.

"Hi, Mrs. Tusiani. It's nice to meet you."

I'm pleasantly surprised at how engaging Pamela's new friend is, and how helpful she is to Pamela, who's unpacking the food.

"Nice to meet you too, Dana. There's enough for the two of you. I hope you'll have dinner together and make sure Pamela is eating," I say, with a wink.

Pamela hears this. "Mom, stop," she says.

"Don't worry, Mrs. Tusiani, we'll eat everything, I assure you," Dana says. She sounds sincere and I want to trust her.

There's a good karma that surrounds Dana. She may be dealing with her own demons, but she seems more stable and normal than any of Pamela's other friends at Riggs.

Maybe this new environment, without the constant flow of doctors, nurses and patients to remind Pamela of sick people, will actually turn out to be the best medicine for her.

PAMELA

June 1, 1999

I talked to Hank yesterday. I'm forever in love with him. We decided to talk again in a month or so. Hearing him made me very happy. He does care about me and I want things to work out. I am going to try my hardest to figure myself out and my relationships with other people.

I'm also starting Eating-Disorders group tomorrow.

June 4, 1999

I just left a message on Hank's machine and feel like an asshole. I did not live up to our agreement. I wish I could be calm, but now I'm worried he'll be mad. I feel like a stalker. What is wrong with me? Ups and downs, I hate them!

I feel sad now. Four months sober though. I ate three meals today, which was hard.

June 13, 1999

I am really nervous about this week because Dr. Frasier is away.

I called Hank tonight and we talked for two hours. I love talking to him. I love him. I'm not sure if I should tell my family or not.

Hank needs two weeks without me calling. I really want to live up to it, if not, we won't be together. It's also a good thing for me to learn that people have boundaries and not everyone is going to do what I want.

BEA

When Dr. Frasier takes a vacation, so does Pamela. She comes home and reconnects with Hank. I'm seething over this and say so at our next family meeting.

"I don't understand how you can be with this person when you have nightmares about him," I say.

"I can't live my life and be fake to please you, Mom. He's been coming up to Lenox to be with me, and no matter what you say, we are in love," Pamela responds with equal defiance.

"You did drugs together, Pamela – I'm not stupid. You've admitted that yourself. Daddy and I are paying a lot of money for you to get treatment, to have an apartment in Lenox, are you going to risk your sobriety for him?" I'm really angry. "Going out with Hank just makes you dependent on someone else for your happiness. You're going backwards, not forward."

Dr. Spellman slices the air with his sharp tongue.

"Mrs. Tusiani, Pamela is a grown woman, and you should stay out of her personal affairs."

What a jerk. I have a right to my opinion when it comes to my daughter and her affairs. I'm the one who has to clean up the mess when there's a problem, not him.

Of course Dr. Spellman is protecting Pamela. She probably painted me in her private therapy sessions as a judgmental mother who won't let her daughter date whoever she wants.

Maybe she even told him about my initial disapproval of Paula's dating Roger. They met when Paula was barely out of high school and he was already out of college and working at his first job. Their five-year age difference concerned me because Paula was going off to college and Roger was interested in a serious relationship. At the time, I tried to persuade Paula to play the field and not date Roger exclusively, but she wouldn't listen.

Is a mother not supposed to guide her children on these matters? In Paula's case, it turned out she was right, and her relationship withstood the test of time. Pamela knows this, and that's her bargaining chip with Hank, even though the foundations of the two relationships are worlds apart.

I realize I can't win this argument with any amount of logic. "Fine," I say, "but you'd better not bring him to the wedding. I don't want to feel uncomfortable – that's Paula and Roger's day, not Pamela and Hank's."

"Don't worry, I won't," she says.

For some reason, I don't feel relieved.

PAMELA

June 21, 1999

Family therapy was a nightmare. I'm really angry with my mother. Sometimes she is just so off the mark. She doesn't understand why I'm so messed up in the head. I suppose this is because I told them that I've been talking with Hank. Mom said she never liked him and never will. It doesn't bother me, I'm just glad to get it out because I'm not going to lie anymore.

I feel so dependent on my parents, I hate it! It's all about money. If I had any, I would be free. I don't think they will ever understand or accept the way I am. I will not tolerate having to put on a facade for anyone. I need to accept myself – fuck whatever anyone else thinks!

God bless my family and everyone in need of Your love. I want Hank to be in my life, I believe he is good for me. I hope I am right.

BEA

"Mom," Pamela's voice sounds weak on the phone.

I brace myself for the "needy" Pamela.

"Is everything okay?" I ask.

"I really want to come home. Dana's out and it's so lonely here," she says.

As an out-patient, living in her own apartment, Pamela is lost without her roommate. It's not as if she can go and hang out with fellow patients in the game room or the kitchen or the library at The Inn, as she used to be able to. She's on her own now, and needs to learn coping mechanisms outside the facility. Loneliness has always been Pamela's greatest challenge. I suppose that's why she attached herself first to me, then to Teddy, now to Dana and Hank.

"Why don't you watch a movie or draw something until Dana comes home," I suggest, trying to redirect her attention.

"I'm really not up to it," she says.

"Pamela!" I say loudly, trying to jolt her out of the blues. "How are you ever going to live by yourself in New York if you can't get through a few hours without Dana in Lenox?"

The receiver clicks.

She could be cutting herself right now in retaliation for my comment, but I don't have the stamina to call her back to find out if she is.

PAMELA

June 27, 1999

11:40 p.m.
I am tired and sick of being trapped in this web of depression and anxiety. Ten months at Austen Riggs has done a lot for me but I would really like to think that someday I will be satisfied.

My life is so messed up. I don't want to be a mental patient in Stockbridge anymore. Why couldn't it have worked out that I could be ready in August to go back to New York? I've been dealing with this shit for too long. I don't want to "hang in there" or "take it step by step". That sucks!

It is torture to feel anything, to be anywhere . . . I need a vacation from myself. I want to be productive. I want to mean something to myself. How long will it take to feel some comfort?

Would going to beauty school or having a pet make me feel better?

I'm scared of staying here. It's too isolative and secure. Getting used to it will just make me want to avoid dealing with life. I have to deal with this shit every second. I want to move on. Spending my time in therapy and talking about my issues all the time is supporting and I am grateful for it, but it's not what life is about.

I do not want to be impulsive. I want a plan. I can't take listening to everybody tell me what is good for me. I appreciate that, but why can't we work on getting me back into some sort of possible lifestyle? Please do not go off on a tangent Dr. Frasier, this is what I want to discuss. Please help me!

BEA

Five weeks before the wedding Paula sends us a long email.

Hi, Mom and Dad. It's 3 am and I can't sleep. I'm so upset about this morning's session. I never said "Mom has bad taste," and last week, she twisted what I said about Dad. Pamela's taking things out of context and using my remarks to drive a wedge between me and you.

I am trying to console myself by saying that she is sick and can't control it, but after experiencing these attacks against me in the last few sessions, I'm fed up. I know I have my weaknesses and that I'm not perfect, but I do love you and am worried these sessions are straining our relationship.

It's obvious this whole wedding is stressing Pamela out. I feel totally responsible for asking her to be my maid-of-honor. I also feel totally selfish for focusing on my own happiness and wedded bliss right now, instead of her pain.

I keep telling myself that if we accommodate her and be flexible, it will be fine. But even if I include her (as I want to do) she is not happy for me. She is not excited. She is nervous. She is angry at everyone who is invited and she will carry that anger with her that day. There's nothing I can do to make the wedding a pleasurable experience for her. She is mad that the attention is on me. She thinks I am angry that she will destroy my wedding, which I am not.

Michael says I should ask her not to be my maid-of-honor, but will that bring more resentment toward me in the future? Rather than make any more mistakes, I'd rather take the risk and include her.

Why does Pamela have to make you doubt my sincerity or my love for you? I love you very much. I have too many things to worry about right now and don't know what do to. Basically, I am writing because I feel so bad about what this whole thing with Pamela is doing to my relationship with you. It's causing so much unnecessary pain. It's not fair.

I hope you don't think this is crazy, but I can't talk to anyone else about what I'm feeling right now. Sorry for babbling. Love Paula

PAMELA

July 11, 1999

Happy Anniversary Mom & Dad!
My weekend went better than expected. Hank came up last night and spent the day here – it was great to be with him. We're both in love with one another. This is a new relationship and is already so different from the past.

July 12, 1999

Family therapy was frustrating as usual. I hope my family can come to accept Hank because he is a part of my life that I enjoy and treasure. I wish that my mother and I could be happy. I don't want to hurt her anymore, but I also can't hurt myself in order to please her.
Tomorrow I start work at Gatsby's. Please help me God.

July 13, 1999

I was very upset to see Cassie being brought out by paramedics on a stretcher. She apparently jumped off the roof. This is something I cannot deal with – I need to get out of here. The sick shit that is going on is definitely not therapeutic.

BEA

I stop in Great Barrington to pick my daughter up at the end of her shift at a new part-time job at Gatsby's. It's a clothing boutique with funky-style clothes for hipsters – right up Pamela's alley.

She's a clotheshorse, whose sense of style is always a step ahead of the latest trends. Custo t-shirts are Pamela's "must haves" at the moment and I offer to buy some for her. Using her employee discount, she flashes me a big smile while ringing up the sale. I smile back. We both recognize the progress she has made.

It strikes me how comfortable Pamela is, as she walks among the racks assisting customers. The owner seems equally comfortable having a mentally-ill patient from Riggs working in her store. I'm so grateful to this kind woman for trusting my daughter and giving her a chance to re-enter society. I hope New Yorkers will have the same compassion.

PAMELA

July 20, 1999

I had a great weekend with Hank.

I don't want to go to work at Gatsby's. It's so boring. All I do is walk around and button shirts and smile and try not to yawn.

What Lies Beneath

Gliding across the surface,
Floating, unaware
Of what lies beneath.
Rather – frightened of the depth –
The creatures, the sand.
Terrorized by the pull tide.

Confront the dark secrets,
The hidden passageways,
The large coral reef . . .
Touch its coarseness.

Look into the eye of each fish.
Start with one slowly.

BEA

We're sweltering through the worst heat wave of the year. It's Paula's wedding day, and the mercury is a record 100 degrees. But you'd never know how stiflingly hot it is looking at Paula – she's radiant. I've never seen her so happy.

I, on the other hand, am trying to stay cool tending to last minute details. What I'm really sweating over is Pamela.

Right up to the last minute, we give her the option of backing out as a maid-of-honor but she remains determined, for her sister's sake, to make it through the day.

Despite some initial jitters at the church, the ceremony went surprisingly well. Now, at the reception though, I'm worried about the free-flowing liquor being served in every corner of the room. It would be so easy for Pamela to fall into her old patterns, especially with all the anxiety that led up to this moment.

Instead, Pamela manages to steer clear of it, choosing to express herself in another way. With the first downbeat of the band's lively rendition of Ricky Martin's "Living La Vida Loca," Pamela flings off her shoes with abandon and takes to the dance floor.

With hips swiveling and hands held high, she becomes what she has always craved to be – the center of attention. Paula, Michael, Roger, Cathy, her cousins, me – we all get caught up in the revelry and dance along with her on the Conga line, doing the Macarena. It feels like old times, when Pamela didn't need to drink and do drugs to be happy, and I want it to last forever.

PAMELA

August 15, 1999

Time passes quickly, especially the last month. Being together with Hank has been really good. I love him so much – we were made for each other.

I wish I liked myself better though, sometimes I just can't stand myself – how I am and the things I do.

BEA

Right after the wedding, Pamela redoubles her efforts to discharge from Riggs. It seems every conversation we have now is about her coming home to New York, starting at Fordham and living on the West Side.

I have my doubts. Though her eating has improved and she's working at Gatsby's and has remained sober all these months, I'm still worried about her adjusting on her own in a new environment.

"If living with Dana has taught you anything, it's that you do well when you live with someone," I say to her, trying to convince her to reconsider whether it's a good idea to live alone in the apartment Mike sublet for her in Manhattan. "Maybe you should think about an arrangement where you have a roommate."

"Don't worry, Ma," she assures me. "I'm an adult. I'll be fine."

I fear what she's not saying is that she expects Hank to keep her company when she finally gets her own place.

PAMELA

August 25, 1999

Feelings are exploding everywhere. Dr. Frasier and I decided on a discharge date of October 1st. I can say at this moment that I love myself.

Tomorrow marks one year here and I'm glad, for my life has totally changed. I have five more weeks to spend thinking about scary things. I feel sad having to leave friends I made here and all the nurses who have been so wonderful to me.

BEA

I just got off the phone with Dr. Spellman. It's our last conversation before Pamela's discharge from Riggs. We spoke at length about the progress she has made over the past 13 months. She's no longer cutting, drinking or using drugs. She's not suicidal or using sexual relationships to escape her feelings. And she's better able to communicate as an adult, through art, writing and language.

I take notes, so I won't forget what Dr. Spellman says about handling Pamela in the future. I feel it's important to share his advice with the rest of our family, so I write them a letter.

Dear Mike, Paula and Michael,

I spoke with Dr. Spellman today, and this is what he said:

At some point, Pamela lost the ability to manage urges and impulses. At first, it was chronic, then it became acute. Over the past year, she has continued to have impulsive break-throughs, though they have lessened considerably in the past six months. What she has been learning at Riggs, is how to recognize these impulses and reduce them by managing and understanding the stimuli that serve as triggers.

At Riggs, the psychiatry and psychological support system have helped her plumb the depths of self-awareness through self-discovery of her unconscious; have assisted her in managing herself and her expressions of behavior; and have helped her develop ways of speaking about her feelings through the use of language.

If there should be a setback, and in the next year, there is a very good chance that will happen, don't flip out. And don't fall into the trap of expecting conditional responses from Pamela – that will only victimize her.

Instead, swallow hard.
Take a deep breath.
Hug each other.
Look to the future, not the past.
One day at a time.

I hope this will serve to remind you, as it will me, how to help Pamela in her continuing struggle to find happiness and self-fulfillment.

Love,
Mom

CHAPTER 5

New York

Q: Let's move on to her high school years. Again, was there any significant change in your work activity or time you spent working during that four-year period?

A: That four-year period would be '91 to '94. I would, upon reflection here, I would say slightly more business activity during the period. Because we had the Gulf War in 1990, and the effects of it. So that period was late grammar school, probably early high school, a little more difficult pressing time.

Q: I understand. From talking to your lawyer and other things you produced, your company is in the business of shipping and has to do with petroleum products. And that would be a time frame that would be significantly stressful and an issue for you during the Gulf War, would that be right?

A: Your question was, I believe, did you spend more time. I would say probably during that period of time the answer is yes.

Q: Did your travel increase in terms of how much time you spent away from home during that four-year period on average?

A: I'm not certain.

Q: Can you recall any events during that four-year period that you were unable to attend?

A: I recall one specific incident, and I think I was reminded of it, and that was missing a father-daughter dance in high school, which she was looking forward to and I missed it.

Q: Was this something, when you say you were reminded, was that something you were reminded of during later therapy sessions?

A: Yes.

Q: During this four-year period, how would you characterize your relationship with your daughter? Obviously it would have changed in some senses because she is a mature young woman. Now tell me how you would characterize it.

A: I think it was good. She was still Daddy's little girl. I probably treated her in a little bit more special way than I did the others because she was the baby.

Q: Your wife told us yesterday about when your daughter had come home and had been drinking and was disciplined for that; do you recall that incident?

A: Yes.

Q: Were you aware before that incident that your daughter had been experimenting with alcohol?

A: No.

Q: Did you have any information, aside from what you later learned through therapy – at any other point in time did you have any information that your daughter was abusing alcohol?

A: No.

Q: When you did learn that in therapy, that was a surprise to you?

A: Yes.

PAMELA

October 10, 1999

    Today is the 10ᵗʰ day home in New York. I'm in my new apartment on West 64ᵗʰ Street. Living on my own is tough. I am very lonely. I do feel a great sense of freedom though, something I have longed for since I was young, but it's not all I thought it would be.

    Freedom to me was being able to have the TV all to myself, then it became being able to have friends over (and not worry about my Mom and Dad). I thought it would be so cool to be able to party all the time in my own place – have lots of friends, drinks, drugs, sex and cigarettes. I couldn't wait.

    Well, Pamela, it pretty much sucks because you can't do all those "cool" things. I am depressed ten days out of a mental hospital. It's like a huge tornado sucking me in. I'm the only one who knows about it, who feels it clenching my throat.

    I can't eat, have no appetite at all. And Hank is going to break my heart, I can feel it coming. He is confused and can't handle a girlfriend – me! I am hurting.

125

BEA

Like Pamela, I'm both scared and excited about this new development in her life. If she were healthy, I'd have no qualms about her moving out and living on her own as Paula and Michael did.

As I did with them, I go to Pamela's new apartment to scrub the toilet bowl and put fresh sheets on her bed, but this time it's very different. There are bottles of pills and prescriptions to be filled. At this point, Pamela is on Serzone, Buspar, Trazodone, Prozac and Klonopin, as well as Retin-A and topical Erythromycin for her acne. Lining up the small plastic containers in her medicine cabinet, I worry how she will keep all of them straight.

I catch myself momentarily and realize she got it straight when she lived with Dana. Dr. Spellman's voice suddenly pops into my head. "She's an adult and you should treat her like one. Don't baby her or set her up for failure."

I need to back off. So I begin to focus instead on the fun part of the move – lining the pantry shelves, filling the refrigerator and organizing the drawers.

Cleaning the big picture window in the living room, I stop briefly, and glance at the tall skyscrapers that will be Pamela's new view on the world. This is no lazy Stockbridge, Massachusetts. This is New York City, full of gray concrete, hectic activity and noisy traffic. It's a tough, scrappy environment. I don't know if Pamela can survive in it alone.

I did it, but I was made of sturdier stuff when I was a fresh-faced 18 year old looking to prove myself at Hunter College. I was the first girl in my family to pursue a higher education. (My dad wanted me to be a secretary like my sister, but I told him I wanted to go to college like my brother.) I was hungry for knowledge and pursued my dreams as if I had something to prove to my father and myself – as Pamela is trying to do now. But is it really the same?

"Hey Mom." Pamela suddenly brings me back to the present.

"I need to get a shower curtain and some lamps. Want to go to Urban Outfitters?" she asks.

I grab my wallet, and we head out the door.

PAMELA

October 11, 1999

I am thinking of calling Teddy. God help me, I just did! I'm sick to my stomach. I hope I don't throw up.

I love Hank but he is scared of me. I would love to meet the woman of my dreams — we would be so close mentally and physically. Maybe, I want a boyfriend as loving as I see my brother is with Cathy.

Pain is such an awful feeling, it fills every cell in the body and can eat you up.

October 12, 1999

So I was right ... my heart is broken, or maybe I'm just pissed that I was rejected (by Hank). He can't handle having a committed relationship right now. Fucking bullshit!

I thought I'd get lucky if I went down the block to Fordham and sat in front of the building, but no one looked twice at me. I buy a Lesbian magazine thinking maybe I just need a new kind of relationship.

I want friends but don't know how or where to make them. Life is definitely a double-edged sword. God, make it worth living. Someone, love me tonight.

BEA

Mike calls me from a cab.

"Bea, Pamela and I are on our way to pick you up. Then, we'll head to her place and get a bite to eat."

Thinking nothing of it, I run downstairs. But I freeze in my tracks when the cab door opens and I see Pamela in the backseat huddled over a cardboard box. In the box is a tiny gray kitten.

Everyone, even the cab driver, who seems to be part of the conspiracy, waits for my reaction. Mike already knows what it will be.

Just last night when he told me he wanted to fulfill Pamela's latest impulsive wish to get a cat, I said, "Are you out of your mind?"

"It'll keep her company, Bea, it'll be good for her, especially since Hank isn't in the picture, you'll see," he said.

I'll see? I'll see what?

"We don't even know yet if she can take care of herself, let alone an animal that has to be fed and cleaned up after and taken to the vet. It's a big responsibility, and if it doesn't work out, there's no way I'm going to take care of a cat. I hate cats and they make me itch," I added, as if he didn't already know that. What a scatterbrained idea.

So I feel betrayed when, 24 hours later, I'm ambushed in a cab with this tiny creature mewing on Pamela's lap. It seems my husband and daughter have found a special way to bond, at my expense. I am not amused.

"I know what you're thinking, Mom, but I can do this, I really can," says Pamela, stroking the little creature's tufted neck.

"I hope so," I say through clenched teeth.

PAMELA

October 20, 1999

Mom is next to me on my bed. She came over to comfort me. I'd rather not be alone since I heard that Eva, a patient at Riggs, committed suicide. She was so nice and loving. Why? Such a horrible, unloving act. Her pain must have been heavy, but such extreme measures? God bless her . . . which is confusing to me because she murdered herself . . . a deadly sin! I pray for her soul.

I got a little kitten yesterday, Angelina (I named her after Angelina Jolie). I love her and hope she learns to love me. She's scared so I guess we're kind of similar.

Pray for Bess' soul.

October 24, 1999

I love my little Angelina, she's so cute. On the other hand, Hank, whom I'm trying not to think about is a real A-hole! Well, maybe not, but it's easier to hate him than to understand him. I want to be happy I don't want to cry! Why am I me?

BEA

With another two and a half months before the spring semester at Fordham starts, Pamela is looking for a part-time job to occupy her time. I'm happy to see she's filling out applications for Barnes & Noble and Tower Records, but Mike soon comes up with an idea of his own.

"I think it would be less pressure for Pamela to work at my office where she'd be in familiar surroundings and people would understand her special needs," he tells me privately. "Don't worry, Zach doesn't work there anymore. He left a long time ago."

"That's not the point," I snap back. "Don't you see, you'd be rescuing Pamela from having to find a job on her own? She needs to think and act independently, that's what Dr. Spellman and Dr. Frasier told us. It's better for her self-esteem."

We both think we know what's best for Pamela. In fact, Mike and I have been fighting a lot about it lately. This comes out in our monthly phone calls with Dr. Spellman, who continues to follow Pamela's case and support us during her transition.

"You and Mr. Tusiani should be in parent counseling to help you figure out how to handle your day-to-day interactions with Pamela," he advises us. "Never respond to urgency with urgency. For instance, it may not necessarily be wise for Pamela to be working in a relative's office. If you were in counseling, you'd be advised to wait a week and think carefully about it before giving her that option."

At his suggestion, Mike and I make an attempt at parent counseling, but after just one session, in which we are told what we need is not "parent counseling" but "couples counseling" to resolve issues between ourselves, we don't go back.

Despite our squabbling, Mike and I actually have a solid relationship. We get our points across to each other without losing our sense of self or being intimidated by each other. A therapist may interpret this as problematic, but somehow, the two of us know that focusing on our own relationship would draw us apart and we need to stay together and be on the same page if we want to help Pamela.

So we decide to seek counseling from professionals in different ways. I switch from seeing my own personal psychotherapist to one who specializes in BPD, while Mike continues to reach out to doctors for guidance about Pamela's treatment.

It's not perfect, but we manage. I still don't think it's a good idea for Pamela to work in Mike's office.

PAMELA

October 26, 1999

I spoke at the Fireside AA meeting today about my loneliness and about how it makes me want to drink. It felt good to talk about it.

Anyhow, something happened at the baseball game tonight ... I smelled weed and my heart started pounding.

October 27, 1999

Couldn't stay the whole day working at Dad's office – FAILURE! I just wanted to crawl into bed.

Hank came over and broke down. He's in a lot of pain. I want to be there for him if he will let me into his life.

November 1, 1999

Okay, so I had a really horrible weekend and didn't cope as well as everyone expected. I drank – breaking my almost 9-month sobriety and smoked a little marijuana. Two puffs got me rocked. I danced all night. Could have picked up a girl. Talked to a lot of people. Met this one guy dressed as a hippie, he was really nice though, stopped me from smoking more dope. Thank you, Keith, whoever you are.

Yesterday I was angry, pissed off and feeling like I was really going to kill myself. My wrists were bleeding and I was sitting in the bathroom yelling at the kitten to "go away!"

I could have cut deeper. Thoughts raced through my mind ... death, life, family, friends. I called Dad and asked for help.

"God, grant me the serenity to accept the things I cannot change, the courage to change the things I can, and wisdom to know the difference." Keep going back ... it works ... you're worth it! You're worth it!

BEA

Pamela has had a setback. Mike tells me she called him two days ago asking for help and he took her to see her therapist.

"You did this without telling me?" I ask, stunned.

"She didn't want to worry you," he says. "She went to a bar and had a few drinks and smoked some pot, but she realized it was a mistake. Don't make a big deal out of it."

It dawns on me that Mike is being fooled by Pamela the way I once was, and that she is pitting us against each other.

I try hard, the next time I visit Pamela, to focus on something else.

"What fascinates you so much about Angelina Jolie?" I ask, looking at the many photos of the actress Pamela has strewn about her. Most of them are of the young, seductive drug addict Jolie portrayed in the movie *Gia*.

"I like how fearless she is," says Pamela, who glues Jolie's evocative photos onto cigar boxes and in scrapbooks.

Pamela has taken up scrapbooking to help fill the long stretch of empty time she spends in her apartment. She's working on multiple projects at a time. I'm drawn to one in particular that's titled "I Love You Daddy."

"What's this?" I ask, pointing.

"Oh, I'm making a Christmas present for Dad," she says, as she rifles through piles of old photographs.

I'm surprised. From time to time, since she's been sick, all I've heard Pamela say about her father is he doesn't give her enough attention, hasn't been there for her, and controls the money. Maybe this sudden outpouring of affection shows that Pamela recognizes the softer side of Mike since he helped her with Fordham, the apartment and getting the cat.

Just the other day she called him in a panic, which is unusual, she usually calls me when there's a crisis. She's starting to lean on her father more and more.

I pick up the black construction paper book and turn each page slowly so as not to smudge the freshly applied glue. It's filled with memorable photographs of father and daughter.

One of them is inscribed with purple ink: "Two imperfect souls exchange joy and laughter. I know I was your little girl. I don't forget that and don't want you to either. I still want to be Daddy's little girl, but can't show it sometimes . . ."

Elsewhere she writes . . ."you are the smartest, most loving, giving, accepting and coolest Father I know." And on the very last page are two Polaroid photographs in which Pamela has written on her face with lipstick: "I (heart) U Dad."

I can't believe I'm jealous.

PAMELA

November 14, 1999

Fourteen days sober! AA rule: no relationships the first year of sobriety. Just found that out an hour ago.

Horrific time last night. Went out with my best friend Cathy to a bar and some blond-haired black boy was touching me and telling me how much we could party with all his cocaine. Not good. It was tempting.

Thank you God! I got out of there with Your help. I am proud of myself. Help me not to feel sorry for myself and want to be dead. I have to learn to live in a different way.

*I went swimming yesterday at the Reebok Club. It felt amazing. I want
to keep doing it . . . day by day . . . first things first . . . easy does it. I am
going to fight this!*

BEA

Michael is about to propose to his girlfriend Cathy. He already
bought the ring, and asked her father for her hand. Anticipating the
big announcement, Cathy's mother invites us over for Thanksgiving
dinner as a way for our families to meet. Michael tells me, Cathy has
a big, traditional Italian family from White Plains and we have a lot in
common. As happy as I am for him, I'm a little apprehensive about how
his prospective in-laws will react to Pamela.

When the day comes, we go and try our best to protect Pamela from
prying questions. Someone in our family remains at her side throughout the day-long feast, and we manage to avoid any uncomfortable
situations. That is, until I get up to go to the bathroom and Cathy's
grandmother, the family's matriarch, surprises me in the hallway and
gently whispers in my ear.

"Two of my nine children have similar problems."

I put my head on her shoulder and we embrace.

PAMELA

November 21, 1999

*Michael and Cathy got engaged yesterday! I can't believe it. It's won-
derful. I think it's a little funny how I just got through my sister's wedding
and now Michael is getting hitched. Guess I'm the only one left (pressure
from myself).*

November 22, 1999

*Hank says I want to be depressed. Can it be true? It makes me mad.
I am very functional, yet really scared to feel happiness. What if I'm let
down? I was very close to taking pills minutes ago, but am calmer now.
Thank You, God. Maybe I do have some strength.*

134

December 1, 1999

Cold, cold, cold! Dad bought me a big, warm coat and a suit-jacket for work at his office. He was so upset today, I wish he could relax for once. God, be with him, please.

Work went well today. I think I was very talkative. I want to go rock-climbing at the gym but don't know if I'll actually go through with it. I haven't talked to my sponsor in two weeks, maybe I'll go to a meeting tomorrow.

BEA

Mike gets a phone call from Pamela. She's hysterical.

"Dad, I can't stand being alone anymore. I want my friends to make me feel special, like I'm number one," she tells him in an infantile tantrum. "I want people to drop everything to be with me."

He tries to calm her down.

"Pamela. You know that's not possible," he says in his pragmatic way.

"Your friends have their own lives, they can't be with you all the time."

"Well, what about you and Mom and Michael and Paula?" she pushes on, knowing she's grasping at straws.

"Haven't we demonstrated that we're there for you over and over again?" her father says, exhausted by the mental gymnastics of another mood swing.

"I know, but it's not enough," she whimpers.

PAMELA

December 4, 1999

DO NOT GET HIGH EVER AGAIN! I am an idiot! I must be insane! I hate myself for everything! I am not normal. I go from fine to freak-out.

December 5, 1999

I feel stupid about how I acted last night. I should not doubt my drug problem. I want to be in control of my life.

I just thought that I missed Teddy or Hank or Zach, but I don't. I miss someone who isn't here and never will be.

December 26, 1999

This Christmas has been my best ever, so far. Dana came down from Stockbridge and we had a wonderful time together. I felt really comfortable with my family and "bestest" friend.

I made Dad a scrapbook and he really likes it. I'm glad.

Saw the movie "Girl Interrupted" and cried really hard. I actually saw it with Dana the other day and with Mom and Dad tonight. I really identified with Suzanna Kaysen, a girl who lived at a mental institution for a year, and felt the same things I did. Maybe I'm a girl who was interrupted too? In fact, I know I was.

I'm attending Fordham's undergraduate program next month and I'm scared but also excited that maybe I do have a chance to make friends and fall in love with learning again . . . that I can be somebody and achieve success. Success to me is that day when I will walk through Fordham with my head up, a smile on my face, and my hand waving to someone I know.

I feel selfish for asking this God, but I have to: please show me the path to living free and I will struggle to follow it, no matter what. Maybe I am already on that path, but I expect some stars to twinkle to gain some supernatural feeling of exaltation. It doesn't work that way, I suppose.

There are some dreams that I don't want to come true – but that's another story.

December 29, 1999

I feel crappy. Called everyone I know. I even told Hank that I wanted him to come over. I am such an idiot! Pretending to be an independent woman, fearless and confident.

I am in a cold sweat. Should I go out to some bar tonight? No! I know that drill . . . but still . . . I think it could be different. I don't want to sleep or watch TV, I want some human contact.

I bought a damn outfit for New Year's Eve and don't have anyone to look good for. No chance of love.

BEA

Mike and I are hosting a New Millennium party for some family and friends in a local restaurant. It's been a while since we've had such gatherings. We used to hold parties all the time for the Super Bowl, Labor Day, Fourth of July – and everyone always looked forward to them. But since Pamela got sick, Mike and I have pulled back. It's too hard to see our dearest friends and their children move on with their lives, while ours is still in limbo.

But now that we've seen Pamela handle Paula's wedding successfully, Mike and I feel we're ready to celebrate like old times. And Pamela's all for it.

We hire a DJ and buy glittery "2000" hats and horns.

Pamela shows up at the party dressed in a form-fitting silver outfit and is in high spirits, dancing and singing karaoke. After she finishes a duet at the microphone, she corrals me into a corner.

" Can I have a little drink, just to get a buzz on?" she shouts into my ear so I can hear her over the booming music.

I remain speechless.

"It's the new millennium and everyone at my table is drinking champagne. I feel like such a freak," Pamela says, trying to garner my sympathy.

She's attending AA meetings three times a week and as far as I know, all this time, she's been sober. I try to think what Dr. Spellman might advise.

"I can't believe you're putting me in this position," I say. There's no way I'm giving you permission to drink." And I stare her down until she backs away from the bar.

I give a heads up to Mike that the free flowing booze is tempting Pamela – it's something we didn't anticipate. We've never actually seen her drunk, and the idea of her being a fall-on-the-floor, slurring alcoholic is hard for us to imagine. But now we are faced with the reality of how serious her drinking problem is.

And we thought we were making progress!

PAMELA

January 2, 2000
New Year's Eve was fabulous. My glitter and outfit were a hit. I danced
a lot and socialized so much at the party of family and friends. I felt re-

137

ally comfortable. I did drink though, but got a headache I could have done without. I really don't need to drink to have fun. Realize this point you made, Pam!

At 3 a.m. Hank calls.

We had a wonderful time today together, but I realize that I also felt good New Year's Eve not knowing what would happen. I still don't know what will happen, but that's okay because I want to focus on myself first.

BEA

I'm filling in my calendar for the New Year. I usually enjoy this annual ritual of getting organized. Along with losing weight, it's one of the New Year's resolutions I try to remain faithful to. But this year in January 2000, no matter where the pen lands on the monthly grid of days, my eyes keep going back to the big "X" marked on the 18th. It's the first day of school for Pamela at Fordham. Everything in her life and my life is riding on that date.

Though it is three weeks away, I'm already noticing a change in her. Her anxiety is increasing as her appetite is decreasing. She's having nightmares, headaches and passive thoughts of suicide. By now, I know she always has trouble adapting to change.

Although she says she's excited about signing up for Victorian Literature, American History and a poetry course, her body language says something else.

It's hard enough for a normal young adult to develop self-confidence in college, I can't even imagine what it must be like after having a nervous breakdown. Pamela is afraid of failing again – at school, at making friends, at living on her own – and she's putting enormous pressure on herself, hoping Fordham will be the answer to all her problems.

Her success though, I feel, will depend heavily on whether her professors recognize her potential as a writer and artist and whether she can make friends.

As I focus on that fateful January day, all I can do is pray that it will live up to all our expectations.

PAMELA

January 13, 2000

A lot of things have been stirring up in my mind and body ... things that cannot be explained. If I can't use words, how will I feel different?

I start school next week and am trapping myself in a web of Pamelization, meaning, I freeze up before I have to do things that make me anxious. I need some self-confidence. It's weird how I think the world is a big game and I'm always the loser.

January 17, 2000

Tomorrow is the day of reckoning. I feel better now than I did all day. I was flipping out. Dad came over and brought me some food. Thank God for his love and help. I am not asking for a miracle tomorrow, when I start classes, I just want some sign of compatibility with the people and the school.

BEA

I'm in the kitchen and can't find a pen that works. I go into Mike's office where I know he has a stash of felt-tip markers and am shocked to find his usually clean and orderly desk covered with bills. Thumbing through them, I see Pamela's rent bill, $3,000, then telephone, $39.60; cable TV, $49.55; medical/pharmacy, $507. Plus, $185 per hour for 4x a week talk therapy, $175 per visit to the psychopharmacologist; $170 per session with a nutritionist and an additional $700 a month for my own sessions with a BPD specialist.

I am astounded by the thousands of dollars streaming out of our pockets for Pamela's living expenses and medical care. Mike and I usually don't talk about the dollar value of our daughter's recovery, but when confronted by it, it's overwhelming. I am so grateful we are able to afford it.

Grabbing a marker from under the messy pile of paper, I can't help but shudder at the thought of what other families do, who don't have the same resources.

PAMELA

January 19, 2000

It went all right, but wasn't all I hoped for (of course). I just went to class and then back home. Orientation is today at noon, so maybe I'll be able to meet people.

I ate three meals yesterday and binged late at night on two donuts and a bunch of cookies. I don't want to gain weight. I'm pretty much happy with my figure now, but to maintain it, probably means not eating very often.

BEA

A day later Pamela calls me at 3 a.m. I hear laughter in the background.

"Where are you?" I demand, in a groggy haze.

"In a phone booth outside some bar on Amsterdam Avenue," she slurs.

I'm really upset. How can she have broken her sobriety after all these months?

"Get yourself home right now, and call me when you get there," I yell, slamming down the receiver.

Mike hears the commotion and wakes up.

"What's going on?" he asks.

"Your daughter just called from a bar. She's drinking again."

Mike shakes his head in disbelief and starts getting dressed to head over to Pamela's apartment. As we discuss this latest backslide, the phone rings again. This time he picks it up.

"I'm home now, I'm sorry," Pamela says.

"That apology means nothing to your mother and me, unless you promise to call your sponsor and go to an AA meeting first thing tomorrow morning," he says, totally in command. "Do you understand me?"

"Okay, Dad," she replies, meekly.

PAMELA

Went out with Cathy last night, dancing, and she got the guy I had my eyes on. But it might have been for the best. I met someone named Ken, he seemed really nice, but who knows with my luck?

January 25, 2000

The past two days have been wonderful for me. I had my poetry class, which is awesome – hard, but a great teacher – and I just felt so good about being there and expressing myself.

Ken did call on Sunday and believe it or not, we just parted 15 minutes ago. What a great guy! We ordered Chinese, listened to some jazz, then went to Starbucks and chilled in comfy chairs. I liked that.

We came back here and he kissed me by the door. It was magical – our first date and it ended with a kiss – that's all – the way all first dates should end! It's been awhile, probably three years since I've had this feeling (with Teddy).

January 31, 2000

. . . so Pam freaks out tonight because of an upsetting day when realizing she hates her body and does not want to feed it. This leads to an angry poetry class, a crying session with Dana on the phone and me on the floor covered in a blanket listening to Alanis M., two burning candles glimmering in the mirror.

That is just the beginning! I made the biggest fool of myself on the phone with Ken. We've been out once and I feel the need to tell him I don't want to be hurt or led on. What was I thinking? I'm an idiot. I can't trust that he likes me, but he is calling and wants to hang out with me so that must mean something. I am not rewinding, please, help me not to. Fast forward, Pam. I will feel better. It's just life. Gotta let go.

Tripping Over Empty Space

Valcar, take me away
On your white feathered back.
Hanging, my body swings around,
Unwilling to fall into the throws of realism.

"Do not go gently into that good night,"

Rather, do not go at all.
Stay pinned down.
Hammer me to that door –
The one that never opens.
Lock me up.
I will be safe from the outside,
But not from my mind.

BEA

The whole time Mike and I are at the opera, I'm hoping Pamela is enjoying herself on a date with the new boy in her life. Things are looking up since she met him.

But, when we get home, before I even take off my coat, the phone rings.

"I need help," says Pamela.

"What's wrong?" Mike and I both ask on the speakerphone.

No answer.

"Where are you?"

"Home," she says, and hangs up.

I grab the extra key to her apartment and Mike and I jump in a cab. We swing into the lobby of Pamela's apartment building and mange to get onto an elevator without having to go through security at the front desk.

Up on the tenth floor, we ring the buzzer over and over again. No one answers. Trying not to draw attention to our urgency among neighbors living along the same corridor, we let ourselves in.

The apartment is dark. We call out to Pamela, hear a whimper, but can't tell where it's coming from. Mike flips the lights on and we search the bathroom and closets before Angelina jumps out from under the square coffee table, where we find Pamela, rolled in a ball, hugging her knees, weeping without sound.

She's in a trance. I try to remain calm as I gently coax her out, but spring back in horror when I see what she looks like. Her forehead is seared with a half-dollar-size cigarette burn and traces of a white substance line her lips.

Pointing to a bottle of scouring cleanser, Pamela whimpers, "I just drank some."

142

Reading the label, I see it contains bleach. Mike calls Poison Control and they tell us to flush out her system with water.

"I can't believe what I just did," Pamela says over and over again, blinking her eyes as if waking from a deep sleep. But she offers nothing more about what caused this horrific scene.

Keeping my own hysteria under control, I move into action, clean and dress her burn, make some tea and rub her back. After we realize the worst is over, around 3 a.m., Mike goes home. I stay, sleeping on the couch. But it's impossible to get any rest after what just happened. Besides, I'm startled every few minutes by Angelina jumping up to lick my face.

As the sun rises, I gaze out the window at the vast sky-scape and wonder why our child, of all others whom I know, has been chosen for such a miserable fate.

PAMELA

February 2, 2000

Guess I couldn't let go. I am so angry for trying to destroy myself last night (after I saw Ken). I drank bleach – what the fuck is my problem? I have to be calm and talk it out – not take it out on myself and my family. God, please be with my parents and siblings and Hank. I put them through agony. Mom, I wish I wouldn't do this to you. I promise I will never make you feel like this again.

Four Corners

It is a mechanical beast, and it screams –
Steel against steel, a heavy thundering weight.

Bones, painted with a flesh base coat,
Continue to ache as my cheek presses
Against the hard wooden floor.

Bloodshot eyes, disturbed by a shimmer of sunlight
Peeking through the cracked basement window.
The roaring second-hand of a rusty alarm clock
Pulses like the blue veins impressed in my forehead.

It is a silence of something about to happen.
Broken, at intervals, by another metallic groan as
The beast moves.

The demon nests inside me.
When it wakes, I fall into a trance of violent paranoia.
Blue and yellow pills line up at full attention.
Tempted by distaste,
My heart pumps with thick muddy rage.

Sweat drips from my clenched skin and those
Round pellets begin to swim toward my watering mouth,
An open orifice, unable to spew its waste,
Yet still willing to swallow more.

Fears, spinning in a distorted circle.
Tick, tock . . . tick, tock . . .
Four-eyed suits pointing and laughing
At a tiny dry poker chip in an enormous room.
Destined to stand and spit on every one of its four corners.

BEA

Mike sets up an emergency family session with Pamela's therapist. We are both anxious to discuss her backslide openly and honestly before it gets any worse, but of course, our disappointment in her behavior shows.

"Pamela, why did you drink bleach? Mike asks.

She sits quietly, looking at him with a blank stare. It's as if she's still trying to figure it out herself. Her impulsivity is so far out-of-control, it's hard for her to recall what triggered last night's ugly chain of events.

"Well, something must have prompted it," I say, my voice rising.

Sensing that we're expecting more than cold-stone silence, she finally speaks.

"Things didn't go very well with Ken," she starts off hesitantly, "and I just couldn't take another guy letting me down." She looks away and says, "I'm sorry."

"Sorry is not good enough, Pamela," I say. We've been down this road too many times before.

Gradually, over the last few weeks, Pamela has stopped going to AA meetings, to the gym and her job – all healthy pursuits – and every time we ask why each of these things is happening, all she has to say is, "I'm sorry." Mike and I always hold out hope that it actually means something, but it never does.

This bleach incident makes us realize, that, along with Pamela's "trying," is the "lying" that always undermines her efforts. She says one thing, and does another, and we don't find out the "real story" until there's a crisis and we have to rescue her.

Ironically, the only thing Pamela has been truthful about is school, it's the one bright light in this whole mess. She's thriving academically and is proud of the glowing feedback from her professors on the many papers and poems she's written. But that success hasn't been good enough for her. She still feels like a failure because she hasn't made friends at Fordham. And this lack of companionship compounds her loneliness, driving her to self-destruct as she did last night.

I glance at my watch. The hour is almost up. We've been talking in circles, and nothing has been resolved.

PAMELA

February 13, 2000
Shaky days. I had a hard time eating today but was able to finally. I cried about it.

I did something I haven't done in a long while – daydreamed. Made pretend lives for myself – some strange ones, but some good ones too!

I know I was only dreaming up some perfect situations . . . I'm allowed to dream though.

Brain Hardware

One screw loose inside my maple chest
Hidden unintentionally, by its varnished stain exterior,
A long, chiseled rod needs to work and may not rest.

That light-provoking shadow across the room is not mine.
It runs as I walk and drinks when I choke.

145

One screw is loose inside my 22-year-old wooden chest.

Looking through the blinded window, flying water appears.
And my dessert pores are lathered as I float over and
under the stars.
A long, chiseled rod fixed on my head, the doctor said, I
need to rest.

So you think my socks don't match?
Purple goes with everything, even tangerine.
That rod keeps turning and refuses to rest.

River flows downstream in every case.
Except the one gushing in my head, it goes up.
One screw is loose inside my maple chest,
A long, chiseled rod is needed and may never rest.

February 23, 2000

Got back from Stockbridge today. Amanda Riley killed herself with a gun up on the hill at Marian Brothers Shrine. Dana was afraid to tell me, so I found out a few days after the fact. I went up there for a memorial service. Mandy, if you can hear me, I want to tell you I wish things could have been different. You had a very positive impact on my life . . . I will always remember you.

February 25, 2000

I am drunk. Why? I can't answer that question. I hooked up with a guy from West Point – very hot – but he ditched me. . . probably for the best. I will try to sleep now and be upset in the morning.

February 27, 2000

Last night I drank again . . . a lot. I didn't get sick though, not that that makes it okay. I had a good time but two weekends in a row there was someone next to me in bed Sunday morning. I kind of feel like last night was okay because it was someone I know. He's nice and sweet and called me this afternoon. I'm just confused as hell about what my needs are and if I should satisfy them.

It's like part of me feels good and all right – the other part feels terrible and bad – sick, even.

146

BEA

It's early afternoon on a Sunday, when Pamela shows up at our apartment unexpectedly. She knocks faintly on the front door, and when Mike opens it, she is standing there with her shoulders hunched over and a troubled look on her face.

"I can't live alone anymore, Dad," she says when we're all seated in the living room. "I need more help than I'm getting."

"Did something in particular make you feel this way?" he asks.

"Yes," she says, but chooses not to reveal what it is.

"How can we help you if we don't know what happened?" Mike asks, hoping to prompt her. I'm thinking she certainly can't expect us to begin the lengthy and expensive process of getting her readmitted to long-term care based on such little information. We wait silently for her to answer the question.

"Well, I haven't been completely honest with you and Dr. Masel about the things I've done, and I feel guilty," she says, looking at us with her big puppy-dog eyes. "I'm having terrible suicidal thoughts, and I'm afraid of doing something stupid if I'm alone."

Mike sighs and goes into his office to look for Dr. Masel's phone number. When he returns, he dials it and hands Pamela the receiver. The three of us wait solemnly to see what will happen when the therapist picks up.

From what I can gather, Dr. Masel tries to convince Pamela to stay in New York and continue to deal with her problems on an out-patient basis.

"I need to go back to Riggs," Pamela tells her. "I left there too soon, I can't do this on my own, at least I know there I have a support system of nurses and friends."

Once again, Mike and I find ourselves hurling at breakneck speed down another blind alley. Not knowing what else to do, we contact Dr. Spellman at Riggs to see if they can take Pamela back.

My heart is beating out of my chest when Mike dials the number. All I can think of is, I'd better not have to take care of that darn cat.

CHAPTER 6

Stockbridge

Q: *At the end of the two-year period but during the three years when Pamela was in college – I guess we were at the end –*

A: *1995 to 1997.*

Q: *How would you characterize your relationship with your daughter during that period of time?*

A: *Good.*

Q: *During that period of time was there any change in your work schedule?*

A: *Not to my recollection.*

Q: *Was there any change in your travel schedule?*

A: *Not to my recollection.*

Q: *Were there any events that occurred during that two-year period that you perceived to cause Pamela any undue stress?*

A: *I think boyfriend issues mostly.*

Q: *Your wife testified later she had regular phone contact with your daughter during the time she was away at school. Did you have any regular contact with your daughter as well during that time?*

A: *I would say yes. Not to the extent that my wife probably but I would call from time to time to check in on her. Even when I traveled I'd make it a basic rule to call, to try to call all the kids at least once from the country where I was.*

Q: *When did you first notice that Pamela was having an unusual amount of stress that required some sort of professional assistance?*

A: *To the best of my recollection Pamela's issues were pretty much surfacing during the sophomore year of college when she was strug-gling with the decision about being in that school, where she was in Baltimore, as compared to somewhere else closer to home. I think this was an ongoing struggle that surfaced during that period of time. Did she make the right decision? Does she really want to be there? Should she be back home? Did that require professional help at that particular time? I was starting to lean toward definitely.*

Q: What events or circumstances cause you to come to that conclusion?

A: I believe she was being overwhelmed by problems and concerns that shouldn't be as overwhelming as they became.

Q: Later on during therapy did you ever learn that Pamela believed she was under unusual family pressure to perform in school, and that she felt she was failing you and her mother in some way because she wasn't performing better?

A: I don't specifically recall Pamela felt pressure to please. Yes, we wanted the best for her. And if she was leaning toward a choice that we felt may not be in her best interest, of course, we would voice it.

BEA

We're in Pamela's apartment going through her "what to pack" list for the umpteenth time. It's a gray and dreary day, sadly unlike the bright and hopeful one four short months ago when she moved to New York.

She is going up to Austen Riggs for a readmission interview today. Mike and I are heartbroken. We want our daughter back. We want her life and ours to be normal again but are beginning to believe she is unable to live outside of a facility. Returning to New York was the big test, and she failed miserably. Now we are back to square one.

It's not fair. Yesterday a friend called with the news that her daughter landed a job in public relations. Much as I wanted to be happy for her, I was resentful because this is what should be happening to my daughter too . . . only my daughter is mentally ill. Her life is at a standstill, and the future remains uncertain.

Mike and I stew as we wait for the outcome of the long interview Pamela is having with Riggs' admissions officer, Dr. Jordan. Mike has a bad feeling, because the short, fair-haired fellow was very cold and detached upon our arrival. It was as if we had never been there, as if our daughter hadn't stayed at Riggs for eleven months, and we never paid thousands of dollars for her care. The least he could have done is say, "nice to see you again," but that didn't happen. Mike thinks he needs a lesson in compassion.

Fortunately, the doctor's assessment of Pamela is better than his superior attitude toward us. According to his intake report, "Pamela is an interesting and challenging woman who is dependent, depressed and Borderline, and recognizes the trouble she is having functioning between outpatient sessions." We are very grateful he has agreed to readmit her.

Before we say our good-byes, I pull an unopened letter out of my handbag that's addressed to Pamela from Fordham's History Department.

"I picked this up from your kitchen counter before we left," I explain. She takes it without interest. "Don't you want to see what it says?" I ask.

"What's the point?

Hastily, I take it back from her and tear it open. It's from her professor, who apparently heard she isn't well and is taking a leave of absence. I read it aloud.

"I will miss you in class – you are clearly one of the brightest students at Fordham," he says, adding his home phone number in case she needs help.

Pamela suddenly drops her bags, collapses to the floor and starts to bawl.

PAMELA

March 8, 2000

I was readmitted to Austen Riggs today. On top of all the other shit I have in my head, I had a fall-out with Dana because I'm involved with another patient – Jake. Dana is so pissed at me, she has so much going on right now, please God, be with her. I feel like I don't know how to be a friend. I screw up relationships all the time and yet, I still don't do anything about it.

BEA

After returning home, I'm in more than a foul mood unpacking Angelina's scratching post and catnip. (Pamela's friend, who lives in Stockbridge, reneged last minute on her offer to take the damn cat.) The phone rings.

"Mom, I did something I shouldn't have." It's Pamela.

What is it now? I just left her a few hours ago.

She tells me she went to her old apartment in Lenox, and met Dana's new roommate, Jake. He hit on her, they kissed and now Dana is in a rage.

My first instinct is to scold Pamela, but I bite my lip. She either wants me to yell or be sympathetic to the mess she's gotten herself into, but I've become wise to this manipulation and remain neutral.

Pamela has zero control over her sexual impulses and is losing her most trusted friend because of it. This rift between her and Dana quickly becomes the topic of peer group discussions and staff meetings and the resulting guilt and self-loathing pushes her into a repeating cycle of acting out and remorse.

Always half-blind as to what's really going on, Mike and I call Dr. Spellman.

"She's over 21, her sex life is none of your business," he counsels, which sounds good if you're made of steel, but doesn't take beating hearts into account.

"You mustn't fall into the trap of rescuing her," he continues in the same stoic vein. To him, Pamela is one case among others in an eight-hour shift, but we are vested in our daughter's well being for a lifetime. It's impossible to stand by and watch as her sexual promiscuity escalates to dangerous levels. It wouldn't be real or honest to make believe this is not happening.

Dr. Spellman is a parent. I wonder what he would do if it was his daughter?

PAMELA

March 12, 2000

My head is a fucking mess! Am I ignoring that? Maybe. Jake is awesome! I am not a sex addict. I just like sex.

I can't take hurting anyone but that's all I do. I'm a selfish bitch! I wish someone would kill me – the easy way out.

I am such a bad person. I don't deserve to live. So what do I do? Break Jake's heart against my will so I can live in misery and keep "working" on my depression? I'm just going to be a distraction for him. I just want to be

151

distracted. I hate myself for thinking this, but in a lot of ways, I don't really care . . . if I can be happy now, I want to take advantage of it.

BEA

Mike and I are reading the Saturday papers on a bright sunny morning, when the call comes.

"I've been raped," Pamela says in a dull, detached voice.

"I just got back from the police station."

Mike calls the nurse's station at Riggs for details, and my hands tremble as I pack a bag. We jump in the car and drive up to Riggs – he banging the steering wheel and me crying all the way.

We find Pamela in a room next to the nurse's station, tightly wound in a blanket, facing the wall. She turns her head slightly when she hears us call her name.

"My panties are still in the hospital," she says, then gives us a copy of her police statement so we can know the extent of her pain.

PAMELA

March 25, 2000

Police Department Report, March 25, 2000

On Friday, March 24th at about 9:00 pm, I went to Lenny's Bar to have a couple of drinks. At about 12:30 pm I was walking up Elm towards Main Street. Two men were walking towards me. They stopped and said "hi". I said "hi" to them. One of them asked me if I wanted to get high. I thought it meant to smoke marijuana and said yes. We went back to Lenny's where a female named Brandy was going to give us a ride. The male subjects introduced themselves as Joe and Rick.

I thought we were going to Joe's house, but instead ended up in a bar in Lenox. While we were driving, Joe and I were sitting in the rear of the car. He started putting his hands all over me and I said "stop it, what are you doing?" When we arrived at the bar, Joe, Rick, Brandy and me, all got a drink. At this point I was introduced to Joe's sister.

While at the bar I said to the bartender that he looked familiar. He said his regular job was as a painter and that he'd seen me around and I said "where?" and he said that he painted at Austen Riggs. He introduced himself as Chuck.

Joe told Chuck he wanted to use his bathroom in his apartment above the bar. At this time Joe, Chuck and myself went upstairs. The three of us passed the marijuana pipe around. We then went back down to the bar and Chuck gave me a bottle of beer.

There was a group of people that were there with Joe and Chuck. Someone said "let's go to Papa's house." Chuck said to wait for him. Joe said no, that I was going with him. I decided to go with Joe because I felt safer with him because his sister was there and she did not actually know if Chuck would take her to Papa's house.

We all went to Papa's house. Chuck then came in and Papa asked me if I wanted a drink. I said yes. Papa took a glass, put ice in it and poured a bluish liquid out of a Gatorade container and gave it to me.

I drank half a glassful and we sat down on the couch. Someone took out a joint and someone else was passing around a marijuana pipe. Chuck was sitting next to me and Joe's sister was sitting on the other side of me. Joe was sitting on another couch with a female whom I think was a friend of Joe's sister. There was another male whom I did not know.

Papa took out a dress that was like a nightie and said to me "why don't you put this on?" I asked him if he had any stockings. Joe's sister took the dress but did not put it on. Papa brought out a pair of stockings and I put them on in his room alone. At this point, I do not remember anything that happened. I felt afterwards, that I must have blacked out.

When I woke up, I was on the couch lying down. I first did not realize what was going on. All I remember is the pain. I kept telling Joe to stop. It was at this point that Chuck started to put his clothes on. I felt like I blacked out again.

When I woke, I had to go to the bathroom and Joe would not let me. He told me to hold it in. I was thinking, "what should I do?" Two other men were sleeping in a different room. My first instinct was to try to get up and leave, but I did not know where I was. I was worried that Joe might get mad and I didn't know what he might do to me. I thought it would be better to try to wait for daylight. I told Joe can't you just leave me alone and go to sleep? I was afraid to get angry because I did not know what he would do to me.

Finally, it started to get light out and I told Joe I was going to get sick. He told me to run to the bathroom. I vomited. When I got out of the bathroom, I was shaking very badly. I was trying to put my pants on. I finally found my shoes in Papa's bedroom. I told Joe I had to go and he said Papa would be up in a little while and he could give me a ride. I said I knew someone in town and didn't need one. Joe said thank you to me and I left the house walking.

I was trying to find my friend Petey's apartment, but was not able to. I called Austen Riggs from a payphone and there was no answer. I tried to call for a taxi and could not find one. This was around 7:00 am. I was sitting on the sidewalk and a man asked if I was ok. I said yes and told this man I needed to get to Stockbridge. He told me where I could get the bus. I went over to Town Hall to wait for a bus when I saw a police car. I stopped the officer and asked him if I could get a ride to Stockbridge. He told me he was on a call and he would have another police officer stop to see me. A short while later, a female police officer stopped and she gave me a ride to the Stockbridge town line, where then a Stockbridge police officer brought me to Austen Riggs.

When I got there, I went to the Alcove Station, which is located immediately next to the nurses' station and slept to around 11:00 am. When I woke up I went to my room, changed my clothes and washed off my make-up, but did not take a shower. Then I went downstairs and called my friend Dana. She said my friend Jake called her during the night and said that I did not come home from Lenny's bar. I told her it happened again and she understood what I meant by this. Dana made me go to the nurses' station and call her from there so she would know I would report what happened.

At first, I wasn't going to say anything, but then I told Patti, who is a nurse and she had me lie down and contacted the supervisor on duty.

They determined that I needed to go to the hospital to be checked out.

SHAME

Shame increases with every corrupt move
Like the tide rises and slams against the rocks
In the whaling town of Sag Harbor Village.

Ironic, the use of the word "wailing."
Two action verbs.
Some say you need to practice one more than the other
Though, it could be argued that each is a skill.
I feel like I'm writing a chapter in an 18th Century Fielding novel . . .
Fiction, storytelling best read at high tea.
I will never be British or male or alive in the 1700s,
So sticking to the subject is probably proper.

BEA

I let loose during a hastily scheduled family counseling session the following day, directing my ire first at Pamela.

"You were playing with fire and finally got burned," I rail. "You have to bear the responsibility for leaving the facility, going out to a bar and taking off with two strange men."

Then I turn to Dr. Spellman and Pamela's new therapist, Dr. Benson ... "You assured me Pamela would be safe at Riggs, and I'm furious that you misled us."

Mike jumps in angrily, "I'm going after those two guys who took advantage of my daughter. What are their names? I'll teach them a God-damned lesson!"

"Mr. Tusiani," Dr. Spellman replies haughtily, "this is Pamela's problem to solve, not yours."

"Well, I'm not sure Riggs is the right place for Pamela anymore and that you are even competent to handle my daughter," Mike counters. This prompts Pamela finally to speak up.

"I want to stay at Riggs and am thinking of pressing charges against the two men who abused me."

"Are you up to that?" Mike asks.

PAMELA

April 4, 2000

OK, so I'm finally writing in here again. I'm angry and out of control (well, not really). I haven't written about what happened, I find it difficult enough to think about it, but I need to remind myself that I was abused. I was raped. I did not consent to sex that night. I wasn't thinking clearly but it's not my fault.

I hate those fucking bastards! I wish they'd killed me in some ways. I don't want to deal with this at all.

Happy birthday Petey and please keep Dana safe in Lenox tonight. I tried to kiss Jake before he left for Paris but was rejected. I guess with good reason!

Pamela contacts the D.A.'s office and presses charges against her assailants. The following account in the Berkshire Eagle: "Two Lenox Men Charged with Rape of Town Woman," sends her into a tailspin.

"According to court records, the complainant is a 22-year-old woman, whose address is is listed as 25 Main St., in Stockbridge, which is the address of the Austen Riggs Center."

She is petrified that the rapists now know where she lives and might try to find her. I go ballistic and call the paper's editor.

"Identifying where a rape victim lives is a breach of privacy protected by law, especially when the victim is mentally ill and living in a well-known psychiatric facility. How dare you make a victim of my daughter a second time! If anything happens to her because of the information in this article, I am going to hold you and your rag of a newspaper responsible!"

The editor meekly mumbles that he will look into it and get back to me. He calls the next day to tell me that after my call, the way this story was reported was discussed at a staff meeting and everyone learned a big lesson from it.

That doesn't make me or Pamela feel any better. I'm angry that no one at Riggs had the guts to pursue this issue with the paper themselves, especially since one of the accused was a painter at Riggs. The truth is, they've totally taken a back seat with anything and everything having to do with the rape. Their lack of action is irresponsible.

While Mike, Pamela and I meet with counselors, lawyers and the D.A., Riggs is building a wall of protectiveness around itself. The stand they've taken is that it's not their problem, it's our problem, and I find that deplorable.

They could be afraid of their image, or a lawsuit, but given Pamela's fragile state, it's like feeding her to the lions. Maybe they don't care as much as I do that my daughter was raped, or maybe we have different ideas about where boundaries should be drawn.

PAMELA

April 20, 2000

*I have to go in front of a Grand Jury next week! Those fucking ass-
holes! Got away with everything!*

April 22, 2000

*My tongue hurts. I had it re-pierced today. It was better than getting
some tattoo on impulse. Tomorrow is Easter Sunday and my whole family is coming to visit. I hope I can pull it off so I don't make a spectacle of
myself.*

*"Rape me. Rape me. Rape me. Rape me. Rape me. Rape me. Rape me.
Rape me. Rape me," screaming in my head. I listened to the Nirvana song
really loud and just wanted to smash things.*

BEA

Mike scrambles to get the best legal team in Massachusetts to represent Pamela, but winds up going with a local attorney who has intimate
knowledge of the Pittsfield Court system.

The attorney assures Mike that it's a slam-dunk, routine indictment,
and it's not necessary for him to make the trip up to the courthouse
where the Grand Jury convenes.

I decide to drive up anyway, to lend Pamela moral support during
the hearing.

Twenty-five local citizens are brought in for this case and it takes a
long while for Pamela, and Dana, a witness by the fact that she was the
first person Pamela told about the rapes, to be called in for questioning.
Three hours pass as we wait in the hall outside the Grand Jury room.
After testifying, Pamela walks out in control and confident, while Dana
is so unnerved, she could very well be mistaken for the rape victim.

Our lawyer convinces us the defendants would be stupid to go before the Grand Jury and risk being questioned by the D.A.

"Their attorneys are way over their heads in this case," he assures
us. "Besides, one of the defendants already has a record."

So we're more than shocked when, the next day, the accused rapists
agree to testify.

"They switched to new attorneys," our befuddled lawyer says.

"Don't worry," he adds, as our fears mount, "it's highly unlikely that Pamela will be called back to testify again."

No sooner do we return to his office than we find out he's wrong. Pamela is summoned to reappear before the Grand Jury within the hour.

As we scramble toward his car, I tell him, "Make sure my daughter doesn't come in contact with her assailants."

Sure enough, as we drive back to the courthouse, the two defendants, dressed in slick suits and in a jovial mood, are walking up the courthouse steps, right smack in front of us.

Pamela gasps and crouches down on the floor of the car's backseat like a frightened animal.

"This wasn't supposed to happen!" I snarl, protecting my cub, and feeling a queasy premonition that something else could go wrong.

Somehow, word spread quickly among Pamela's friends at Riggs that she would be making a second Grand Jury appearance, and they start showing up at the courthouse. They're a motley crew who might be considered "on the fringe" with nose rings and pink hair, but it's heartwarming to see them. Even though they're mentally ill and struggling with their own problems, they care deeply about my daughter, and their presence gives her strength.

Their support means the world to me too.

When Pamela comes out of the Grand Jury, her legs buckle under her like a newborn foal, and she collapses against the wall. Something that transpired in that room left her so stunned, she looks like a zombie. Her glassy eyes are fixed in a piercing stare.

When the short, intense-looking D.A. finally enters the small, nondescript room where we're waiting for the verdict, he takes a long time to shut the door.

"The jury agreed something happened in that apartment with Pamela and those two men," he says, carefully choosing his words, "but there was not enough evidence to prosecute."

A vacuum sets in, sucking the air out of the room.

"No one believes me," Pamela cries out. "Now those two jerks are out there celebrating."

This ignites my own fire.

"You didn't try hard enough!" I fume at the D.A.

"And YOU, I say pointing to Pamela's sheepish attorney, "told us this case was a slam-dunk and my husband didn't have to be here." I feel completely undermined. Both of them told us Pamela's case was indictable.

"What kind of people served on this jury?" I demand. "The words 'no,' 'stop,' and 'let me go' mean nothing in Berkshire County? Pamela did not see the defendants in the street, offer them pot, or take them to a stranger's apartment and rape them. My daughter was held against her will," I say, "but I guess that's not a crime in Berkshire County. The jury saw their sons in that room today, not their daughters, and I feel sorry for a community that doesn't protect its young women."

Trying to quell further outbursts, our attorney leads Pamela and me into another room for a private discussion. Out of the blue, Pamela lets out three blood-curdling screams which brings security running to the door.

My troubled daughter has every right to howl. She always felt like a loser, and the Grand Jury decision just confirms that feeling.

Those twenty-five jurors most probably doubted the story of a mental patient, over 21, who goes willingly into a bar, walks off with these guys, gets high and undresses when they tell her to. They do not factor in the medications in her system, combined with the drugs and alcohol she was offered, all of which clouded her judgment and fueled her impulsiveness.

Pamela may like sex, but she's smart enough to realize when it gets out of control. I guess these jurors don't know this about the troubled Riggs girl who pressed charges.

The atmosphere in the car is frigid as Pamela's attorney drops her and me off at Riggs. I haven't the strength or desire even to say goodbye to him.

PAMELA

April 30, 2000

Sunday morning 1:38 am. I've been up late the last two nights trying to be somewhat creative with my hands.

Cathy called today, I have to call her back but should I just leave out what happened? That two fucking assholes are rejoicing after getting off the hook for forcing themselves on me!

I can't believe I was raped and nothing happened except the increasing anxiety in my chest where a raw, black heart pumps disgust through my entire body.

Am wondering if I should call Mom again and ask if she's thinking of me. I'm lonely but I don't know if that would help. What do I do in therapy now? What do I do period? I feel like I don't exist. What is my damn problem?

BEA

People call and ask how Pamela is. I take a deep breath and choke out, "She's still struggling," with the hope it will satisfy their curiosity. There are very few, other than my spouse, children and therapist, with whom I can share the horrid details of rape and a grand jury trial. It's just too painful . . . I'm not really sure they understand the mental illness that's driving this dysfunction, and I'm very protective of my daughter's reputation.

Although Pamela's life begins to revert back to some degree of normalcy, her therapy sessions have now expanded to include Post-Traumatic Stress Syndrome. She is an emotional tinderbox.

PAMELA

May 2, 2000

I was a hair away from using tonight. Jeremy was going to drive to Boston to get coke but his connection failed. Thank God I didn't go. I can't believe how fragile I am. When will this ever stop? I also came close to drinking and the only thing that stopped me was that I didn't have ID. Talk about shame . . . my family should be ashamed of their fucked-up daughter!

In family therapy, Pamela displaces her anger at the accused rapists on us. It's like a boxing match.

Round one.

"Mom, you never should have pushed me to work or attend a dance or babysit, because, all those things made me anxious."

Round two.

"Michael and Paula never treated me as equals and don't take me seriously."

162

Round three.

"Dad, your hugs always made me extremely uncomfortable."

For the most part, we roll with the punches, despite the knock-downs and left hooks. But Mike is deeply hurt over the hugging remark and doesn't understand where it's coming from. Could she be projecting the sexual assault perpetrated against her on her father?

We've become the family who can't talk to our daughter or sister without stepping into a ring and getting pummeled.

PAMELA

May 5, 2000

Well, I did it! I used two nights ago. Jeremy and I drove to New York and got $200 worth of coke. We went to his house in Connecticut and snorted it all night and the next day. It felt good in the moment and I am craving for more but I have to get through this weekend.

I met with lots of people today about the future of my treatment. They're recommending a rehab for me. This may be my last Friday night at Austen Riggs.

BEA

"I'm afraid Pamela is going to die if she continues on this self-destructive path," the head administrator at Riggs tells us. "She's in a serious struggle with her family that could cost her her life."

I'm dumbfounded. How could all of Pamela's troubles be pinned on the very people who love and care about her the most? What kind of portrait of us is Pamela painting to her therapists? Do they factor in that it's filtered through the perceptions of a person whose reality is distorted . . . and who is repeatedly encouraged (by them) to express her anger at somebody???

The family is an easy target for people suffering from mental illness. Its members are made to feel like "enemies" throughout the therapeutic process, and it's wrong!

It's not as though we haven't learned a lot about the effect of our words and actions on Pamela, but deep in my heart I know something more profound than the four of us is the cause of Pamela's unrelenting torment. Why don't the psychiatrists recognize this?

PAMELA

May 9, 2000

Hot, sticky, spring in Stockbridge. The fan is directed at my exhausted body. I want to stay up tonight and think about the one person that I might love enough to be able to be without someday. Does that make sense? I feel so asexual – don't feel like I need a boyfriend or even want one. Getting close to someone feels freaky but that's okay though because there's no chance of that anyway.

May 14, 2000

Dana thinks I don't care about her or our friendship. I don't know what's going on in my head except I want out of everything. I drank a lot Friday night and made out with Jeremy and Krissie and I've been involved with Rex too – a new patient from Texas. He's cute and very sweet, I hope I don't fuck him up.

Tomorrow at 8:30 a.m. my parents and Drs. Grayson, Spellman, Benson and myself will meet and I will be <u>shaking</u>! God, I hope it isn't as bad as I think it will be. I hope I'll want to get better one day instead of wishing for the end. I'm so morbid. Happy Mother's Day, Mom.

BEA

Riggs is now telling us Pamela has to leave.

"She needs to be in a closed facility that treats dual diagnosis patients – those with mental illness and substance abuse," the administrator intones like God from on high.

I want to flail at him for leading us down the wrong path these past four months. When they readmitted Pamela to Riggs, they knew she was struggling with drugs and substance abuse, yet they continued to recommend an open setting for treatment.

A large part of Pamela's deterioration this second time around, has to do with her being able to walk right out the door to the nearest bar and get into trouble. Had she been in a closed setting, she would not have been raped, and she would have had a better chance of making progress in her recovery.

Now, Riggs is putting pressure on us to get Pamela out of there as soon as we can.

Mike and I are desperately searching for a closed psychiatric facility for Pamela and we quickly realize her history of self-mutilation is an issue. Some promising possibilities – Sierra Tuscon and The Meadows in Arizona – refuse to take "cutters." Mike is leaning toward a highly respected treatment facility in Topeka, Kansas, called Menninger's, when Dr. Spellman comes up with another option.

"I've just learned about a place called Road to Recovery," he tells us on speakerphone. "It's a dual diagnosis facility in Malibu, California, that admits patients who self-harm and has a strong alcohol rehab component."

"We looked at its website, Mom," Pamela pipes up, apparently sitting beside Dr. Spellman in his office. "It's a residence – just a regular-looking house in the hills overlooking the Pacific Ocean. I really want to go there."

What gives her strength makes us weak.

"I need to find out more about this place," Mike says cautiously.

"I already checked, and it's JCAHO-affiliated," says Dr. Spellman.

"What does that mean?" asks Mike.

"The Joint Commission on Accreditation of Healthcare Organizations requires certain standards of treatment that Road to Recovery satisfies," the social worker explains.

When we hang up the phone, I feel stunned. California is 3,000 miles away. I wonder if Pamela can manage being so far away from us and our support.

Mike calls his growing list of psychiatrists to inquire about RR. None of them has heard of it. He calls the facility and speaks at length to its administrator.

"I've got to go there, Dad," Pamela pleads in a follow-up phone call. "I just can't stay here because every minute that passes is wasted. Nothing is being done to help me here anymore."

Coincidentally, the intake person at RR calls to say a bed has miraculously become available. On the strength of JCAHO-accreditation, Mike wires a deposit, and within 24 hours Pamela manages to get to the Albany airport with a supply of Serzone, Prozac, Neurontin, Trazodone, Klonopin, Thorazine, Ativan and Buspar packed in her luggage.

It amazes me how, in such a short time, my daughter transitions from being withdrawn and dependent to someone in control and decisive.

CHAPTER 7
Malibu

Q: Were you able to appreciate any special relationship between your husband and your daughter, a phrase that is popularly referred to as daddy's little girl, was there –

A: Yes.

Q: You got a sense he was particularly close to her?

A: Yes.

Q: What sorts of things did he do with her that, for example, he didn't do with the twins during that first grammar school period of time?

A: Well, he went out buying her CDs. They had this music thing. He was focused on her eyes – all the time Pamela had trouble with contact lenses. He always took her to his doctor in the city. He gave her a job at his office during the summer, but he did that with my son also. I really don't – I can't – it's hard to measure when you are a parent. You will have to ask him those questions.

Q: I realize some of the questions I'm asking might be difficult or impossible to answer. If that's the response that's what you should tell me. I'm doing what I can to try to be a good advocate for my clients. I don't want to be rude, but I have to ask these questions. Did your husband and daughter's relationship change in any way when she moved into the junior high school, somewhat like your daughter's and your relationship changed?

A: No more than my relationship. It's the same.

Q: From two years of college, the same kind of question. Was there any change that you noticed in the relationship between your husband and daughter Pamela?

A: No.

PAMELA

May 17, 2000

I am on a plane right now flying into Chicago and then to Los Angeles. I am so scared to go to Malibu . . . oh, my God, I'm starting to sweat! I love Dana and Petey, I hope they can forgive me for being such an awful friend. I also hope that Road to Recovery will help me get on the right track. I really hope it's a good place and the people are nice. I love you God, please keep me safe.

May 18, 2000

I am so alone! Malibu is beautiful but it's right on the water and that scares me for some reason.

I can't call anyone for five days. I wish I could talk to Mom. I feel like I don't have problems with drugs like the other people here. I mean, I know I have a problem but I'm not going through detox. Just ate a Snickers Pie in one piece and feel so gross now. Maybe I'll try to write some poetry or figure out my timeline – something you have to do here. I have to go through my past and figure out what the hell happened to me!

I love my sister for picking my stuff up at Riggs. I love her anyway!

Malibu

A house in the Malibu mountains,
   The crystal green and blue sea spread across the sand.
Breaking waves crash just like my sobriety.

A question ringing in my swollen ears:
"What is your drug of choice?"
Anything, I think to myself . . .
But dare not let the word through my tightly wired lips.

May 19, 2000

I just found out that I'm in treatment with a famous actress from "That Seventies Show!" I had a better day. Spoke up a lot. Feel like I'm making things up, but I do experience things seriously – I think I'm scared of examining it.

Mike and I are nervous wrecks.

After her initial call to let us know she arrived safely, waiting a week – five simple days – to talk to Pamela, when we used to stay in daily contact, seems like an eternity. Not knowing whether she might be hurting herself, bingeing or having mind-splitting headaches is torturing us.

We feel so oddly disconnected. After being in the driver's seat for so long, we have been relegated to the back, and are now in the hands of a strange driver taking us in a new direction.

Mike, who needs to feel like he's in control, even when he's not, calls the facility's director for daily updates.

"How's Pamela adjusting there?" he asks Dr. Emil Shiraz.

"Don't worry, Mr. Tusiani," says Dr. Shiraz, "Pamela's case is not unique among the patients we treat here."

PAMELA

PSYCHOSOCIAL ASSESSMENT
INTAKE INTERVIEW — ROAD TO RECOVERY
May 20, 2000

Q: Do you use alcohol or drugs? If so, what is your history?

A: I started drinking at 16, and up until a week ago, drank seven to eight alcoholic beverages three times a week. At 18 I began using marijuana, and at 19 started snorting cocaine: my last $100 binge was three weeks ago.

Q: How did you support your habit?

A: From others, parents, work.

Q: Do any members of your family use or abuse drugs or alcohol?

A: My brother, my Uncle Eton and my maternal grandfather Eton.

Q: Have you ever been the victim of sexual abuse? If so, when?

A: Yes, father raped me at age 22.

I am here. I am strong. I am taking care of myself. I'm told positive affirmations are good to recite over and over even if they're not true. I went to a great AA meeting tonight – one that makes me want to keep coming back. I know I have to live one day at a time. I am two weeks sober – am craving but not using right now.

Having a hard time also, because I want that closeness that offers me love. Matt is so cute and he's attracted to me too but we're both addicts in treatment.

I think I am feeling better overall, though still have bad dreams and down time, but I feel really energized. Tomorrow is Sunday and we get to go on an outing. I hope we can shop.

I love you Uncle Joseph and all of my family. I want to be closer but I want independence – I need to learn how to live for myself. I want to be healthy, pretty, imaginative, grateful, smart, and stand up for myself. I want to live in a great house with a pool in the sun and I do want a wonderful partner and children and I want to write and create and dance and laugh and love.

I can't believe I just wrote all that! And I mean it – at this moment, life seems wonderful.

June 6, 2000

I want to die! Please God, what help is there for me? My mind is psychotic. I need help. I want Mom!

I had a severe flashback last night and then kissed and cuddled with Maddie on the couch.

June 10, 2000

I am very scared that I will fail. I went to a good meeting tonight where Craig T. Nelson spoke. He said only 2% of the people in the meeting will recover. I want to recover, I really do. Tomorrow I get my 30-day chip. I am in control of my behavior . . . I just have to keep repeating that.

June 11, 2000

I got my chip!

I miss Mom – she was funny today – asked me if Craig T. Nelson is a former alcoholic. I said that an alcoholic is for life and she was shocked. I wish I could take away all her pain and protect her but she has to start to understand more of my problems better.

June 16, 2000

God, please be with my Dad because he is sick. I didn't call him today and I feel bad, but I felt like I would only be calling out of guilt and I didn't want to do that. I am concerned about him though, and do love him very much.

Tonight's AA meeting was good. I really feel like these alcoholics are my family right now – they're there for me every day. Tom made a bracelet for me and Barry is so sweet, I really like Annie too. How am I going to leave these guys? They are so sweet. HALT! I've got to take it one day at a time.

God, please guide my heart to love myself right now. I want to make something of and be proud of myself. I want to make the right choices. I did today so I'll work on it again tomorrow.

BEA

Pamela calls and asks for her father. She's panting and sounds panicked. I hand him the phone.

"Dad, I'm freaking out. The cops should take my pants for evidence." She is rambling hysterically. "I feel like I'm choking."

"Pamela, calm down," Mike says, trying not to panic.

Then, out of the blue, she asks, "Why did Paula always lock her bedroom door?"

He pauses, not sure where this is coming from, and measures his words carefully. "Probably because she wanted privacy."

I'm listening in. Why is she asking about this? It's so strange. As a teenager, Paula locked her door when she was studying, so she wouldn't be bothered. What is Pamela insinuating?

"There are cameras in my room," she goes on.

This is delusional.

"I can't function and don't understand what's happening to me. I'm in a fog, like I was at the very beginning, in Baltimore, and don't feel safe from myself."

"Pamela, you have to share these feelings with your therapist," Mike says, "and if you don't feel safe, go talk to the nurse on duty."

After he hangs up, he immediately tries to get through to RR. The young counselor who picks up, tells him they are aware of Pamela's bizarre behavior.

"She's having flashbacks of the rape, causing her to be disoriented," he tells Mike. "We're monitoring her closely, adjusting her medications and not allowing her out until she acts normally."

PAMELA

June 19, 2000

I totally flipped out Saturday night at the speaker's meeting. They had to carry me out. What is my head doing?? Am I just making this up? I can't get this rape out of my head. I have a lot of anger and need to explode. Stan thinks I'm not motivated and I'll end up staying here nine months! That pissed me off because I'm trying and just starting to get in touch with my anger and what's behind it.

I love Assam so much – he's the greatest caretaker. I wish he could adopt me. I do love Dad, though sometimes he just makes me so mad. I miss Angelina, Lulu, Mom, Michael, Paula, Roger, Cathy, Dana, Petey, Allie, etc. I wish things with Dana could be resolved. I am such a hateful person for giving our friendship up for drugs and alcohol.

June 24, 2000

I'm not allowed to go to the meeting tonight because they're afraid I'll have a fucking convulsion. I need an AA meeting tonight and every night. I'm trying so hard. Saturday nights are so difficult for me – I want to get wasted so badly. I don't really want to. I just ate four big cookies and then threw them up in the "porcelain God."

I am powerless and my life is unmanageable.

Rainbow Showers

Confined by black see-through bones
Choked by bile, stapled gums and a burning throat,
Constantly drinking the waste from her past.

Holding her head down
At the bottom of a dark pit –
An empty well rotting in the desert

Nails clenching at her face
Trying to cleanse her used and filthy body.

A ray of light shines
Through a world of darkness
Breaking the chains that bind her.

Rainbow showers shoot from her heart . . .
Pink, blue, yellow flash by illuminated eyes.
Butterflies fly from her mouth
Love enters her soul and freedom pours out.

(Inspired in the shower where rainbows appeared to be exuding from my body.)

BEA

Mike and I travel to the west coast with eager anticipation. We haven't seen Pamela for seven weeks – I can't wait to hug her and see for myself if she's okay. I wonder what she looks like now? I'm curious about her living arrangements at Road to Recovery and am anxious to meet the doctors we've been talking to on the phone for the past several weeks.

When we pull up to the facility, just off the Pacific Coast Highway in trendy Malibu, we're pleased to find a normal looking house nestled on a hill just above a scrubby canyon. Surrounded by the warmth of the sun and salty sea air in such a modern setting, it's the antithesis of the cold and austere Riggs in Stockbridge, Massachusetts.

My first instinct, when I get out of the rented car, is to run and throw my arms around Pamela. But I stop short when I realize she is not alone. Someone – a counselor – is lurking nearby.

Mike and I exchange wary glances. It takes us by surprise. We've never had to be monitored before when greeting our daughter. Why is it necessary now?

173

The way this counselor is looking at us makes us feel like we've done something wrong. What do these people at Road to Recovery think of us?

The fact that our daughter feels she needs protection around us signifies that something dramatic has changed between us. We are anxious to find out what it is.

PAMELA

July 5, 2000

Mom and Dad came to visit yesterday. It has been hard in group and in therapy but we've been having a good time shopping and went to the movies tonight. I'm supposed to communicate better in WORDS with my parents (and everyone else, I suppose). How do I do that? God, please support me in finding a way.

BEA

On our second day in Malibu, Mike and I are asked to attend one of Pamela's peer-group sessions. Although the only kind of group therapy we've participated in is family therapy, of course we agree to go, if it will help her. But once we have joined the circle in the common room, with eight pairs of eyes staring at us, we start to have second thoughts. It looks like it will be more about us than them.

The facilitator breaks the ice by asking Pamela if there's anything she wants to say to us and the floodgates open.

"You told me I'm not welcome in 'your' home," Pamela says, squinting her eyes angrily at me. "Well it's 'my' home too!"

I'm floored.

"Pamela," I squint back. "You called me six months ago in the middle of the night, outside of some strange bar, totally drunk. That was very scary. I'm a parent. What do you expect me to do?"

She bites her lip.

"On top of that," I continue, "I find out you're doing drugs. I will not tolerate that, ever. What I said was, I will never allow anyone in 'my' home who uses drugs."

Filling the empty silence that is her response, the counselor prompts: "Pamela, is there something you want to say to your father?"

She shoots Mike a look of intense resentment. "You never pay attention to me. All you ever care about is your work."

"I'm sorry if I made you feel that way, Pamela," says Mike repentantly. "I never intentionally neglected you. I've always worked hard to provide for my family. Now that this has happened to you, I hope I have demonstrated how I will go to the ends of the earth to help you." He leans further out of his chair. "I love you deeply . . . I hope, in your heart, you know that and can forgive me."

Pamela looks stunned. It's not common for Mike to be so emotional. She's not used to seeing her father like that – vulnerable – especially in front of a group of people. It's almost as if she's embarrassed by his openness.

After the session ends, a fellow named Alec, who seems to be in his late thirties, comes up to Mike in tears.

"I wish my father would say those things to me," he says. Mike puts his hand on Alec's shoulder to comfort him.

How ironic that someone who Mike doesn't even know gets his message, while his own daughter is still knitting her brow, trying to make sense of it.

On our way out, I'm relieved Pamela's peers see us as more nurturing and less threatening than they did when we walked in.

The tension we felt at the beginning of our trip has dissipated, and we are all in a relaxed mood, hanging out in the family room among other residents on our last night there.

"Does anyone want coffee?" Pamela asks, knowing our usual evening rituals.

"Sure do," we respond at the same time. She heads off to the kitchen. When she comes back, she places two still-steaming cups of coffee on the table in front of us, and before we can reach for them, her body suddenly lurches and crashes to the floor.

Startled, we run and huddle over her.

"Pamela, Pamela," Mike and I scream over one another. "Are you okay??"

"Quick! Get help," Mike yells to one of the other residents.

It looks like Pamela is having some kind of seizure. Her neck is arched, she's twitching with her hands extended in front of her, and we can only see the whites of her eyes. Her toes are curled under, and spittle is sliding out the side of her mouth.

After an excruciatingly long minute, she comes to in a drowsy stupor. Mike and I are kneeling on either side of her.

"It happened to me when I was 16. I was choking," she says in a trance-like state, then adds another flashback. "My pants . . . no one stopped. They wouldn't let me call the police. They were choking me!"

Mike and I exchange glances, horrified.

"My daughter just had an epileptic fit," I scream when a staffer runs toward us, "and she's hallucinating."

"Calm down, Mrs. Tusiani, it's not an epileptic fit," he says. "Pamela's been having these episodes recently. They're caused by post-traumatic stress."

"Episodes and fits are two different things," I say, starting to get hysterical. "We've been told she's been having episodes recently, but we had no idea they were this bad." I turn to Mike, and he puts his arms around me.

"I can't possibly leave on a plane tomorrow with Pamela like this," I whimper in his ear.

The counselor moves us away from Pamela, fearing she may get more agitated if she sees us upset.

"You have to. Trust me," he advises. "We have it under control."

How can we leave? Mike and I don't know what to do. We can see from a distance the familiar puppy-dog look on Pamela's face, begging us to stay, but the professionals, who've now collected around us, are urging us to leave.

We've been down this road so many times before. I know I could stay in California to help Pamela work through this. But the doctors say she needs to deal with the trauma of the rape on her own in order to heal.

We make our decision early the next morning, when Mike speaks to Pamela's psychiatrist from the motel's phone.

"It's not a good idea to change your plans, because that just adds confusion to the situation," he says, encouraging us to leave.

"I'll increase Pamela's anti-seizure medication. The goal is to reduce her PTSD episodes to three times a week."

PAMELA

July 8, 2000

I hear the ocean. I'm glad I stopped and listened. It scares me because it's so huge and unpredictable, just like the rest of life I suppose. I'm lost and alone in Malibu and can't believe where my life is and how I got here. It seems like it used to be so controllable and I get mad about losing that life . . . when I was in college with Teddy, doing well in my classes, in love with John Milton. I must have been in hiding.

The summer of my senior year in High School, working at a Day Camp, I was a wrapped-up anger-ball scared to roll in any one direction. I had so many friends to choose from and yet I hated my life. I wish I could go back and figure out why . . . No! Don't!!

July 11, 2000

I know I shouldn't be super thin and I am fine at my weight now, but I still feel really fat and the problem is, I just keep eating – chocolate, especially and now nuts, which I never liked.

Dad called from Japan earlier. It's my parents' 29th anniversary. I love them so much. I hope Michael and Paula's relationships last like our parents'. As for me, I'm still floating. God, I know you will pull me into a dock some day – even if I become my own dock, that's okay.

BEA

I'm home, but in a daze. I can't get the image of Pamela, writhing on the floor, out of my mind. It's like a non-stop video running a continuous loop, and I feel guilty every time it repeats. I still can't believe I left her there.

The only recourse I have to escape its penetrating effect is to schedule an emergency session with my own therapist.

"Pamela had a seizure, twitching on the floor right in front of us," I tell the young, blonde psychotherapist whose clear-headed advice I've come to trust. "We feel like we've completely lost control of our daughter's care."

She jumps out of her chair and puts her face directly in front of mine.

"You'd better take back control right now," she says in a burst of uncharacteristic determination. I'm startled. It's not her role as a therapist to tell me what to do, but given the desperate situation I'm in, I welcome her sane advice.

"Demand that Pamela be tested by a neurologist immediately. You have to get to the bottom of this," she says, her flushed face clearly indicating disapproval with Road to Recovery's management methods.

I relay this to Mike, and it propels him into action. He finds a reputable neurologist at UCLA-Westwood who immediately sees Pamela and has her undergo an MRI and an EEG.

PAMELA

July 16, 2000

Oh, my fucking God (not meant to be derogatory)! I cannot believe how bad I've been! Friday night Maddie was frazzled, ready to drink, fuck, cut, die. I got in her car and she took off like a maniac right from a meeting. I broke RR rules and lied to staff, told them I was coming right back, but I knew I wasn't going to. (I don't want to be a liar, but that's what alcoholics are . . . I will . . . must . . . work on that).

So anyhow, we went to West Hollywood and I thought that I was going to get wasted. I was scared but in my out-of-control mode. It felt like old times in NYC. Now I see how dangerous and horrible it would have been if my plan went through. I mean, that's how I was raped by two motherfuckers four months ago. It was also how, before that, I was brought to some field by two assholes and was dropped off at Austen Riggs Center. And how I wound up bringing strangers with dope back to my apartment in NY.

I am a complete and utter crazy person who is a raging alcoholic!

Maddie and I did not drink or use. We went to a club and danced for ten minutes then went straight to the car and drove back to RR at 2:00 am.

I got shit in group and couldn't go on an outing today. I deserve it

178

though and am so thankful I didn't fuck-up. One little thing Maddie and I did was get tattooed. She paid. I just felt wild and upset enough to finally get my tribal band – actually, a barbed wire band on my arm. Mom and Dad are totally going to flip. Can I hurt them any more?

Another action of mine that I feel anxious about is I made love to Alec a few hours ago. He is so sweet and we just let loose I guess. It's wrong because we're both in treatment and it's definitely against the rules. I'm also supposed to be afraid of men, and I broke a plan of mine not to have any sort of relationship.

What am I doing to my life? I mean, this isn't a bad, bad thing, it's just a distraction from the work I'm doing. I'm worried about my life – how long will I be here at RR? Am I going to live here in Malibu after that or go back to NYC? I wish I had some idea. God, I have messed up, but at least I did keep my sobriety – I owe that to You living in Maddie tonight.

July 22, 2000

I've been having seizures – at least the doctor said that my EEG showed seizure activity. I'm still not sure what happens and why. I'm scared as hell about them and hope the medicine he gives me works. I'm so glad to be off Prozac and do feel better in my depression.

Alec has been coming to my bedroom and waking me up every morning. God, that makes me wild. He's got this girlfriend he sends money to but he told me he wants to live with me. I know I still have my treatment to deal with. PAM, it's YOUR life . . . I need to know the difference between right and wrong.

Dark Chocolate

Perched on the roof of an empty heart,
Like a hollow piece of chocolate melted in the sun.

I care about being rejected
And prey on the footsteps of strangers.

Those scented by Banana Boat Dark Tanning Oil
Send shivers through my body . . .
Leaving each black hair on my arms at attention.

"What do you mean, you got a tattoo?" I hear Mike yell furiously into the phone. "Who paid for it?"

My hand shakes as I pick up another extension.

"A friend," Pamela answers defiantly.

"If it's that Alec, get rid of him," Mike screams . . . so loudly now, I'm afraid he'll have a heart attack. (He just learned, through his daily contact with RR, that the resident who cried and fawned over him at group therapy has recently been paying early morning visits to Pamela's room).

"I'm going to kick his ass," says Mike, full blast.

"Fuck you!" Pamela hurls back.

"Pamela, I know you are lying! I love you and will pay for your treatment and medication, but nothing more," he says, before slamming the phone down.

The next time Mike talks to Dr. Shiraz, the director tells him Pamela is angry because of perceived neglect.

"She's holding you hostage," the doctor says.

"Yeah, I'm the bad guy, but what she doesn't see through her warped sense of reality is, I'm spending hours on the phone with doctors, trying to get to the bottom of this seizure problem."

I'm beginning to feel sorrier for my husband than my daughter.

While I hate to think Pamela can be so manipulative, I'm starting to believe it's true. She is capable of hurting those she loves far more than I ever imagined. I just wish it wasn't directed at Mike. He doesn't deserve it.

PAMELA

July 25, 2000

A lot has gone down the last few days. Rachel [the Program Director] told my father about the tattoo and the Alec relationship and we had a big argument. He said I'm not serious about my treatment. We both told each other off!

I can really only deal with this day by day. Alec's leaving for Arizona tomorrow to get his stuff and see his kids. He has a 16-year-old daughter! Now, that is freaky! He's supposed to come back in a few days.

I was taken by ambulance to the emergency room today. Had a bad seizure last night and threw up. I don't know what causes them. I need to work on myself and they are getting in the way. Am I trying to stay sick?

BEA

"You should see what I look like! I'm wearing a helmet with wires sticking out of it like Medusa," Pamela tells me in her usual off-beat, self-deprecating way in a phone call from the hospital.

I don't know whether I'm supposed to laugh at her joke or cry at the image of her being hooked up to so many wires.

It brings back the pang of guilt I feel for leaving her in California. It's much too far away, and I'm beginning to question the choice we made in sending her there.

"Well at least they're trying to figure it out," I respond, trying to convince myself of that as well.

"In a way, I'm so relieved to be in the hospital. . . but I can't believe," she begins to sob, "just as I'm getting sober, something else drags me down."

I cry along with her.

We have eight phone numbers taped to our refrigerator, for: UCLA's ER, the nurses' station, a general hospital number, direct line to Pamela's room, the neurologist, epilepsy expert, RR, and a psychopharmacologist. Mike is constantly juggling calls with all of them.

I, meanwhile, am tossing down Excedrin for the throbbing headaches caused by the pressure of having to deal with one crisis after another.

They come to a pulsing crescendo when the doctors tell us Pamela's seizures are psychogenic, caused by emotional trauma, not epilepsy. She's immediately released from the hospital with a prescription for more psychotherapy.

I'm relieved . . . but have no idea where we go from here.

PAMELA

August 2, 2000

As slow as the day is, time travels pretty quickly sometimes. Pain, guilt, happiness. I ate more than I wanted, went to the AA meeting, my treat-

ment. I lied for attention. Why did I fake seizures? How does that benefit me? Sometimes I can't tell between reality and fantasy.

I know my parents have suffered but I continue to make them feel my pain. They must hurt as long as I do. I want to let that go. WHO AM I? I have to find that out. I can't communicate correctly if I have nothing to convey. There is no substance behind me.

My father did not sexually abuse me. I didn't like him hugging or touching me (I still don't) but I made up that he molested me. He never got in bed with me. God, I'm speechless now that I let it out – I'm trying to be honest with You.

About my drug habits, I snorted cocaine two times – once with Teddy and Cindy in Baltimore and once with Petey from Riggs. At Riggs I had two bouts with crack. In college I did ecstasy with Hank and Cindy about 5-7 times and smoked pot with Cindy almost every day. Over the last year, I drank mostly and smoked pot.

BEA

I'm in bed, tossing and turning. It's impossible to sleep. I look at the clock. It's 2 a.m. All I can think about are psychogenic seizures. I'm sick with worry that they will plague my daughter for the rest of her life. There has to be some way to prevent them. What if she's driving a car, or walking across the street?

Tired of staring at the ceiling, I get up and go to my computer. As it loads, which feels like an eternity in the stillness of the night, I'm wondering if someone will need to be with Pamela at all times to keep her safe. I pray a quick search through the vast resources of the World-Wide Web will give me the answer.

PAMELA

August 5, 2000

I just binged on chocolate-covered pretzels and purged it back up! I am dizzy and shaking and don't know why I did it.

Paula and Roger are leaving tomorrow. I already said goodbye. Dana called and we had a great talk. I feel really split though. It's like I have three lives, one in NYC, one in Stockbridge and another in Malibu.

Alec is supposed to come back and I'm so confused. I've been dreaming of Hank and Teddy almost every night.

I'm scared of myself – my thoughts, words and actions.

God, grant me the SERENITY to accept the things I cannot change, the COURAGE to change the things I can, and the WISDOM to know the difference.

BEA

"Hey, Mom." Paula walks through the front door, flings her backpack on the chair and gives me a peck on the cheek. It's an unexpected visit. She's making a pit stop after her grad school classes before heading to her home on Long Island, but by the troubled look on her face, I can tell she's come by to say more than hello.

She and Roger just returned from Malibu, and I'm all ears. I haven't seen Pamela since July, and am anxious to hear what Paula has to say.

I perk some coffee and we sit across from each other at the kitchen table.

"We spent a lot of time together and Pamela did a lot of talking," Paula says, and takes a sip of coffee. "Considering what she went through, physically she looks pretty good. We walked all over Malibu, went to Santa Monica Pier and she had a good appetite –we ate out a lot."

"What about the seizures? Did she have any?"

"You're not going to believe this, but she told me that she can start and stop them when she wants."

"What do you mean?" I'm incredulous.

"She controls them, she makes them up," Paula says softly.

"Why?"

"Who knows? Maybe it's for attention, because they always seem to happen when other people are around. Or, it could be some sort of survival tactic to cope with the trauma of the rape," Paula says.

After all the sleepless nights, conversations with therapists, neurologists and repeated hospitalizations, she's making them up? Why is she doing this to herself? Why is she doing this to us?

"It's a real sickness," I say. "I read all about psychogenic seizures on the internet, but it's still hard to imagine this is what Pamela has."

"It gets worse. On Saturday night, our last night, we went to PF Chang's for dinner. Roger was with us. And right in the middle of our meal, out of nowhere, Pamela's tone changes, she gets very quiet and says, 'I have something very important to tell you and you can't tell Mom or Dad.' But I feel I have to tell you, Mom, because it's really upsetting me."

"What is it?"

"Pamela said Daddy raped her."

I'm dumbstruck. "Pamela said that? To you? And Roger?" When she was at Riggs, she said her father was inappropriate with her because she didn't like the way he hugged her. Now she's saying he raped her?

"I know it's not true" Paula says. "I know Daddy never did anything to hurt Pamela, but she somehow believes it. She's having flashbacks, that he came into her room when she was younger and did something, but she didn't know what. She asked me why I kept my door locked when I was in high school, implying that it was because of Daddy, but I told her Daddy did not rape me, and he did not rape her." She is visibly upset sharing this with me. "I thought you should know in case it comes up in family therapy," she says.

How could Pamela spread such a terrible lie about her father? I know in my heart, Mike could never do such a thing.

Since her breakdown in Baltimore, Pamela has made Mike the target of her anger, blaming him for all of her problems, but this outrageous accusation is the last straw. I can no longer defend her when she's threatening to destroy her father – my husband – and our family.

Mulling it over, suddenly the haziness of the last few weeks comes clearly into focus. Pamela's needing a monitor to greet us, her lashing out at Mike in group therapy, and the coldness of the other patients toward us on our visit, are all beginning to make sense – the people at RR have been told Pamela was abused by her father.

They may have believed her, but thank God Paula didn't, otherwise we never would know the extent of Pamela's sick mind. What makes me angry, and less empathetic toward Pamela, even as she remains mentally ill, is her attempt to turn Paula, the sensitive, sympathetic twin, against her own father . . . had she told my son Michael, he would have dismissed it at the outset. And placing a grain of doubt in Roger's mind is unforgivable. He's new to the family and might think it's true.

There's no way I can keep this from Mike. But I know it's going to kill him. "Let me talk to Daddy before you do," I say.

PAMELA

August 7, 2000

I was able to start a poem yesterday on the beach and hope to finish it tonight to send to Uncle Joseph. It feels good to create again. I wonder if my friends are right when they tell me to try to get my work published. The disappointment would be unbearable, but guess it's worth a shot.

A White Lily Leaks

It is a beginning, the journey of a solid seed,
Ensconced in cherry-glazed cement.
The inner world where a single life grows
Surrounded by cold, hard, blackened earth.

Light will ultimately push it to break through.
Colored rays will stripe its heart in nature.
Vibrations will give rise to its growing soul.
Doubting, Doubting, Doubting . . . its simple power.

BEA

"I have to tell you something and it's not going to be easy," I say to Mike when he returns from work that night.

"What is it now?" he asks, throwing his attaché case on the floor and loosening his tie. I take his hand and walk him over to the living room couch. I have no idea how he will react.

"Pamela told Paula and Roger that you raped her," I say barely audibly.

The sad look on his face alarms me. His mouth falls open in disbelief at the latest twisted turn of events. He doesn't rant or rave, but shakes his head.

"She said it happened when she was a child," I add.

Mike paces the floor, trying to think of what he could have done that Pamela thought was inappropriate.

"I hugged her a lot and tickled her feet, but I did that with all the kids," he says, continuing to wrack his brain for logical reasons for this accusation.

It's Mike's nature to give bear hugs and exude warmth among people he loves . . . something his all-embracing Italian mother taught him early on. No one, except Pamela, has ever thought this behavior is sinister.

After a long night of soulful searching and self-recrimination, we conclude that Pamela must be confusing affection with sexuality. It's the only thing we can think of that makes sense and allows us, eventually, to fall asleep.

PAMELA

August 15, 2000

Another month and I'll be 23 years old.

Everything was all right until I talked to Dad about going home to NY this weekend and he is scared that I'm not ready, and I can't really blame him. I would love to see Angelina, LuLu and Uncle Joseph and am dying to go through my writings and drawings. But Dad wants to talk to Dr. Shiraz and Mac [therapist] to see if they think it's a good idea. Now, I don't really want to go. Then I ate a bunch of food really quickly and tried to throw it up but couldn't. Felt sick and stayed in bed all afternoon.

BEA

"I did something very bad," Pamela tells me.

"What is it," I ask with the usual trepidation.

"I can't tell you," she says, baiting me.

"Well, no matter what it is, it's in your past, and tomorrow will be another day," I reassure her, hoping she'll tell me what she told Paula. "God is all-forgiving and after all that you've been through, nothing will surprise Him or me," I say, trying to convince her to share the deep, dark secret that's festering inside.

She gives a slight hint. "It involves a family member."

This little game is getting sick.

I feel like an elastic rubber band stretched to the breaking point.

PAMELA

*This morning I woke from a dream not unlike those I've been having.
I was in high school . . . a loner . . . fumbling around in the background
while my best friend, Kristie, was the more competent student. In one of
my classes, I wrote a poem that won me a spot on a TV game show. I gave a
speech after the reading and said, "thanks to my mother and Uncle Joseph
who are great writers and my dad is too, kind of." For some reason, saying
that about my dad was treated like a terrible sin.*

BEA

Mike, still torn up about Pamela's rape accusation, is anxious to get it
out in the open and exonerate himself. He calls Dr. Shiraz to sort it out.

"What exactly did my daughter say happened?" Mike asks.

"Well in her intake papers, she said her father raped her when she
was 22, but I don't believe what your daughter said about you is true,"
Dr. Shiraz says. "She also said she took drugs with her brother, her
Uncle Eton and her Grandfather Eton."

"These are all lies! This never happened. I never raped her. She's 22
now! My son never took drugs and there's no one in my family named
Eton," Mike angrily replies.

"Mr. Tusiani," the doctor says in a patronizing tone, "the best thing
to do is wait until our next family therapy session, and I will try to coax
it out of Pamela."

"But that's a month away," says Mike, left hanging in the air.

Trying to put him at ease, the doctor points to positive signs of Pamela's progress. "The seizures have stopped, her mood is picking up
and after three months at RR she's sober and faithfully attends AA
meetings. She's even mentioned returning to New York recently. Let's
give it another month, and we'll see what happens then."

In the meantime, we continue to wire $22,000 a month for Pamela's
care and keep in touch with Dr. Shiraz, who constantly reassures us,
"Pamela is halfway there."

CHAPTER 8

Malibu

MR. DAVIS TO MR. MICHAEL TUSIANI (WITNESS)

Q: *I would like to talk to you about the time just before May of 2000. This is the time when your daughter has had the incident at Austen Riggs and you are considering a different facility. Ultimately she ended up going to Road to Recovery?*

A: *Right.*

Q: *Tell me about that time in terms of what information you gathered to decide where she was going to go next.*

A: *To the best of my recollection, we had a meeting with the administrator and Pamela was there. He was saying to her that your behavior needs a different type of facility. I think she said to us that day or later on she was upset with the conversation because she felt the administrator was blaming her for the rape, and she wasn't pleased with that.*

    They suggested she go to a place where she could work on her drinking, drugs, substance abuse and also get psychiatric care. They felt they didn't have the adequate program to do that and we needed to find another place. We were told that the social worker there, his name was Roy Spellman, seemed to be an experienced individual and would help us locate the right facility. And they assured us they would not let her go until she could go to a place to get proper help. We appreciated that, of course, we were frantic. Dr. Spellman came up with some suggestions.

    I think my wife testified yesterday that we went through a process of exchanging faxes. And my wife was pretty much the point person there. Although, I did get involved in some conversations certainly.

Q: *Did you do any independent, you personally, any independent investigation of Road to Recovery before you applied for your daughter?*

A: *I don't recall.*

Q: *Did you call anyone at Road to Recovery before the application process to find information out?*

A: *Yes.*

Q: *Who did you talk to first of all and what did you find out?*

*A: The director of intake, Patricia Samms. She had all of Pamela's paper-
work from Austen Riggs, and she [said she had] been approved, and
meets the criteria.*

Q: Approved for what?

*A: For Road to Recovery. She said they have been in business for ten
years, only one year in Malibu. A husband and wife own the facility.
Dr. Shiraz is the top person. It's a team approach, a twelve step program. The average stay is thirty, sixty, ninety days. Family is involved
by phone, updated regularly. It's very individualized treatment. And
scheduled family visits are important.*

    *They said it was $22,000 a month, with the exception of medication.
She said have two separate checks sent to her. I said could you [do]
wire transfer, and she said yes. And that was it.*

*Q: This was the information you had obtained after you learned she was
approved or information you obtained before you submitted your application?*

*A: According to my notes here I spoke to Samms and she said – I remem-
ber it was a big relief to me – she said we can handle her. Pamela's
diagnosis was common.*

BEA

I stare at the calendar. September 14, 2000. On it is written, Pamela's
23rd birthday. This is the third time in a row she's celebrating in a mental health facility. It's my daughter's first birthday in the new millennium, and I want to be with her. Mike and I miss her terribly and use
this birthday as an excuse to fly out to Malibu for a three-day weekend.

    When we arrive, we are surprised to find Pamela in a happy mood.
She looks great, her eyes are sparkling and she seems to exude uncharacteristic confidence, which causes my heart to flutter.

    Maybe the California lifestyle agrees with her? Driving along the
Pacific Coast Highway, I begin to fall in love with California myself.
The salty smell of the ocean on the left and the vast scrubby cliffs on
the right, filled with carefree surfers and volleyball players is surpris-

ingly restorative. I can understand why so many rehab places and art colonies are located here – it has a transcendental aura that radiates calmness and peace, and that's what I now see reflected in our daughter.

But what strikes me even more is how comfortable Pamela is with Mike. She isn't at all upset when he hugs and kisses her. In fact, she seems to enjoy his undivided attention. He and I don't know what to make of it, especially since her rape accusation looms in our minds, and we're anxious about bringing it up in family therapy.

Her attitude continues to surprise us as she initiates the conversation once we arrive at Nobu for her birthday dinner.

"I want to move back to New York and give my therapy with Dr. Masel another try," Pamela says confidently. "I'd like to return to Fordham at some point too."

Ever cautious about a mad rush to make quick changes, Mike harkens back to an old mantra: "What do your therapists have to say about this?"

"They want me to stay in Malibu, but I don't understand why. Everyone is so encouraging about the progress I've made. I'm starting to feel different from all the others who come to RR and leave after a few months. It's like I'm stuck here and can't seem to move on like everyone else," she says.

"Well, are you sure you're ready to move on, Pamela? Do you have a plan?" Mike asks.

"I'm sure I can keep my sobriety, I've done it for 5 months now, but don't know where I'd live. I can't come home, because there are too many memories of all my failures there. Maybe a community-living arrangement?" she says.

Call it a mother's instinct, but I've come prepared with some literature on an out-patient program at New York Presbyterian Hospital in White Plains, which runs an off-site housing program in the nearby suburb of New Rochelle.

"Take a look at this," I say as I place a brochure of the facility in front of her. My biggest fear is, Pamela will leave her current in-patient care without the necessary support systems in place to help her succeed. We've been down that road before.

PAMELA

My parents came in tonight and things went well. We talked about my plans to go back to NY. I'm not sure I'm confident about that. I thought I was. It's going to be hard.

I just read this pamphlet on a residential program in White Plains that might be a better option than moving right in with Mom and Dad. Wow! Ants are crawling everywhere! Is this a sign??? They are freaking me out! Calm down, Pam, please. Oh, oh, I'm going to start crying. God, what direction do you want me to go in?

BEA

In our therapy session with Dr. Shiraz and Mac, we learn Pamela is being monitored again at meals. After fifteen minutes of talking about food issues, Mike jumps in and steers the conversation in a new direction entirely, and I can feel the walls closing in.

"Have I ever offended you in any way that I wasn't aware of?" he asks, in a gentle yet straight-forward manner.

Pamela's eyes widen, but her mouth remains clamped. Silence is the only sound in the room.

I break it, for Mike's sake, to get this out in the open and have it over with.

"What is the 'bad thing' you've told me about that's upsetting you so much?" I ask, trying to draw it out.

"I'm not ready to talk about it," she says, averting her eyes.

Dr. Shiraz changes the topic. We've accomplished nothing.

How could Dr. Shiraz, of all people, sabotage us like this? He assured us he would bring up the accusation of rape in our family session, and now he's sweeping it under the rug. He had a chance to help us clear the air. Why didn't he pursue it? It doesn't seem right that a therapist would backpedal from something so vitally important to his patient's recovery and to our peace of mind, especially after we traveled such a long distance.

We leave California extremely frustrated. How can Pamela ever move on if she's spending so much energy holding deep, dark, fabricated lies like this in? How can we support and embrace her, when there is such a sham going on – even with the therapists.

PAMELA

September 19, 2000

What a horrible mood I was in today. The meeting with Dr. Shiraz and Mac made me feel hopeless, like I'm going to be a patient for a very long time. That's not good because then I can't think of myself as anything but a patient. Confused, and very sad, demoralized, outraged, doubtful and weak. Can I make it work in NY? Do I want to? I am lost.

This made it hard to enjoy the time with Mom and Dad. I hope I didn't disappoint them. Please keep them safe on their flight home. Home is such a sketchy concept for me now . . . but my gut instinct is to return to NY.

September 20, 2000

I called NY Presbyterian Hospital and asked about the residential program there. Deena used to work there and told me that compared to RR, it's still an inpatient, very structured program. That makes me a little wary so now I'm leaning toward a way of stretching my time here and getting my car sent out to me in the meantime.

I'm so grateful for Paula's recovery from Hepatitis C. I know she had to go through hell injecting herself every day to try to get rid of it – thank You God, for allowing the treatment to work. Dad told me that now she's probably thinking about starting a family!

Imagine! Me an aunt – or – my sister a mother! Aunt Pam or Aunt Pamela? I guess, Aunt Pam, would be more hip. I do want to be a cool aunt!

September 23, 2000

I felt so lonely tonight, that I thought of calling Hank – God, I hate saying (writing) that, but it's the truth and honesty is important. At least I didn't act on it.

I called Matt instead. He might go to the Musician's Picnic tomorrow with the group. I am kind of apprehensive about going because I get nervous in crowds. I see myself freezing up while walking around, scared to talk to anyone. Hoping, no one will talk to me, then wondering why no one is talking to me. I wonder why I set myself up like this? My intention for tomorrow is to have an open mind.

September 24, 2000

Do I have to be in a treatment center or hospital for the rest of my life? It seems that way if I can't start being able to enjoy this life. I don't want to be here but there's no place that I do want to be. I need some relief. Drinking or using just can't be the answer. Someone else can't be the answer either. Self-pity will get me nowhere fast. Maybe I'm asking for too much.

September 26, 2000

Just got back from the Narcotics Anonymous meeting. Unlike the AA meetings where I know most people and feel part of the group, I get nervous at NA. Maybe it's because the crowd seems tougher.

God, I feel really ugly. I'm breaking out all over, my hair is at an awkward length and I hate being 135 pounds! Oh, poor me!

I need to work the "Steps." My 4th Step in particular (make a fearless moral inventory of yourself) has been sitting around, waiting for me.

September 27, 2000

I finally spoke with the intake person at NYP Hospital and set up a day I can go visit the program. I talked to Mom and Dad about it and I'm going to go home next week for a few days. I feel like this is a well-thought out plan to go check the place out and spend some time in NY to figure out if I can live there. Go Pam! Sometimes I need to give myself credit when credit is due.

Trying to restrict my food intake – tonight I was able to skip dinner. I had a brownie and 9 calorie Carbolite ice cream instead. If I'm not around food, I don't eat – that's how I diet. Not so good, but I want to get down to 130. I'd really like to be 125, but I can start with 130. I weighed myself today and I'm down to 134. This is the only way I can lose – two meals a day is too much.

October 1, 2000

Great AA meeting tonight. I love the unity in Malibu, people are very welcoming to newcomers and are so committed to their sobriety.

Matt and I left early and went to the beach. We had a nice talk and I felt very comfortable with him. I didn't feel as though he could take away all my pain or that he carries all my happiness, we just talked like friends. I was able to open up and didn't feel anxious. I had no urge to jump his bones either. It feels I've come a long way.

BEA

A week later, Pamela calls and is dropping hints about a new special friend.

"Mom, I met this really nice guy named Matt."

"Oh?" I say, trying to hold back judgment when deep inside I know it's there. "Where'd you meet him?" I ask, hoping to disguise my concern.

"He's an outpatient at RR, and we see each other at AA meetings."

My antennae go up. If this guy Matt is in AA, it means he has some kind of addiction. I wonder what demons he's fighting and why he needs treatment at RR? I hope he's not another Alec, just looking for sex.

I know I shouldn't care, or at least the therapists tell me I shouldn't care, about what happens in the privacy of Pamela's bedroom. But given her erratic past, I can't help but feel troubled.

Why do I have to worry about this in the midst of planning Michael's wedding? Even though Pamela has made significant progress since Paula got married – she's sober, confident, gained some weight and looks healthy – I still feel that I can't go to Michael's wedding and enjoy myself without worrying about her. I wonder, if she ever gets married, will I be happy then?

PAMELA

October 2, 2000

I'm in knots and feel like I'm going to crawl out of my skin. There's a big power struggle between me and Mac [P's therapist] and Dr. Shiraz [the director]. I told Mac when I get back from NY, I want to look for an apartment and his reaction was confusion over my impatience.

What is the problem with me wanting to move on? I'm scared as hell, but what do I do stay in this protective environment just because I'm scared? I would think that my progress shows I'm ready.

Why is RR different from Riggs? My freedom wasn't constrained at Riggs, I just wanted to be back in NY too badly. This time I am choosing to stay out here for my recovery. I just want the freedom I've worked so hard for. I can see how I might want to move back to NY only because of my frustration with RR and that's not the right reason for doing so.

I don't know why I'm afraid I will lose myself in my home environment but I am. If I didn't admit that, I'd be as sick as my secrets!

My parents did say they support me in whatever my decision is. You think I want to screw up?

October 4, 2000

So, I'm here – home in NYC. Angelina is lying on my leg just like old times. Of course, I'm a new me so these are new times. I got a very warm reception from my family. Dad and Paula picked me up from JFK. Michael, Cathy and Uncle Joseph came over and Mom made chicken cutlets. Yummy! I felt pretty calm and comfortable. I did get a little shaky and tearful when I checked out all my clothes. The ones that are too small for me bummed me out. I can't believe I felt that I was fat when I fit into them.

I am a beautiful woman. I am healthy and carry myself well. I accept myself as I am. I have the strength to overcome unhealthy thoughts. My emotions are valid.

I did not get to a meeting tonight. I feel okay, but maybe I should have pushed myself to go.

October 5, 2000

Went to the "Atlantic Group" meeting tonight with Maddie and Lily who were in Road to Recovery but are now living back in NYC.

I had to say I was from the Malibu meetings and people came up to talk to me afterward. I guess that's a good thing.

I'll get into the NY Hospital thing another time, it was basically another treatment program – probably not worth it. New York is hard to be in. My anxiety is above the calmness I strive for.

BEA

When Pamela and I pull up to the facility in White Plains, the sprawling green grounds that immediately sweep into view deceptively promise the same lightness of spirit inside. But the atmosphere beyond the main entrance of the facility is less welcoming with its high ceilings, somber walls, wide hallways and antiquated décor.

"What's wrong with your daughter?" The mother of another young adult who's also being evaluated, strikes up a conversation.

"She's had a nervous breakdown," I respond, much to her surprise.

"She's such a beautiful girl, who looks like she has it all together," she says, then goes on to tell me about her own child, who looks as if she has developmental problems.

When both young women walk out of the Dialectical Behavioral Therapy session they were sitting in on, I see they're having a conversation. I'm surprised how easily Pamela socializes with this stranger, and realize there is much I don't know about how my child relates to others. She wishes the other girl good luck as we exit the elevator together, and I marvel at her kindness and maturity. This is a good sign.

Back in the car, I ask how the class and interview went.

"I can get the same type of therapy at RR," she says.

We drive on to the community living residence where she has another interview with a social worker. Afterward, the young, plainly dressed woman takes us on a tour of the house where we find enough bedrooms to house eleven residents. A chart on the refrigerator lists daily chores for each resident and outside, on the deck, I notice tin cans overflowing with cigarette butts. It's co-ed, but at the time of our visit, the only residents are four women – two are mothers, and none is as young as Pamela. All are absent during our mid-day visit, which makes the activity level of the house hard to gauge.

We jump back into the car and find a place to have lunch and discuss our impressions of the morning's events. Pamela sits facing me with her back to the bar in a small bistro-type restaurant that serves light fare.

"New York is just too busy for me, it makes me anxious," she says, as she tries to sort through her feelings about the program she's just seen. "It's warmer and calmer in California, and besides, I know what I have there – living in a beach house with strong support from my AA group is a better way for me to step down. I don't know that I can fit in here in White Plains, the people in the house are older than me, I'm afraid I'll be lonely."

At that very moment, a single white bottle among the shelves behind her head pops out at me.

"Look behind you," I say.

When she does, she sees what I see – a rum called "Malibu." Both of us take it as a sign that could very well determine Pamela's destiny.

PAMELA

October 6, 2000

Just got home from a Yankee game. They won! It was nice to be there with Michael ... he took us to his office and gave me some souvenirs. I hope he likes it there. It did make me a little nervous because a lot of people were drinking.

I went into the bathroom and puked up the cookies I was eating. It was scary that I could do it so easily after not doing it for a whole month.

Dana is supposed to stay over tonight – oh, she's here!

BEA

Dana drove down from Lenox, MA for the weekend. Although Pamela is initially excited to see her former Riggs roommate, the atmosphere slowly becomes thick with tension as Dana brings back memories of a time and place Pamela would rather forget. She doesn't see her friend making any real progress with the anorexia and OCD she suffers from, and senses Dana's striving remains stagnant.

After Dana leaves, two former friends from RR, who have since moved back to New York, offer to take Pamela to an AA meeting in their neighborhood.

"Isn't it great you have friends here who understand what you're going through?" I say.

"Mom, you just don't get it. These girls aren't any better. They're still suffering from bulimia the same as they were when they were in RR. If they didn't recover, what chance do I have with all my problems?"

Her mood has dipped dramatically with this realization.

Mine dips too. What makes me so sad is, after five months in California, Pamela is beginning to consider it home – her friends, AA and the lifestyle in Malibu have created a safety net for her to run back to – and I worry she might land there permanently.

Even though she's 23, she was never able to take the traditional route of graduating from college and establishing herself in a mature way before separating from the rest of the family and moving out of the house. Of course, I want to see her leave home and succeed as a young adult, gaining her independence, as all mothers do, but it should be based on emotional stability, not on a need to escape.

PAMELA

October 9, 2000

God, I need some spiritual healing. Thank You for getting me back to Malibu safely. My mood swings have been in full force since I went back home. Where is home? I've been feeling so depressed. Somehow, I feel more centered now, lying in bed, looking out at the dark ocean. Could I be more connected to You here? Well, I know the connection is inside of me, not exterior, so that doesn't make sense.

Why do I shut off when I'm upset? I couldn't talk to Mom or Dad, it's like I'm in my own world and no one else can enter. I couldn't even communicate with my parents. What is wrong with me? I hate that so much! I can't even think about the money my parents are spending on this, probably over $100,000 by now! I have so much to be grateful for, my parents love me incredibly and I love them immensely and can only promise I will do my best.

I like the support system and familiar faces at RR but I get the feeling that some think I should be gone already. I need to learn how to deal with my scariest enemy – myself!

I want to be on my own. I've done it before and I did survive, except for the bad behavior. Why am I so anxious about my next move then? Does it mean I'm not ready? I see it as my pattern of fear of doing things on my own. . . work, school, sports, camp . . . but once I did them, they turned out all right.

I am a wonderful person. I deserve to have a wonderful life. I will find happiness one day. I just have to keep working on it one day at a time.

BEA

Just before Pamela's trip back to California, she comes down with a cold, which delays her trip twenty-four hours. I'm nursing her with hot tea, when she startles me by jumping out of bed and heading toward the kitchen.

198

"I need to get a haircut before I leave," she says, flipping through the Yellow Pages.

"What do you mean? Your hair looks beautiful. Why do you want to get it cut?" I say, trying to short-circuit this impulsive act. "It's cold out, and you're feeling miserable. You're in no shape to go out," I plead with her.

But she's on a mission, and ignores what I say. Before I know it, I'm heading down Third Avenue to some new hair salon with her, because she's afraid to walk there alone.

I start working on a crossword puzzle while she is escorted to a stylist on the second floor, and when she reappears, her hair is very, very short. It leaves me speechless.

Her brother Michael's wedding is a month away, and not only do I have to worry about how to conceal the crown of thorns she has tattooed on her arm, but she now looks like a boy! For sure, all eyes will be on her instead of the bride.

Why does she always do this? Draw attention to herself in a negative way? I'm incensed, yet hold my tongue. I know she's waiting for my reaction, but I won't give it to her. In fact, neither of us says a word on the ten-block walk back to the apartment.

Pamela is profoundly sullen and non-communicative until I drop her at the airport the next day. When I return home, I sit at the computer with my scattered thoughts and torn feelings and write her a letter.

October 10, 2000

Dear Pamela,

Yesterday was a hard day for both of us. You left for Malibu feeling badly, and while I respect your privacy in terms of revealing exactly what factors caused that, I can only communicate to you my own feelings about this past weekend.

I need to share some thoughts with you. I felt very uneasy, as if I was being used, pushed ever so gently into old patterns of needing to rescue you from making decisions, particularly about your ambivalence in going back to RR. I feel as if you have a way of manipulating me into feeling sorry for you.

I also regret not having said no when you asked me to accompany you to get a haircut because it was an impulsive act, decided by you in a split-second, and in retrospect, my going along with it was unsettling. Everyone told you how beautiful your hair looked this past weekend, but cutting it, I've learned, is still a way you act-out to show what you can't express verbally.

Closing yourself off from me and everyone else in the house without some indication as to why, made me feel like a victim in my own home. It's uncomfortable to feel avoided by a family member where we all live. I don't like it. Direct dialogue is a better means of communicating.

I love you very much, but love doesn't equate with feeling sorry for you. There's a difference. It occurred to me while driving back from the airport, and afterwards when I thought about it, the only real help I can give you is to let you fly away to a place that will help you to express yourself in a way that won't be damaging to you, me, and others in your life. There were many indications to me this weekend that you are certainly on that path. It made me happy to see a glimmer of your old self with a newfound strength and self-awareness.

I hope you understand these thoughts needed to be expressed, to perhaps open up a meaningful exchange between us in the future. They are written with honesty on my part and admiration for the enormous efforts you have made and continue to make in your recovery.

Always wishing you the best,

Love,
Mom

As soon as I drop the envelope in the mailbox, I want to retrieve it. Dr. Spellman's warning flashes back. "You shouldn't praise Pamela for what she should be – an adult." Did I just do that? Can I even utter a word anymore without it being picked apart by therapists or even myself?

PAMELA

God, please help me call apartments tomorrow, I really want to find a place and move in with Amber. She is a good, sweet person and we could help each other out. I really want this and don't want my fear to get in the way.

I really want to have a Twix bar . . . really badly . . . it's only a few feet away. Why do I feel so guilty? Anyway, art class was good tonight, oil painting is hard, but fun. I also had a massage today – wow, it was awesome! I really like Matt – I'm starting to get butterflies in my stomach and my heart is fluttering. Rationally, I know it's perfectly human to experience longings for someone I'm attracted to. Hopefully, I will think before I act and be better able to deal with the consequences.

October 20, 2000

I did it! I actually did it! I went to the housing complex in Calabasas today and left a check to hold the apartment I saw yesterday. It wasn't that nerve-wracking either. I'm happy for myself!

Matt and I went for an ice-cream after the meeting tonight. I feel like I'm really falling for him. God, please guide me in a healthy direction.

October 22, 2000

I had a great time with Matt at Universal Studios today. I was worried I wouldn't have a good time. I hate feeling that way. It's like I'd be more comfortable just staying home by myself. I don't want my life to be like that.

I ate a bunch of garbage – chocolate and candy – and feel fat as hell (if hell is fat, that is).

BEA

Within two weeks of returning to California, Pamela is adamant about her plan to step down from RR, continue there as an outpatient, and get on with her life.

She quickly finds a two-bedroom apartment at Malibu Canyon Apartments in the suburb of Calabassas for $1300 a month.

"It's unfurnished and I get it Nov. 1st if I leave a $150 deposit," she tells her father excitedly. "I'll need to buy furniture, get a phone and cable hooked up."

"What's the rush?" Mike asks, trying to temper her spinning wheels. "Can't you wait until after your brother gets married?"

"Don't worry, Dad, I don't plan on moving in until after I return from the wedding, but I need to get it ready and guarantee payment now. I already found a roommate. Amber, from AA, says she can move in with me after Christmas."

"What does Dr. Shiraz have to say about this?"

"He's totally supportive, Dad . . . did I mention I need a California bank account, a credit card and my own checking account?" she says, on a roll. "Oh, I almost forgot, can you ship my Subaru, TV and stereo out here?"

"Draw up a monthly budget. Show me what your plan is for managing your money and living on your own," Mike says. This time is not like her apartment in New York, where he was in charge of paying all the bills. He has to know Pamela recognizes the expenses she has, and determine whether she's responsible enough to handle them by herself.

I find it interesting that RR is supportive. Just two weeks ago they discouraged Pamela from stepping down in New York, but in California, it seems to be okay. This change of attitude troubles me.

"I think they just want our money," I tell my husband.

"I spoke with Mac, and he said Pamela is confused about making a decision," Mike says, "and that's normal. He advised her to slow down, take it day-by-day for a month and visit other treatment places in New York when she comes back for the wedding."

Oh, the wedding! All I can think of is table seating, planning the rehearsal dinner and worrying about guests coming into town. How can I be expected to visit more facilities with Pamela when she'll be home for such a short period of time? She's not my priority right now, Michael is.

I take the bottle of valium out of the medicine cabinet and put it in my purse.

PAMELA

October 24, 2000

Less than two weeks until I move into my new apartment. I'm thinking of doing outpatient Monday, Wednesday and Friday and change my art class to Tuesday, Thursday and Saturday so I'll have something to do every day.

Afternoon group put me in the worst place ... so depressed. Assam thinks it's because I have a pattern of doing something new and then getting upset over it, like I did when I moved back to NY from Riggs. Then I started crying because I wanted to see Mac and found out he'd already left. What an asshole! He was supposed to see me today! God, let me let go of this anger.

Matt was here today too, but he spent most of the time with the two new girls, which of course, bugged me too. I was already in a bad mood, it just twisted the screw a little harder into my side.

I went to art class and was painting grapes when Matt showed up and scared the hell out of me! He came up right behind me while I was painting, and reassured me he doesn't look at any other girls but me. He told me he was worried I didn't like him because I left without saying good-bye and we both laughed at our insane insecurity.

November 1, 2000

Had a little flashback episode on All Hallows Eve. I don't really know exactly why I flipped out except for the stress of change and getting freaked out when I was alone at the Cross Creek meeting. I felt someone rubbing my back, but no one was there.

Anyway, Dr. Shiraz and Mac want me to stay at RR until after I'm back from Michael's wedding in NY, but I've decided to go ahead and move this Saturday. I believe I'm making a good decision. I am not a mental patient but a strong and capable woman, ready to live a healthy and happy life. Whatever happens, God, I know I am not doing this alone. You are with me. I love You tremendously.

BEA

"It's madness for her to move a week before the wedding," I tell Mike as he walks in the door and drops his briefcase. The poor guy hasn't even taken his coat off and I'm already bombarding him with my own frustration.

"Bea, you have to understand, she feels like an adult now and we can't control every little thing she does," Mike replies. "It seems the only power we have over Pamela is her budget. See for yourself." He goes into his bag and tosses me a piece of paper. "She faxed me one today."

To Dad
From Pamela
11-02-00

Monthly Budget	
Rent	$687
Phone	125
Electric	25
Gas	25
Cable	31
Appliance Rental	26
Groceries	300
Gas for Car	80
Art Class	400
AA Meetings	30
Cigarettes	135
Movies/Restaurant/CDs	300
Clothes/Spending	300
Total:	$2,464

"This doesn't even include the mattress and furniture she bought!" I say, with a sour taste in my mouth. It makes me sick to think of Pamela taking advantage of us.

"I don't think she's focusing on the money we're spending. This move is actually going to bring our costs down," Mike says. "The bills from RR will drop from $22,000 a month to $8,000. I know Pamela's in a rush to move on, but she's also showing signs that she's capable of handling it."

"I just hope you're right," I mumble warily.

November 5, 2000

Guess where I am? It's day two and I'm alright! Yippie!

I went to AA this morning and saw my sponsor Teri. She bought me a housewarming gift – a really cool candle and card. I am really blessed.

Good news . . . Paula went to her doctor and found out there's no Hepatitis C detected in her system and if it remains that way in 6 months, she's cured! Thank You God for that! Faith is such a beautiful practice! Please help me be conscious enough to separate from my self-centeredness and pick up a card for my loving sister. Oh, and I need to get Michael and Cathy a wedding gift. Why am I always so wrapped up in myself?

Went to RR to pick up the rest of my stuff, did some grocery shopping and rented two movies (not a good thing for me that I left my driver's license and credit card at Blockbuster!).

Food continues to be the devil, I'm convinced. I ate a chocolate chip muffin tonight instead of dinner. I am not anorexic anymore. Please God, remove this obsession with my body from me.

November 6, 2000

Matt ran out of his meds today and was freaking out. He was manic and paranoid. When he walked over to me and put his head on my shoulder, I swear I thought someone died! I took him to the pharmacy and then he wanted to buy an Abyssinian kitten just like Angelina for $100. Thank God his check didn't go through! And I thought I was impulsive!

It felt so good to take care of him. All we've done is hug, talk, hang out and kiss once and a while. I haven't felt this way about someone without physically fooling around with him.

November 8, 2000

I just heard that Maddie's husband killed himself. I'm very sad for both her and him.

I'm kind of flipping-out because Macy's and Barnes & Noble called to set up job interviews for tomorrow. I am very nervous.

November 10, 2000

I stayed over Matt's yesterday. We kissed and then some. I want to tell him I love him, in a romantic way, but that doesn't mean I'm totally and utterly in love with him. It's too soon.

We went to see Robby's Drag Queens at a lesbian club last night. The show was awesome and I wasn't incredibly tempted to drink though I did feel a little uncomfortable around liquor.

I got the job at Macy's and will be stocking the first floor hosiery section from 6-10 am from Monday to Friday. Thank You God for the courage and confidence I had in that interview.

November 12, 2000

Oh God, why am I feeling this way? I am irritable and want to be alone . . . to hide . . . because I don't feel I can communicate with anyone.

Went to the movies with Matt. It was nice, but again, my instinct was to crawl inside my head when words got caught in the vise neatly tucked away in my throat. I really hate that!

I want to eat, eat, eat. Bad, bad, bad! I'm tired but I don't want to get up in the morning so I don't want to go to sleep – does that make sense? Please help me help myself.

November 13, 2000

Six months sober!!! Yeah baby!!! I've worked so hard to achieve this! I took my chip tonight and people were really happy for me. That they do care made me feel good about myself.

I went to Macy's today and prayed the whole time that my papers were in order. And what do you know? I met the woman who hired me and she took me to the office to work things out. God, You were there for me and I should never doubt that. I love having You in my life. Miracles do happen. I start work when I get back from NYC.

I'm getting nervous about going home for Michael's wedding just because I don't want to be in a funk, even though I know that getting depressed is okay and very normal. I can feel and think, but not act on those feelings and thoughts.

I'm anxious about seeing all those people I haven't seen in awhile. Plus, I've gained weight since then. Hopefully they will see it as a good thing.

BEA

Mike calls the house after I pick Pamela up from her red-eye flight at JFK. "How is she?" he asks.

"Hold on a minute," I say as I put the receiver down and glance toward Pamela's room. The door is closed and I hear the water running, the coast is clear.

It's amazing after all this time, I'm still on edge. I don't want her to think her father and I are talking about her behind her back, but it's nearly impossible for us to communicate when she's in the house, so we have to be secretive.

Picking up the phone, I quietly fill Mike in.

"I honestly didn't know what to expect, but she handled herself well. She picked up her own luggage and was surprisingly upbeat about her move to the new apartment in Calabassas. The only thing that seems to worry her is the job at Macy's. It's from 6-10 a.m. and she's anxious about getting there on time.

"I have to tell you, Mike, I'm worried about that too. She's on so many meds, I don't know how she's going to get up that early.

"Bea, remember what Dr. Spellman said about setting up situations for failure before they exist?" Mike says.

I remain subdued.

Changing the subject, he asks, "did she mention anything about the wedding?"

"She seems excited. She already set up hair and make-up appointments with Paula and is also planning on going to an AA meeting. And, get this – she's even thinking about taking Angelina back with her!" I say, marveling at the thought. "If she can be responsible for the cat – now, that would be a sign of real progress."

PAMELA

November 16, 2000
I am home in NYC and very anxious. I took a bath and am calmer.
The rehearsal dinner was hard. There was tons of alcohol everywhere and I smelled the red wine. It would have been so easy to take a sip of it but

thankfully, God's will did not have me picking up a drink tonight.

I felt awkward with people all around me, which scares me about how the wedding will be Saturday. Talking with my brother-in-law Roger, really helped me feel better about myself. I am very grateful to have him in my life.

I'm able to tell people about Matt – that I have a boyfriend now. I'm happy about that. Went to a meeting today, which put me in a good frame of mind. Took my "Angel" to the vet – she's all ready to fly back to Malibu with me on Sunday.

BEA

"Damn! I can't see the street names," I sputter as Pamela and I circle the same few blocks in Westchester, trying to find the restaurant where the rehearsal dinner is taking place. We just left the church, and since Mike came straight from work, we drove up in two cars. Of course, Pamela decided to ride with me and within minutes, I'm lost . . . in a strange neighborhood . . . just as the sun is setting.

"Don't worry, Mom, we'll find it," she says. It's a complete role reversal. I'm cursing and ranting, and she's trying to calm me down. I have good reason to be upset. Mike and I are hosting this special dinner for our son, and I'm already twenty minutes late.

As we drive past the same corner for the umpteenth time, Pamela stops me in my tracks.

"I need to make a call," she says, picking up the car phone. Out of the corner of my eye, I can see her leg shaking.

Watching her dial her AA sponsor in L.A., I'm ashamed that my impetuous behavior is causing her to reach out to a support system clear across the country. It makes me realize just how handicapped she is. Like most people, I can vent my anger and anxiety when I need to, but she can't. She becomes overwhelmed and shuts down.

I guess calling a stranger 3,000 miles away is a healthy way for her to handle the anxiety of the moment, but it still stings. I'm her mother – the person who's supposed to comfort her when she needs it – but not anymore. I feel lost in more ways than one.

When we finally arrive at the restaurant, Pamela takes a seat at the bar and starts talking to my daughter-in-law's friend. Michael gives me a look and motions for me to come over.

"You've got to make sure she doesn't drink, Mom," he whispers nervously, before turning to greet another guest.

PAMELA

November 17, 2000

Oh, God, I need strength now. I am coming up on a difficult . . . not impossible . . . situation . . . the wedding. What worries me most is my comfort level, anxiety-wise, not my obsession with alcohol and drugs, although I know it could lead to that easily.

Why am I so quiet??? It feels like I'm weighted down. Life is good and happy — why can't I express that? I don't understand myself, but I trust You do.

I am a calm spirit. I float above the world with a twinkle in my eye and a smile on my face. I accept myself for what I am, a growing woman, recovering from a depressive addiction. You are watering me everyday with love as I change to a healthy life. I am a FREE SPIRIT! I am a FUN and PEACEFUL woman! I am a companion to myself and others. I intend to remain grounded tomorrow. I will breathe in the air of tranquility and look at life around me to remind me of the beauty of God. I intend to dance and talk and enjoy myself . . . focused on the joy in my brother's heart.

BEA

"Who decided to put Penne alla Vodka on the menu?" Pamela asks as she walks over to my table during the reception. "It's an AA no-no!" she says, shaking her index finger at me.

I'm momentarily stunned. The wedding so far, has gone off without a hitch. I've greeted over two hundred guests on the receiving line and am just sitting down to enjoy the meal when Pamela makes me aware of this faux pas. Of course, after all the painstaking decisions I had to make about the menu, this single detail just seemed to slip off my radar.

"I'm so sorry, I didn't realize . . . " I say contritely to my daughter. "Would you like me to order you a dish of plain pasta."

"No, that's okay," she says, sauntering away.

She seems annoyed, and I feel terrible about it, but as soon as the band strikes up the Macarena, Pamela's up on the dance floor with her cousins. It's almost as if the rhythmic beat allows her to escape to another, more visceral place, where she doesn't have to ruminate about every remark someone makes, or dwell on her own problems.

The only time I see her mood shift, is when a set of slow songs is played, and she reverts to being a wallflower. My eyes are locked on her receding image as she slinks back to her table and sits there all alone. Though I pray some fine, compassionate young man will ask her to dance, it does not happen. Maybe they've heard stories about her flipping out or taking drugs . . . maybe they're afraid of her.

Sensing my daughter's need to be rescued, I walk across the dance floor to her table. No sooner do I pull up a chair, than she drops another bomb.

"I've decided to cut my trip short and fly back to Malibu tomorrow," she says, finding an antidote for her loneliness.

"But what about Thanksgiving? It's only a few days away. Aren't you going to be home for that?" I ask, trying to talk her out of an impulsive act.

"It's no big deal, I've already seen the whole family, and besides, I've got a job and an apartment to get back to in California. And I miss Matt."

My stomach sinks. So this sudden change of plans is really about her boyfriend and the need to be loved and wanted by someone.

I'm happy to see Pamela's life stabilizing, but I'm sad it's happening so far away, and dependent on a boy. Mike is right, we're losing her. New York is not home for her anymore.

She returns without the cat.

PAMELA

November 18, 2000

Michael and Cathy's wedding was wonderful! I had an amazing time with the love of my family and God. Thank You so much! I was calm and had lots of fun. It was great to see my cousin Lauren – everyone said we look alike – and we do!

I intend to have a good flight tomorrow.

I miss Matt. It would have been great to dance with him. . . I'll just have to fantasize about it!

November 21, 2000

Went to RR and saw Matt today. Am blessed to have him in my life. He makes me smile. Thank You God, for my sobriety, for NA meetings, my house-mate Amber, Matt, Assam, Angelina, my apartment, my car, my emotions, my peace. I make the effort, You make the outcome.

November 23, 2000

Happy Thanksgiving! I'm so grateful for this day. I realize how precious my life is and am very happy now for where I am in my world. I have received so many gifts and hope to use them well.

I stayed over Matt's. Am feeling really good about our relationship. I like the pace it's going at because I'm nervous about the whole sex thing and hopefully when we do, do it, we'll both be closer and more comfortable with each other.

Keep Michael and Cathy safe on their honeymoon.

November 28, 2000

I've been slacking off a little, especially when I stay over at Matt's. God, thank You so much for everything I have in my life. I mean, I have a life! It's amazing! Even though things are hectic lately with work and meetings and groups – I don't feel like I have time for a breath of air, that's not good. But, I'm also scared of having free-time on my hands – what would I do with it? Relax, somehow, I guess. Work is going well. I'm off today and tomorrow.

I think I'm falling in love, is it possible? Is it all right? I like Matt too much to obsess over our sex life before we even have one.

Please God, watch over Sherrie. She's struggling and I do care about her. Help all those in recovery and everyone in need of my love and the world's. I love Amber, my family and all of my friends. I keep all of them close to my heart.

BEA

Mike calls.

"I just spoke with Dr. Shiraz and he said Pamela's doing absolutely great." Mike sounds elated, and I can just picture him in the office, swinging backward in his chair.

"Her Subaru arrived in Calabassas, the hosiery department job at Macy's is going well, and she's negotiated her out-patient status to four half-days a week."

I haven't heard Mike sound so optimistic in a long while.

"The way Dr. Shiraz explains it," Mike says, "Pamela will go to RR for individual and group therapy on her appointed half-days, but won't be allowed to visit or eat at the facility at any other time."

I cringe. This restriction makes me nervous. Pamela won't be allowed to visit her friends and staff at RR for support if she needs it. What I fear most is she'll have no place to go to socialize, especially in the evenings, when she tends to be loneliest. This will be a drastic change for her, but I guess for RR, it's all about what money buys.

"It seems harsh – like a form of punishment," I point out and can hear his happiness bubble pop.

PAMELA

December 3, 2000

HELP! I'm pissed, angry, hopeless, confused, unhappy . . . very un-normal, like an open-wound, raw, crazed! What is happening? Why am I so emotional? Why am I so fucking tense, uptight, anxiety-ridden?

Am I mad at Amber? She's got it all, plus the body to go with it, but like my sponsor, Teri, says, I don't want her problems. But I see her getting what she wants and I'm angry because I'm not getting what I want. It gets confusing here because I don't know what I want. I know I'd like to have things go my way more, change Matt a little bit to fit my perfect image of a boyfriend or not have to eat so much so I could be thin again. It annoys the hell out of me! Nothing fits me.

You know how people talk about "God Shots" and spiritual awakenings? I want to know You're here with me. I need to know You feel my pain. I have to know it's going to get better. I want to know that I will have a life that I can enjoy. I want to be able to have fun!

How can I have fun when I'm fat and hardly feel comfortable around anyone? How can I do that without drinking and drugging? How can I let people in when no one seems to want to be in. Please, please, show me You're here.

December 6, 2000

Down and out in Calabasas! Today was very hard. I am grateful for my sobriety but feel it was in great jeopardy as I wanted to drink badly. I slept till noon and stayed in my pajamas till 5 pm. Very productive day! I don't know what's going on with me.

December 10, 2000

The other night, Friday to be exact, Matt and I made love for the first time. I was nervous to expose my body but he said the exact thing I needed to hear. He told me my body was beautiful. I don't know how convinced I was, but I loved hearing it.

I told him I loved him and I meant it. It doesn't matter. Well, maybe it does feel a little awkward because he hasn't said it back to me but I don't expect it.

I've been feeling pretty normal the past few days, which is a relief. I think I may want to go to beauty school. Please dear God, You'll have to help me with that one.

December 15, 2000

I've been dishonest and feel soooo guilty. I called in sick at work the last two days just because of FEAR. Fear of being outside, in public, fear of boredom at work, and that the day will go slowly. I don't want to be a liar or lazy and unproductive.

I intend to have a productive and peaceful day tomorrow. I intend for time to pass quickly at work. God, be with Amber as she faces her demons with her husband tomorrow. My mom is struggling with a stiff-neck, I wish I could be there for her more. Please relieve her pain. And also, help Matt's migraines to go away so he can get some rest and peace. Thank you for another day . . . sober. Amen.

December 18, 2000

I quit work today! I feel shitty! I'm a liar. I feel so guilty. Or, maybe I should feel bad as hell?

Things That Make Me Happy
   Soothing music
   Lit candles
   Drinking tea
   Writing in my journal
   Daily intentions
   Talking to staff
   AA meetings
   My sponsor, Teri
   Reading AA literature
   Writing poetry
   Painting
   Dates with Matt
   Talking to Amber
   My kitty, Angelina
   Eating Ice-cream
   Watching movies
   Praying to God
   Having a job
   Shopping on the Internet
   Exercising
   Walking on the beach

BEA

"I quit my job today," Pamela mumbles into the receiver.

"What happened?" I say, biding time to collect my wits. This is such a letdown.

"It was just impossible to get up at 5 o'clock every morning," she says apologetically.

I knew it!

"Well, what made you take such an early shift?" I ask.

"I had no choice, Mom, it's the only time I could fit it in with my therapy sessions and AA meetings.

"Does Mac know about this?"

"Yes, I just had a session with him and he's starting me on a different anti-depressant called Paxil." Nortriptyline, Lithium, Zoloft, Effexor, Prozac, Serzone . . . now Paxil . . . half a dozen anti-depressants in three years. Will this one be the magic pill? What if, like all the other meds, it doesn't work?

Of course, I don't share my disillusionment and frustration with Pamela even though a stiff neck is making me very cranky.

I'm wearing a collar and taking steroids, and now this additional stress is giving me a pounding headache. Seeing me suffering, and with Christmas just a week away, Mike cancels our planned Dec. 26th trip to Malibu, and instead, offers Pamela the option of flying home for the holiday. To my great relief, she takes him up on it.

I am so happy to see my Pammy walk through the front door and drop her duffle bags, like she did when she used to come home from college during winter breaks. When we embrace, it's not forced or restrained, as it was in Malibu. Here, it feels natural . . . like two pieces of a puzzle inter-locking in a familiar fit. Taking advantage of this spark of the "old Pamela," I linger to nuzzle her soft cheeks and drink in her essence. I try to hang onto this moment as long as I can.

Having my daughter home, in my arms, makes me feel complete. She looks healthy, robust even, and her dark, thick, short hair is fashionably pointed with bangs. Silver earrings and bracelets and a black coat with a tie-belt, indicate to me, she's making the effort to take care of herself.

But within 24 hours, that image fades. The butterfly that I saw arrive at the airport yesterday has regressed back into a caterpillar cocooning on the couch. She stays in her pajamas all day under layers of thick blankets with empty soda cans strewn among the pillows. Her hair is unwashed and her eyes look blank.

I ask her repeatedly if she wants to go out, and she says no. She doesn't want to shop or go to a movie or get her nails done. The only time she gets up off the couch is to go outside to smoke, or take Matt's calls.

It's clear to Mike, Paula and Michael too, that despite the progress Pamela has made by living independently in Malibu, she is still suffering from depression. I pray this Paxil is going to kick in soon and elevate her mood so we can enjoy Christmas. But halfway into the holiday week she tells me she wants to take an earlier flight back to California."

I could have predicted it. Her pattern of solving problems is to run away from them. It's clear the only thing she could be running away from this time is us. Logically, we know she needs to separate from her dependence on family, but emotionally, it crushes us to feel rejected.

"This time, I'm definitely taking Angelina with me," she says.

This leaves me with mixed feelings. I can't believe I'm even admitting this, but, after feeding, scooping up after and playing with this four-legged critter for the past six months, I will actually miss the little imp. I also worry that Pamela is not as stable as she should be to take full responsibility for her pet right now.

Even though I don't want to fall into the old trap of setting her up for failure, I start to protest. But she cuts me off.

"This isn't about you, Ma!" she says adamantly. "It's my cat."

PAMELA

January 2, 2001

Why are things like they are? Why am I sad? Why is life so drab?

Why do I hate life?! Why do I have to go back to Road to Recovery? I don't want to go back! Things are supposed to be great ... sobriety, love and "happiness" is supposed to come next, but it doesn't. I've been through this so many times. Why? Why am I depressed?

BEA

Mike approaches me as I'm stepping out of the bathroom. I can tell by the look on his face, something has happened.

"Bea, don't get upset. I just got off the phone with RR and they want Pamela to go back as an in-patient for a few days to stabilize her."

Before I have a chance to react, he fills me in.

"It's nothing serious. We're not terribly concerned," Rachel, RR's program director, told Mike when he called for a regular weekly update. He was not expecting to hear bad news.

"What exactly happened?" he asked.

"Well, Pamela called last night and said she was having suicidal thoughts," Rachel explained. "So I told her to come in to RR to talk about it."

"Did she?" he asked.

'Yes, she came in for a session, but went back home," Rachel said.

Two days into the new year, and 2001 is already off to a shaky start.

I could sense this was coming. Pamela called me yesterday and told me the New Year's Eve party she attended in Malibu was a disaster.

"I was miserable, but had to put on a happy face," she said, when I asked about it.

She felt awkward and out of place, she told me, and her friends, including Matt, didn't understand why she left early.

Knowing her so well, I do understand. Although she looks good, and seems stable outwardly, on the inside, social anxiety is paralyzing her with fear and forcing her to flee.

She was in her apartment when the bells chimed, all alone – a state of hell for her – where new resolutions are pointless.

PAMELA

January 3, 2001

RR wants me back in and I refused. Dr. Shiraz is pissed to say the least. I'm just having a rough time. I'm angry at myself and the world. I need to express that anger and give it a LOUD voice. I don't feel like writing about it.

I love Matt and some part of me wishes I could float on that cloud and that would make the difference, but experience tells me otherwise.

Even so, I accomplished a lot today – I cried, opened my mouth, let people into my world – and cleaned my space.

I intend to work hard tomorrow in therapy. I intend to be free with my voice and try to connect with others. I need connections. I intend to be free and enjoy the elements.

BEA

"We shouldn't make Pamela feel like a failure," Paula says to Mike and me from across the kitchen table. "She went to a safe place New Year's Eve, didn't drink, and reached out to RR when she needed help."

"You're right. But it's so hard to watch her slide backward again," I say.

"What more can we expect of her at this point?" Paula continues. "She handled herself like an adult. When she felt a bad situation coming, she took action to help herself. Remember when she came back to New York after Riggs, she acted on her impulses and got in trouble? Well, in Malibu, on New Year's Eve, she acted responsibly by calling for help – which is more than she's ever done in the past."

Paula's positive take on the situation is eye-opening and comforting, but something in the pit of my stomach tells me we're in for more bad times.

PAMELA

January 4, 2001

Alcoholics Anonymous – Step One Exercise

1) *What has kept you from recognizing your powerlessness and your life's unmanageability?*

Family expressing confidence in me, functioning on a daily basis, achieving good grades, jobs, friendships, hiding my behaviors.

2) *What area of your life has caused or is causing you the most sadness?*

Emotional life: rejecting myself and therefore thinking others reject me; being antisocial.

3) *What events in your life caused you to realize the extent of your pain?*

Attempting to kill myself, using my body – giving it away for drugs or attention. Attention-getting behavior toward my parents.

4) *What specific pain is your loudest signal?*

Loneliness is torture.

5) *What are some of your survival skills?*

Cutting, burning, faking seizures, drinking, using, ignoring, smashing, breaking, starving, puking, sex.

6) *How has this blocked you from seeing real problems?*

Covers my problems up and sets an alarm for emergency from my family/friends. The behaviors are not the problems, they are the so-called, solutions.

7) *What specific behavior causes a problem you have been avoiding?*

Playing the one who needs to be taken care of helps me to avoid being independent.

8) *How do you do this?*

Act incapable.

CHAPTER 9
Malibu

Q: *Bearing in mind that when anyone fills out a form the information that's placed on the blank page doesn't necessarily always reflect the answer to the question that precedes the blank. Given that, though there is at least a suggestion there that Pamela believed at some level that you had, that she had been the victim of sexual abuse by you and had the rape. There's a suggestion that both things occurred.*

A: *Right.*

Q: *My question is, first of all, I want to give you the opportunity to respond to this because I think —*

A: *Relax. Ask the question.*

Q: *Did you ever have any inappropriate physical contact with your daughter?*

A: *Absolutely not.*

Q: *Do you have any idea why Pamela might have filled this out the way she did?*

A: *Absolutely.*

Q: *Please tell me.*

A: *This was a very trying time for me. As you know, when you go into any facility they give you the psychological, you have to answer questions at each facility. To the best of my knowledge, this did not surface, this statement, in other admission forms, but it did surface in conversations that we had at Austen Riggs.*

Q: *I didn't see any reference to Austen Riggs either, including the discharge information. But it was —*

A: *You asked the question, I'll answer, I'll give you a full answer.*

Q: *Okay.*

A: *During therapy Pamela made a statement that I hugged her too much, okay. And Italian families, they express emotion. All my kids knew very well when I came home from a trip they would run up to me, and*

I would say give me a hug or come on, tighter, you can do better than that. It came up, and I think Pamela didn't like that. And she felt for some reason uncomfortable. Of course, she didn't say anything, but she felt uncomfortable.

Then a very, very disturbing thing happened to me. My daughter Paula comes to me and says, "Daddy, I have to tell you something. I went up to see Pamela at Riggs and Pamela said to me that – I don't know, I don't remember her expression. I think she said something like he fondled me."

Q: *She said you fondled her?*

A: *I was shocked. You know, when a kid comes to a father and says something like that, I said Paula, she is a sick girl. I mean my wife was there in the room when she said this. I said you got to believe me there's nothing to it. And my daughter said and my wife said of course not. We would have seen something. Even though you deny these kinds of things there's always that doubt and it just bugged the shit out of me.*

And I went inside – and I remember the incident very well. I sat in my den transfixed at the wall, just saying to myself I can't believe this happened. And then trying to say what could I possibly have done to give her that impression. The hugging, this I said, playing with her feet, teasing her about it because she had big feet, things like that.

And then I lived with this, you know. And I tried, at every session I would bring it up at Austen Riggs and at Road to Recovery. I remember one of the groups we had on our visits, these kinds of things you try to raise. I said Pamela, if there's anything you need to say, anything that I have done wrong, please say it. I wanted her to say that yes, I think you did this to me, Daddy, or you are mad at me because I did drugs, whatever it was. I was trying to put that puzzle [together]. There was something trapped in her. But nothing was said.

PAMELA

January 10, 2001

I hate You God! My life sucks! I'm just a fucking, fuck-up! I will never feel good. I hope I die! I don't know what's going to happen now. I'm sweating, my heart won't stop racing. What did I do? Who cares?

My thoughts are just too crazy! I hope I don't puke!

My family is so far way. I want my Mommy to take care of me.

I am three years old. I am ten, playing basketball all wrong. Why am I here? God, take me to a good place. I am a fool . . . an asshole . . . a piece of shit! Scared of everything! Stop now!

BEA

"Hello, Mr. Tusiani?"

"Yes, this is he," Mike says, not quite sure who's calling.

I'm standing within earshot and shrug my shoulders as if to say, "Who is it?"

"It's Amber, Pamela's roommate."

"Is something wrong?" Mike asks, as his eyebrows arch.

My antennae go up. It's about Pamela!

"She's fine now," Amber explains, "but earlier, I found her vomiting in the bathroom. I asked her what was wrong, and she pointed to a bottle of Trazodone on the floor. She couldn't remember how many she took so I called an ambulance, and they rushed her to West Hills."

"Is she in the hospital now?" Mike asks.

"They pumped her stomach and released her after three hours. She's at RR now."

Hearing the word "hospital," I grab Mike's arm desperate for details. He turns toward me.

"Calm down, Bea. She overdosed on a tranquilizer, but she's okay and is back at RR."

I feel faint. Mike sees me stagger and hangs up with Pamela's roommate. He makes me sit down and immediately phones RR's program director.

"Can I speak to my daughter?" Mike asks.

"She's still coming out of it," the director tells him.

"Do you know what caused her to do this?" he presses on.

"This was not a suicide attempt, just a cry for help. Pamela is very angry at herself because she acted out after doing so well for so long," she says. "Now is not a good time. She's not ready to talk about it yet."

She reassures him, "we'll keep her here until she stabilizes."

Mike hangs up the phone. "At least she'll be safe at RR," he says. But will she?

PAMELA

January 22, 2001

Slept well last night, except for a new nightmare. Stayed up the night before reading chapters 2,3,4,5,6 and 10 of the Big Book.

Am working on the 4th Step – my fear list. My biggest fear right now is Teri's direction for me to get a job somewhere that has a lot of people around like Starbucks or Blockbuster. That scares me because of my anxiety around people, and I am comfortable not having a job right now. Problem is, I do need to stay busy. I need to bring this up with Mac. I did have a meeting with Dr. Shiraz and Rachel. I prayed beforehand and it made all the difference . . . I am learning, God . . . it works. Anyway, they agreed that I could stay over at my apartment Thursday night as a kind of experiment. Part of me is afraid to leave here so we're slowly trying it out.

The meeting tonight was really depressing. People are in really tough spots. I suppose it helps me to hear that others are struggling, just like me. I am definitely not alone or one-of-a-kind. We all share the pain of life's tragedies but we also share the hope of fellowship.

BEA

"Mom, it's really hard being back at RR," Pamela says, calling me a few days later.

"They have me seeing a new medical doctor, who's not familiar with my case, and it's so frustrating. He's supposed to reevaluate my medications and might be changing them."

"Make sure you tell him everything you've been on," I tell her, worried that this new doctor might not be aware of her history of seizures and low blood pressure.

I'm frustrated too. This is the third doctor overseeing her medical care in ten months and I'm not so sure he'll be able to understand how complicated her case is just by reading her chart. It takes time to develop trust and confidence in a doctor, and the one thing Pamela needs above all else is continuity. She is backsliding right now, and having to adjust to a new doctor is not a good thing.

I'm thinking of telling Mike to call this new doctor, but don't know whether it's the right thing to do. The lines of communication at RR are not as clear as they were at Austen Riggs.

At Riggs, we were only allowed to talk to one person about Pamela – her social worker – and she was always present during every conversation. There were strict rules and boundaries between family members and staff, in an effort to protect the patient's privacy.

But at RR, communication is more scattershot. Everyone on the staff takes our calls, and it's not clear who exactly is in charge of Pamela's overall care. Is it the director? The administrator? The residential coordinator? The social worker? The medical doctor?

Mike thinks having contact with all of these staff members is good because we can get "background" information about Pamela we otherwise wouldn't be privy to. But I'm beginning to question whose interests are being served, the "buyer" (us) or the "client (Pamela). I sense Pamela knows this too.

Within days, she makes a strong case for herself and convinces Dr. Shiraz to let her go back to her previous half-day schedule at RR. But she is only back in her apartment a few days when she lands in the emergency room again for "misusing" pills.

PAMELA

January 23, 2001

Matt's father died and my emotions were on a roller-coaster ride today . . . from hyper-actively anxious to upbeat. Matt is struggling and I don't know exactly how I'm supposed to help. I'm better now though, after a meeting. I hope my love can offer him some comfort.

January 25, 2001

This girl came to RR today from Riggs. It brings up a lot of bad memories of myself and where I've been. They overwhelm me. I freaked out this afternoon thinking about what I was like then. I am not there – I am a totally different person! Wow – I guess that's a good thing to discover about myself. I am not sleeping in the same room with her though because I need to be alone and don't feel comfortable.

January 28, 2001

Matt is worrying me. He hasn't called since he left to go home for his father's funeral and I'm worried about his mental state and that he will relapse. Please, God, help him think rationally. I just don't need to deal with this anxiety.

I'm going back to my apartment tomorrow night and am excited about that.

February 2, 2001

I spent last night with Matt. It was really great to be with him but we didn't make love. I was disappointed. I'm so selfish.

Started feeling weird: panicking, shaking, feeling totally hopeless about my life, thinking about going back to Riggs. Thank you God for bringing my head back, there's no way I'm going back there. I called Mac and he told me to call the psychopharmacologist: the med withdrawal is causing it. That's a big relief.

BEA

"Guess what?" I tease Pamela playfully during one of our nighttime chats. "What do you think about having a family vacation in California?"

She squeals with delight!

"Daddy, Michael, Paula, Roger, Cathy and I have all been talking about it, and we've come up with some dates that might work."

"Really? Everybody's coming?"

We haven't all been together since Christmas, and Pamela's recent overdoses have us thinking she needs something fun to look forward to. Plus, we miss her and are worried about her.

"There are so many places we can visit . . . Disneyland, Universal Studios, and go shopping . . . it'll be just like one of our old family vacations."

"You can come to see my apartment and Angelina too! And I can take you to one of my AA meetings," she says, with growing excitement.

The very next day, she petitions the administrators at RR and negotiates her way into staying with us at our hotel when we make the trip.

PAMELA

February 7, 2001

I guess You can tell I've had a rough day. I was supposed to go home tonight but wasn't allowed because of Matt. He didn't take some drug test and the staff decided I shouldn't go home because of that . . . to be safe. I'm pissed as hell, but dealing with it.

Mom, Dad and the whole family are coming out here next week and I don't know how to feel about that. I want to call Mac, maybe I will. God, help me get through this. One day at a time, right? It sucks sometimes.

Please keep Amber and Matt safe. I pray for Avis, Juri, Maddie, Kathleen, Leslie, Ted, Mel, Kirsten, Deborah and all those in need of my prayers.

February 9, 2001

Went to the bank to deposit some long overdue checks from Macy's. Now I have some money in my account. I went to the Santa Monica Mall and bought Matt an engraved lighter for Valentine's Day. It says "miss you always". I hope he likes it. I bought some stuff for me too – a cool bag, a wallet, sunglasses, face lotion, shimmer, aromatherapy for my temples and a pair of Gap jeans (hopefully they'll fit the next time I try them on). I'm gaining weight. It must be because I eat much more when I'm at RR. The food is too plentiful there.

I'm getting excited about next weekend because I do want to see and spend time with my family.

BEA

"Oh, wow! Pamela looks like her old self," Michael says as we pull up to RR. Her hair has grown longer and her bony-frame is filled out. "She looks so good," he says again in my ear.

We're all so relieved to see Pamela looking healthy and in control as she jumps into the van and directs Mike up and down the canyon roads to her apartment in Calabassas, a suburb of Malibu. Once there, she gives us a quick tour of the place, while Angelina weaves her way through all of our belongings. It's small, but nicely furnished and the cupboards, I'm happy to see, are well-stocked.

"Is this your roommate?" I ask, picking up a picture frame on the bureau in the living room.

"Yes, that's her."

"I hope we didn't scare her away by descending on you like this," I say. "I thought we'd be able to meet her."

"Maybe later . . . she's working at RR. They just hired her as a cook, and she prepares lunch around this time."

I do a double-take when Pamela takes us to her room next. It's quite a contrast to the rest of the apartment. The bed is unmade, clothes are piled high on the floor, and the litter box is filled with many days' worth of Angelina's poop.

A light-bulb suddenly goes off in my head. Dr. Spellman from Riggs once said that a disorderly environment reflects a disorderly mind. I realize that even though Pamela looks good on the outside, an internal struggle is still taking place.

She's oblivious to my concern and seems unperturbed as she steps over the mess to retrieve a large sketchbook.

"These are incredible," Paula says of the still-life charcoals Pamela has made in her new art class.

We all notice how her drawings have evolved over the past year. At Riggs, her blood-dripping, self-destructive images were indicative of the chaos in her life. In contrast to that angry period, this sketchbook is more sophisticated, with realistic renderings of nude figures, animals and floral vases, that are well-organized and muted in color. And most of them are signed.

Maybe these nine months of sobriety have made the difference? We're all amazed that someone who struggles so hard to get through every day, can be so artistically expressive and gifted.

233

After seeing where Pamela lives, much else of what we do on this trip is driven by her vacillating mood swings. We ask, "What do you want to do?" or "Where would you like to go?" But she answers by shrugging as if she's a child again, incapable of making such decisions, and the burden is on us to fill every empty moment.

Thinking he's doing a good thing, Mike makes a reservation at Dar Magreeb, a Moroccan restaurant where we ate during a family vacation to L.A. in 1987, and one the kids enjoyed. Though well-intentioned, this trip down memory lane backfires because Pamela is not the same person she was back then.

As a 9-year-old child, she was thrilled by the belly dancers in their traditional costume, undulating amid the diners, but as an adult, the sexual atmosphere disturbs her. She becomes agitated and goes out for a cigarette every ten minutes, so we get up and leave before the meal is over.

With the two sets of newlyweds heading back to their respective hotel rooms, Pamela once again finds herself in an awkward position staying in a room with her parents. At 23, she wants to be treated like an adult, but her dependence on us keeps her stuck in the role of a child.

The following day we're filled with high spirits as we head for a day trip to California Adventureland. But ten minutes into the van-packed ride, Pamela turns from the front passenger seat and asks Cathy, who's sitting next to me in the back, "Can we switch?"

We all look at each other. We're driving 60 mph on the freeway and are wondering what's going on in Pamela's head.

"Sure," Cathy says, in her usual agreeable manner.

Mike pulls off onto the shoulder and as soon as the change is made, Pamela nestles her head on my lap and I gently stroke her beautiful, thick, black hair. You could hear a pin drop. We're all silent for the next several miles. We know she needs comforting, but don't know why.

Pamela's more in control on the last night of our stay, when she invites Matt to have dinner with us.

"Sorry to hear about your father," I say, when we first meet. His eyes start to tear-up, and Pamela puts her arm around his shoulder to comfort him.

234

In that moment I realize, Matt's just as broken as Pamela. Although I don't know what he's being treated for at RR, or how he landed there, I can see he and Pamela need each other for support.

Of course, I want what every mother wants for her child. I want her to fall in love with someone who is mentally stable and settled. But I'm deluding myself. Why would someone like that want to be involved with a girl who is so unpredictably fragile and mentally-ill?

I guess, for now at least, it's a good thing that Pamela has a steady boyfriend, because I know how desperately she needs to feel loved. What I fear is, she will carry the burden of Matt's problems too. From an early age, she has always had enormous empathy for people who are suffering, but she never seems to derive the same degree of empathy for herself from others. This void consumes her.

After dinner, it's hard to detach and say our good-byes when we bring Pamela back to RR. Standing on either side of her, Mike and I plant a parting kiss on both of her cheeks.

PAMELA

February 18, 2001

Why did I ever take those fucking pills? I want out of here! Being an inpatient at RR sucks! I can totally do the same things living in my apartment. It will be difficult, just like life is most of the time.

I need the strength to talk clearly and confidently to Mac and Rachel and Dr. Shiraz (if that's what it comes down to) about leaving inpatient care. I've been going to my apartment anyway, and doing well there. I don't want to feel disappointment over and over again.

Please God, I totally have faith in Your judgment and trust You will lead me in the best way possible. I intend to be open to compromise, if needed.

My weekend with the family went so much better than I imagined. Everyone was great, except a little guilt from Mom and annoyance from Paula, things went well. We went to California Adventureland next to Disney and it was lots of fun.

BEA

Flying back on the plane, I use the quiet time to reflect about Pamela's progress and jot down my observations.

Pros:
- Pamela stayed with us for two nights and didn't bolt to the safety net of RR.
- She appeared healthy.
- There was no evidence of shakiness.
- She didn't have to take pills for anxiety.
- She went along with the group dynamic, making compromises at the theme park, movie and shopping mall.
- She didn't have to call her sponsor to rescue her.
- There's no evidence of self-destructiveness: cutting, body piercing or anorexia.
- She's concerned with grooming her hair, make-up and clothes.
- She is committed to sobriety, with nine months substance-free.
- She drives back and forth to meetings, apartment and the gym by herself.
- She expresses herself creatively through artwork.

Cons:
- Poor self-image: she continues to think she's fat.
- Mood swings: she is bored easily. Her excitement typically wanes after a short while.
- She expresses herself verbally, after the fact, rather than beforehand, when she could make a difference about the outcome.
- Communication is physical rather than verbal: she curls into herself with her head down when she's upset.
- She leans on one person to feel whole within the group: like Matt or me.
- She splits people: expresses dismay to me about her father when he makes plans without listening to others; and tells him she's angry with me when I question her habitual shopping.
- She changes plans on impulse, and that sets up roadblocks that impede her own decision-making.
- She has a lax attitude about responsibility: she left bath water in tub, didn't renew her license plate on her car and left the litter box full.

When we land, I make a copy of this list and immediately mail it to RR's director.

PAMELA

February 20, 2001

I'm off Serzone. No antidepressants for the first time in 3 years!

And I feel good. I mean, not great, but a whole lot better being off meds. Everything is going well with my sobriety, with Matt, with my moods. The only thing that's getting to me is my weight and being here at RR. The new compromise is I can stay at my apartment four nights a week. It's better than nothing, but of course, I want to be totally out of here!

I tried very hard to diet today although I might be doing it wrong. I didn't eat all day until dinner and then I had a small piece of chicken, salad and grilled veggies. Now I'm in bed to avoid food even though I'm not hungry.

I also went to the gym today and did 15 minutes of stair-master, and then some sit-ups and 3 sets of leg machines and had a good work-out. Everyone was talking about weight and body issues today and it really got me down.

BEA

Pamela gets her computer working and e-mails me with a hopeful message.

"I'm totally off all anti-depressants and I feel better than ever. Isn't it strange, but good at the same time?

But within hours of my receiving this, Pamela calls in a jittery voice to tell me she's not doing well.

"Call RR," I tell her sternly, fearing she might do something stupid again.

"I can't do that, they'll want me to go back full-time," she says.

"I know you don't want to go back there Pamela, but maybe it's the best place for you to be to get through this rough patch," I say, trying desperately to convince her. "I thought you were doing well off the anti-depressants?"

"I've been having nightmares and can't sleep ever since they took me off Serzone, and I'm confused about whether I should start another antidepressant," she says.

On and off, up and down.

Of course it's exhausting for her. It's exhausting for me too, and I'm not the patient.

How is someone who is so confused, going to talk rationally to a new doctor about taking yet another medication? I'm sure she doesn't even remember half of what she's already been on, especially with the memory loss from ECT treatments and post-traumatic stress from the rape.

I feel compelled to step in and stop the process from spinning out of control. But how can I possibly help from 3,000 miles away?

I pour through "The Essential Guide to Psychiatric Drugs," by Jack M. Gorman, and make copies of the pages that indicate which meds have already been prescribed for Pamela: Nortriptyline, Zoloft, Wellbutrin, Lithium, Paxil, Effexor, Ritalin, Risperdal, Mellaril, Neruontin, Trazodone, Buspar, Xanax, Ativan, Klonopin, Depakote, Ambien, Restoril and Serzone.

Then I note the antidepressants Pamela hasn't taken: Elavil, Ludiomil, Tofranil, Luvox, Nardil and Parnate. I highlight the following passage: "Parnate almost always works, so the major issue is usually surviving its side-effects."

Looking up what they might be, I find drowsiness, dizziness, sleeplessness, increased anxiety, migraines and nausea.

I add that information to the 58-page packet I put together and mail it off to Pamela with the attached missive: "This material is from a book about medicines used to treat depression. I compiled it with the hope that it will help you have a meaningful discussion about them with your doctor."

PAMELA

February 24, 2001

RR is so totally boring. Groups are redundant, people are crazy, I can't take it anymore. But I need to replace it. Anyway, tomorrow I am free again. To do what, though?

238

I heard a speaker tonight who has really inspired me and helped me believe going to beauty school is the right thing to do. I'm scared as hell, but I can do it, I know I can.

The Enemy at Hand

I sleep to stop the chatter in my head.
I sleep to not eat, to avoid pain, to waste time.
I sleep to dream about things that aren't true,
To feel the warmth of something new,
To drown the hurt and end the rain,
To wake up someplace new.

The enemy is at hand.
When to savor life?
I can't wait to stop the fight,
Too much energy is spent in the struggle.
That is my way of living.

One day at a time is slow enough.
But, why the suffering?
I can't see why a life like mine should be lived.
It's going to end, the time is near.
Please, God, take away my fear.

February 28, 2001

Today just sucked. That I have to sleep at RR 3 days a week is soooo stupid! I need to get a job or go to school before I can leave there. It's something I want too!

I intend to go on the Internet Thursday morning and look up schools, both academic and beauty and get catalogues and information so I can TAKE ACTION IN MY LIFE!

Amber said Mom left me a message today and told her that she feels lonely and isolated out in the Hamptons all by herself. She reminds <u>me</u> of <u>me.</u> We are alike in a lot of ways. I can't call her because it's too late and I don't have a calling card, besides, I don't even know the area code. God, please let her know how much I love her and miss her and that I wish I could talk to her. I love my Mommy and do not want her to suffer! Please relieve her loneliness.

While I doubt Pamela thoroughly reads through and digests the entire 58 page manifest I send her, the quote about Parnate obviously catches her attention.

"I've been talking to Dr. Vasily about going on it," she says.

"Did he tell you it has many food restrictions?" I ask.

"Yes, they gave me literature that says no ripe bananas, avocados, soy sauce, aged cheese, caffeine – and just my luck – chocolate!"

"That sounds really difficult. Do you think you'll be able to do it?" I say.

"What choice do I have, Mom? Stop worrying!" she says.

I'm on pins and needles. After all, her favorite snacks are chocolate chip cookies and Kit-Kat bars. How is she going to stay away from these forbidden foods given her track record for impulsive behavior?

I search the Web for information about Parnate and pull up stories about users winding up in emergency rooms. Apparently, patients on Parnate who go off their special diets can get severe headaches caused by elevated blood pressure, and in rare cases this can prove fatal.

I delve back into Dr. Gorman's book and find that some psychiatrists who prescribe Parnate, also give their patients a blood-pressure lowering pill called Procardia, to carry with them, and put under their tongue at the first sign of a headache.

Should Pamela get this pill if she goes on Parnate?

I agonize over whether to share this information with her. My instincts tell me I should, but the thought that I might be setting her up for failure holds me back. The cerebral part of my brain tells me, if she carries this pill around with her, it could give her a false sense of security and actually encourage her to eat chocolate ice cream or dip sushi in soy sauce.

In the back of my head, though, I hear Dr. Spellman telling me to "stay out of it . . . don't be a meddling mother . . . it's not your business." So I stay out of it.

PAMELA

Thank You God for keeping me sober and alive today. I've been strug-
gling with my life and it's attachment to RR and my depression.

Tomorrow I start Parnate, which has serious dietary restrictions. No
more chocolate or caffeine! How hard is that? I just hope it will be worth it.

I signed up to get catalogues from Pepperdine University and Califor-
nia State in Northridge and Newberry Beauty School too.

Well, it's a first step. It will probably benefit me to find out about Santa
Monica College too because it's a community school where I'd be more apt
to take a class or two without having to enroll for a full semester. I need a
part-time schedule, at least at first.

Grief Letter

In this writing I will recall the person I used to be and who I
never want to meet again.

After school, when I was around ten, I locked the door to my room
and looked out the window. Through the vertical blinds I watched
the neighborhood kids playing catch, riding bikes and skateboarding
and found myself being angry at them. I told myself how pathetic
they were and imagined people ridiculing them because that's what
I thought would happen to me if I did that.

So I hid in my room and wrote in my journal about how God
failed me and how life would be so much nicer six-feet underground.

The same fears plagued me later in life while in college, when I
would walk along the street to get to my classes instead of taking the
campus route. For me, the center of campus was like going head first
into a blazing fire. All the people looked nice and were talking, but
I avoided it along with the lacrosse boys and their gorgeous chicks,
at all costs.

These long-held social anxieties are a part of me that I need to
say good-bye to. I am no longer that same, shy girl. I am a woman,
free and secure in a wonderful world of opportunities that I will not
pass up.

My lifestyle from a year ago is something I need to put in the
past instead of dwelling on it day after day. I romanticized my life
back then, and tended to overlook the real horror film it had become.

It was actually long before a year ago when I started destroying myself. I had been clean and sober for a few months when I lost my appetite. I got high from feeling so empty and became anorexic.

Then my sobriety ceased and drugs and alcohol re-entered my life more destructively than ever before. I could go on and on but my point here is to say good riddance to the old me... the Pamela who didn't care about herself, but only the high she could achieve. I am done with her. She got me nowhere fast. I will move forward, but remember always the bottoms I have hit and the heartache I have caused.

March 3, 2001

I slept a lot today which could be the result of many things. I spent last night at Matt's and he didn't sleep at all. He woke me up early, ranting and raving, he was pretty angry and I don't blame him.

The Parnate may also be causing my drowsiness. I slept during lunch and before dinner, but of course, got both meals anyway. I have been eating salad and meat and I had some cereal tonight . . . and oh, I had eggs this morning with Matt at Mort's but no bread! I feel fatter than I've ever been. I hate it. I want to be happy with myself. I want, I want, I want. Things could be worse. Isn't that the truth? God, take this obsession away, please!

I'm trying to remember all those I've harmed for my 8ᵗʰ Step.

BEA

"Did you get the care package I sent you?" I ask Pamela, eagerly anticipating her grateful response.

"I got a notice that something was delivered when I wasn't home, and I have to go to the post office to pick it up," she says.

My spirits are deflated. She's been complaining to me about not knowing what foods she can eat while on Parnate, so I went to the supermarket and bought whatever of her favorites I could find that are legal . . . Stella D'Oro cookies, peach-flavored iced tea, popcorn, peanut butter, crackers, pretzels, Honey Bunches of Oats Cereal, Jolly Rancher candies. I threw in some toys for Angelina and a book or two, lugged the heavy box to the post office and sent it priority mail.

Pamela senses I'm annoyed that she doesn't appreciate my effort, and blows me off.

"I need to talk to Dad."

Without even saying goodbye, I toss the phone to Mike. Listening to his end of the conversation, I can hear they're discussing money.

"What was that all about?" I ask, when he hangs up.

"There's only seven patients living at RR now, and Pamela thinks they're keeping her there because of the money I'm wiring them every month," he explains.

"Well, she does have a point," I say. "Do you think they're taking advantage of us?"

"As you just heard me tell her, I think her instincts might be right, but until she either goes to school or gets a job, I'm committed to her care there," he says. "She has to prove she can function in society, before stepping down and living independently. She seems to understand that."

PAMELA

March 6, 2001

I'm very frustrated because I need to get a job or volunteer position and I don't know which to do. Do I apply to places? Do I ask permission first from Mac or Rachel? Do I work or volunteer? Mac wants me to volunteer. I don't know what I want. My mind is side-tracked, thinking about Matt actually. I need to take action and make a decision.

March 8, 2001

Prayers are needed tonight. Sandy is suicidal. She needed 43 stitches last night and a charcoal shake.

Paula just called. I kind of want to go home to NY to visit. I miss my Mommy. I want her to rub her fingers through my hair while doing the NY Times Crossword Puzzle. Am I being a baby? I don't think so. I just want love.

I haven't been with Matt for a week and even then, he's so preoccupied with his own shit, I don't feel much love.

Last night I had a terrible migraine and was nauseous. I got back from

243

painting and lay in bed for a few hours with the pain until I finally fell asleep. I dreamed I jumped into a muddy ocean and saved a baby from drowning. I like that I was able to save that baby. Maybe it was a sign that I can save myself too.

March 13, 2001

I feel disconnected. I'm 146 lbs. again, just like in 8th grade. I'm on a good diet but because of the three drugs I'm on, I'm not losing. They are all weight-gainers and lower metabolism, cause dizziness and drowsiness. Oh, God, help me! Should I get off the drugs? I need to exercise, but I'm so tired.

My sex drive is down too. I'm totally avoiding intimacy and sex with Matt. What the fuck is going on with me? I hate it! Yes, I use the strong word HATE!!

March 15, 2001

I've been up for 36 hours! I didn't sleep at all last night and my exhausted body needs some restful sleep tonight.

I haven't gotten my period in 6 weeks and I'm getting anxious about it. I doubt I'm pregnant, I mean I don't remember the condom breaking the last time we had sex. I don't really want to think about it. I miss Matt. Things have been pretty distant between us. I want to be with him but because of our sleep patterns I only stay over his place once a week.

It's the Ides of March again, and I'm glad I'm where I am now as opposed to where I was three years ago . . . in the emotional and physical gutter. I am blessed and very grateful for that.

BEA

"Mom, I've been doing a lot of thinking and I'm considering applying to beauty school," Pamela says in her latest phone call.

My heart sinks. I think of the song "Beauty School Drop-Out," from the musical, Grease, and gulp hard. Pamela is so much more talented than that. She was an honor student, she writes poetry and is a lover of nineteenth century English literature. Her potential as an artist is unlimited, and her recent illness and talk therapy have unleashed an incredibly keen intellect and a perceptive mind.

"Are you sure this is what you want?" I ask rather lamely.

244

"Yes, I've already looked into it. There's a Newberry School of Beauty nearby in West Hills and tuition is $3,300 for the year."

"Well, you'll have to talk to Daddy about that. But first, don't you think you should volunteer at a beauty shop to see if you actually like doing this?" I'm trying to slow her down. Mike and I have already laid out money in advance for a gym membership and the classes at Fordham that she never saw through to the end, and we are not likely to do it again on a whim.

PAMELA

March 18, 2001

I feel a strange energy inside. My heart beats fast. Every pore tingles. It feels weird. I wonder if my depression is lifting? I ask You, what do I do to take action? What is my first step? I am anxious to begin. I feel something curious, like juices flowing, that I haven't experienced in a while.

March 20, 2001

Well I slept until 11 a.m. Did a work-out today and it really felt good. I was really tired and didn't think my legs would move, but I was able to break a sweat. I know that I need to live for today and the results will come later, just like AA.

I called Newberry Beauty School this morning to ask questions and they're supposed to get back to me.

I did an EMDR (Eye Movement Desensitization and Reprocessing) session with Barbara and actually got into some stuff from the past . . . maybe it will help.

Matt still isn't sleeping at night and I never see him anymore. He did give me a nice good-bye when he left RR today and I'm glad about that.

March 21, 2001

Art class was pretty cool tonight. I finished one painting and started another impressionist painting of flowers in a vase. I remember thinking how long it would take before I was able to paint standing-up and now I am doing it! Progress . . . not perfection. I even remember how much anxiety I had over coming to this class and now it's nothing. I even enjoy it.

March 25, 2001

I feel pretty crappy, physically. My hair is messed up, my nails are falling apart and my skin sucks, but I'm not doing anything to help matters so it's basically my fault.

Matt and I went for dinner to Travestere last night in Santa Monica. We sat outside. It was really nice. But someone broke into his car and he was rightfully upset. They took his walkman and gym bag with his weight-belt in it. To top it off, this afternoon we went to Mort's – he had a double order of French toast and I had a Spanish omelet (this is for posterity, just in case we do end up together, these are things I want to remember) – the piece of shit car wouldn't start and we had to wait for AAA to come.

When I got back I watched the Oscars at RR . . . I'm still here . . . it sucks. Rebecca is supposed to take me to Pierce College to talk to a counselor about classes tomorrow and I'm nervous about it. I wish I could just disappear from this world just because I don't want to have to deal with this at all.

March 27, 2001

I want Matt to think I'm a "Classic Girl" like Jane's Addiction. Maybe he does, but he doesn't let me know it and that's the sad part. Am I special to him? I wish I was more connected to him, it's not intense. I guess that's good for now, but not forever. I can't live like that. I don't want anyone to settle for me and that's what it feels like.

Assam told me that Matt doesn't care about himself right now, so how is he supposed to care about me? I guess it makes sense. I know he cares about me, I'm just so needy.

I'm mad at Mom. Well, she's pissed at me because she sent a package that I needed to pick up at the post office and I didn't because, oh, I guess I'm scared to because where is the post office? Plus, I have anxiety about new places. According to her, how can I make it in the world if I can't go to the post office, which I feel is totally true and I hate that!

Mac wants me to visit the beauty school even though Dad thinks it's a "waste of talent." I do want to go to the beauty school. I do and I will and then my life will have a purpose. I will try new things and not worry about whether or not I will succeed.

March 31, 2001

I went to the Newberry Beauty School on Thursday with Rachel, met *the director, and took the exam to get in. It was easy . . . like a dummy-version of the SAT. Anyhow, am I going to beauty school?*

I really want to do this, but at the same time, I want everything to stay the same – change is scary. No more RR if I go to beauty school because classes are 8:30-2:30 Monday to Friday. But I'd be cutting, coloring, braiding, blowing-out hair! So much fun! Actually, I feel happy right now!

BEA

Pamela is confused and frustrated and so are we. She wants to go to beauty school, but scheduling is a big problem. If she goes to school during the day, she can't participate in RR's programs, and if she goes at night, she can't attend AA meetings. Either way, she'd be losing a support system, and she's paralyzed about making a decision. Besides that, school is a long-term commitment and she's not sure if she should do it in California or in New York.

That leaves her in a Catch-22 situation. RR tells her she can't leave without having a plan for work or school in place. And although Rachel promises to help her find a beauty school program that would fit with RR's schedule, she never quite makes it a priority. So Pamela is floundering in uncertainty.

Paula tells me she is fed up with the way Pamela is being jerked around.

"It sounds like RR is just not set up for a step-down program," she says to me after I explain her sister's dilemma. She points out that at Riggs, they helped Pamela find jobs, first cleaning out the van, then at a nursery school and finally at the clothing store. But RR doesn't seem to have the same transitions in place. "They want Pamela to succeed," she says, "but they don't realize that the restrictions they're putting on her and their lack of support are actually holding her back."

I agree with her. "I also don't like that she seems so drugged up," I say. "It's not helping her beat the depression."

Because there's no clear-cut resolution for Pamela, the first day of classes at the Newberry School of Beauty comes and goes without her, and she falls into a funk.

PAMELA

April 3, 2001

I don't feel that grateful for being alive and sober today. Actually, I cried a lot in bed and feel suicidal. I am not happy with how I don't see my life getting better. I want someone to take care of me.

Will You take care of me, God? Please hold me in the palm of Your hand and whisper into my ear how much You love me and how I am going to be a success in this world. Tell me how pretty I am and how I will get married some day and have beautiful children who will love me endlessly. I need You so much.

I don't want to want to die. I want to want to live.

BEA

"Hi, Mom, is Dad there?" Pamela says.

"Is something wrong?" My hand is already starting to shake.

"Well, Rachel thinks I should stay here in California rather than come home for Easter," she says.

"Why?" I ask. I'm disappointed. We haven't seen her for nearly two months and I've been looking forward to her coming home to spend the holiday with the family.

"She says it's better for me to stay and face my difficulties rather than run away from them," Pamela explains.

I know the therapists fear she will fall into old patterns in the family dynamic, but I'm tired of them calling all the shots. It's hard for me to believe it could be a bad thing for her to be home for Easter, a holiday we always share together.

I take a deep breath. The last thing I want to do is make Pamela feel guilty about not following the staff's advice.

"So why do you need to talk to Dad?" I ask.

"I just found out my roommate's son is staying at our apartment during the holiday, and I don't feel comfortable being there with them," she says. "I need to see if Dad can arrange for me to stay at RR for a couple of nights."

248

"He's at a meeting now, I'll tell him to call you later.

Luckily, an empty bed is found at RR and Mike is able to negotiate what Dr. Shiraz considers a reasonable fee, $1000 a day, for Pamela's stay. Pamela thanks her father for rescuing her from an awkward situation, packs an overnight bag and relocates to the facility.

PAMELA

April 10, 2001

Nothing much going on. I'm trying to write a letter to my Dad for my ninth step. I miss and love Matt. I miss my family too, but I'm not going home this weekend for Easter. I think it's best I stay here.

April 12, 2001

I was in a pretty bad mood today for no reason really. I even made love this morning thinking it would make me feel happier. Of course, being with Matt does make me feel better. Whenever I stay over, I love to watch him sleep at night. He looks so handsome and in peace. He told me I was beautiful despite my acned face. I hate it!

Amber's son is visiting with friends tomorrow for a week so I need to vacate. It won't be a big deal but I'll have to stay at RR during that time.

I'll Fly Away . . .

> *Naked minutes tripping through hours*
> *Marking each movement it slowly rewards.*
> *Drifting vines entrap the dull sun,*
> *As devastating clouds choke the sky.*
> *Relaxing breath*
> *Sways harshly against powdered wind.*
> *Concrete punishes where spirits tread,*
> *Back and forth, swallowing dust.*
> *In the mirror your eyes to stare,*
> *Into the past that our conscience relishes,*
> *Bringing warning of what is near,*
> *Too close to change,*
> *Too far to fear.*

The sheet recoils, the dream dies.
Crash.
Down I lie with thundering tears.
Don't come to me, I'll fly away.
Toward empty fields, I'll go and play.

April 14, 2001

Thank you God, for keeping me alive and sober today. Tomorrow is Easter and I don't want to think about it. Holidays suck. Sundays are hard enough and I can't go back to my apartment.

I stayed at Matt's last night but didn't sleep very well and he was in a bad mood. I thought I got my period but didn't, it was just spotting. What's up with that?

I haven't called Teri and feel guilty. Serves me right, I suppose.

I need to call home and Uncle Joseph tomorrow.

I feel like my life is a never-ending circle of blah. I really hate it and part of me doesn't want to get better because it won't matter.

I don't want to live. I don't want to die either. Maybe I'll just stay in bed forever. I'm in a billion pieces. I'm scared. I feel like I'm going to burst soon. God, help me! Please help me!

BEA

Somehow, Pamela manages to get through Easter Sunday on her own. But Monday she calls early in the morning. I'm surprised to hear her voice, because glancing at the clock, I realize it's only 5 a.m. in California.

"I just can't sleep and this insomnia is driving me out of my mind," she tells me. "I'm up all night and exhausted all day. I don't know what to do anymore." She sounds very depressed.

"Insomnia is a side-effect of Parnate," I explain. "Did you tell Dr. Vasily you can't sleep?"

"Yes, he upped the Parnate from 40 to 60 milligrams yesterday and added Thorazine to help me sleep. But people in group are accusing me of "med-seeking," she says.

This sends a jolt through my spine. I don't understand what it means.

Is Thorazine a drug dealer's drug? And why more Parnate, if it's not helping the depression, and causing such bad insomnia?

After listening for half an hour about how trapped Pamela feels at RR, I try to think of a way to rescue her.

"Don't worry, we'll get to the bottom of this," I promise. "Mother's Day is in a few weeks. Daddy and I will fly out and arrange a 'sit-down' with the people at RR to determine the next step in your treatment. Whether you go to beauty school or come back to New York. . . we'll figure it out."

"Thanks, Mom, that would be great," Pamela says, her spirits rising. "I'm glad we talked."

She pauses, then says, "I love you Mom."

"I love you, too, Pam," I tell her, relieved I was able to help her through another crisis.

Immediately after hanging up, I head back to Dr. Gorman's book, to look up Thorazine. It says it's not to be prescribed for sleep to patients other than psychotics. I'm confused. Is Pamela psychotic? Why did Dr. Vasily give it to her if she's not?

I decide to call him myself to find out.

"No, no, no," Dr. Vasily protests. "Pamela is not psychotic."

"Then why are you giving her Thorazine?" I ask.

"I've already taken her off of it," he says.

"Well, what about the Parnate? It doesn't seem to be working. She's still very depressed and complaining she doesn't have the energy to look for a job, or exercise or do anything because of insomnia," I say.

"She's on 60 milligrams. The top dose is 80. I'd like to keep her on Parnate one more week, and I'm sure I can find another medication that will help her sleep," he says with a large dose of confidence.

I tell him my husband and I are planning to fly out next month for a meeting to reassess Pamela's treatment options. "I ask only one favor," I say. "If and when you decide to take her off Parnate, please look into what new drugs are being tested for depression, since Pamela has tried everything that's already out there, and I don't want her to lose hope."

"I'm going to do my homework on this, Mrs. Tusiani," Dr. Vasily reassures me.

When I relay all of this to Mike, he quickly arranges for us to fly to L.A. on Friday, May 11th. He sets up a meeting with Pamela's therapist, Mac, the facility's director, Dr. Shiraz, and Dr. Vasily, who is her medical doctor, for Monday, May 14th, at 2:30 p.m.

CHAPTER 10

Malibu

Q: *So let's return to your notes. You are now, I assume, in New York, and this next page is a phone call with your daughter?*

A: *Yes.*

Q: *Could you review it and tell me what the substance of the phone call was?*

A: *Right. Pamela called, and she said she is not sure that Road to Recovery is helping her. There were several times she said that, especially in 2001, when she questioned whether or not they were serious. A few times I might add, she did say to me, and I'm sure the notes somewhere will reflect this, that Road to Recovery was taking financial advantage of me. And she warned me. She said, "Dad, they are taking advantage." And this call I think was questioning what they were doing for her there.*

    She said one of the counselors worked in White Plains, and she was referring to the New York Presbyterian facility there. And they said it's much more intensive than Road to Recovery. They can help you more.

Q: *Did you share her view at that point in time that Road to Recovery was taking advantage of you?*

A: *As I told you, Mr. Davis, Dr. Shiraz was part doctor, part businessman. The man never called me unless it was returning a call, or it was for money. Money was a big issue.*

    The facility started out with a home, and then they bought another one. They closed it down because, according to what we learned, they didn't have enough patients or they couldn't make the mortgage. I don't know the details, but there were financial issues. I think they were focused on money. Now, I'm not saying that they weren't focused on care, because let the record speak for itself, but I can tell you money was a major issue.

Q: *When your daughter said she thought at some point in time, they were taking financial advantage of her, it was an issue you were con-*

cerned about. Whether you necessarily agreed with her conclusion or
not, you were concerned with it?

A: *I was concerned. But let me comment. Remember, you are dealing*
with a mentally ill person. Whenever you deal with a mentally ill per-
son, the one thing I learned is, as Dr. Shiraz said, reflected in one of my
conversations, she never tells a full story, but never lies. I was never
sure. And she manipulates. Manipulation is one of the traits of Border-
line Personality. Playing one against the other, again, Dr. Shiraz told
me. I wasn't sure and I gave the benefit of the doubt to the institution
because she was ill.

BEA

The next night, when Mike and I return from the opera, the red light
is blinking on the phone. It's a message from RR.

"Mr. and Mrs. Tusiani . . . this is Penny. I am calling to let you know
that Pamela was taken by ambulance to UCLA Medical Center in Santa
Monica because of a food interaction with Parnate."

It's 11:20 p.m. New York time, 8:20 p.m. in California. Tuesday, April
17th.

My body stiffens and blood rushes to my head as Mike's fingers dial
the hospital.

After being on hold for what seems like an eternity, the operator
finally connects him to a nurse in the emergency room. She tells him
Pamela's heart rate is low. She's lethargic and disoriented. "Call back in
a few hours," she says.

A few hours? Mike and I stare at each other in disbelief. We dare not
move from the phone.

At 2:30 a.m. EST, Mike calls the hospital again. I'm hovering by his
side, anxious for an update. Another nurse tells him, "We're waiting
for a bed to open up on the ICU. Her heart rate is low, in the 40's. She's
incoherent, and not able to follow directions."

"What is her heart rate supposed to be? It must be serious if you are
sending her to intensive care," Mike says.

254

"I'll give you Dr. Sharif's phone number. He's covering here and is on duty all night. He can give you more information."

Mike and I are listening on different extensions when Dr. Sharif picks up. "Pamela is responsive and knows she's in the hospital, but doesn't want to talk. She isn't answering questions or cooperating. They're monitoring her pulse rate, which is low and that could be because she's a former cocaine user. I will order a cardiac review and consult with a psychiatrist from UCLA in one or two days."

I know my daughter, and she always cooperates… does this stranger think she is a drug addict, deliberately misbehaving in some way? Is anyone from RR at the hospital with her to explain to him that she hasn't touched drugs for 11 months?

Mike, sensing something is not quite right, brings up the issue of Parnate. "We were told that our daughter was rushed to the hospital because of a food interaction with Parnate, which she is taking for depression."

"I am not familiar with that drug," Dr. Sharif admits. "I'll try to get some information about it from the hospital pharmacist."

This is madness. The doctor treating my daughter doesn't know about Parnate? I knew it was bad, but now it's suddenly worse, knowing Pamela is in the hands of someone who doesn't know a thing about the drug she's on and its life-threatening side-effects.

We call back at 4:45 a.m. and are told Pamela is more awake than earlier in the evening. Her heart rate is fluctuating between 48 and 56, and they're still waiting for a bed to open up in the ICU. Despite our worries, those we speak to assure us Pamela is experiencing a normal drug reaction that needs to pass through her system.

Mike goes into our bed and lies there with his hand over his head. Not to upset him further, I go into the guest room, clench my arms over my stomach, and vacillate between crying and praying for my child.

It is the longest night of our lives because we're not there. We don't know what's happening. We can't even talk to Pamela. And every time we call RR, the overnight staff, who were not on duty when she was taken away, keep telling us to call back at 7:00 a.m. PST, which is 10:00 a.m. in New York . . . are they crazy? It's insane to expect us to sit here, three thousand miles away, and not have any communication from the doctors at Road to Recovery where our daughter first exhibited symptoms. How can they sleep peacefully, because we certainly can not.

After an unbearably long and arduous wait, I finally reach Kathy, the nurse who was on duty the previous day at Road to Recovery.

"Pamela is at UCLA Medical Center, with a very low heart rate," I say, finally able to vent my frustration, "and is waiting for a bed in the ICU, and I've been waiting all night to speak to someone at RR to tell me what exactly happened."

"Mrs. Tusiani, please calm down," Kathy says. "About 45 minutes after lunch yesterday, Pamela came to my office and said she was nauseous and had a headache and that she'd just eaten the pizza that was served for lunch. I took her blood pressure and it was high. Dr. Stedman was there, and he gave her shots of Vistaril and Vicodin. I advised her to rest in a bed down the hall from the nurse's station. After a couple of hours, a staff monitor took her blood pressure and it was back up. She notified Dr. Stedman who told her to call 911."

The questions that have been swimming in my head all night start tumbling out of me.

"Did she do this intentionally? Could she have had a stroke? Is that why she's not coherent? Was Procardia put under her tongue to lower her blood pressure? Why did you wait so long to call an ambulance?"

"No, Mrs. Tusiani, I don't think this was an intentional act. As for a stroke, I never thought of that. And no, we didn't give her Procardia."

"Are you kidding me? Even I know you should use a blood-pressure-lowering drug at the very first sign of hypertensive symptoms, and I'm not a doctor. How can you prescribe an MAOI-inhibitor and not have an antidote for it?" Blood is rising to my temples.

"We used what we had," she says, icily.

That gets my back up. Vicodin is a pain-killer and Vistaril is an anti-anxiety drug. Who's in charge there? Do they know what they're doing? Not only am I mad at her, I'm furious at myself for not following my instinct to suggest to the doctors that Pamela carry this drug around with her when she first started Parnate six weeks ago.

Even though I don't like what I'm hearing or the way it's being said,

I have to keep my anger in check because this is the only lifeline I have to my daughter right now, and I can't afford to lose it.

"Should I be there?" I ask Kathy in a less abrasive tone.

"That's not necessary," she assures me. "Pamela would feel guilty if you travelled 3,000 miles for a drug interaction. Your daughter is getting the best possible care she could get at Santa Monica UCLA."

There's no way I want to cause guilt. One thing I know Pamela doesn't like is the guilt I seem to instill in her. So, once again, I succumb to the advice of a professional over my maternal instincts, and decide to wait it out.

I contact the hospital and they tell me she's been moved to a room in ICU, but when I call that room, someone tells me there's no one there by that name. In sheer frustration, I phone Mike and tell him to find out where the hell our daughter is.

I'm a complete mess.

Trying to sort it all out, I call a friend who's chief of psychiatry at Lenox Hill and describe what happened to Pamela and ask him about her confused state. He looks in his drug reference guide and says a reaction from a hypertensive crisis with an MAOI-inhibitor is violent headaches with confusion. It's not unusual to be disoriented, but he also notes, it could lead to a stroke or death if left untreated.

My heart can't take much more of this.

We discuss whether Parnate should be continued, and he says, given Pamela's severe reaction, her doctor has to make a careful assessment of effectiveness versus risk, in terms of future use. I ask if we can engage him as a consultant for our upcoming meeting with RR to discuss Pamela's continuing treatment, he says he'll make himself available to us at any time.

After a day filled with many upsetting conversations, the last phone call, late in the evening, comes from Dr. Vasily.

"Pamela has been placed in a regular room," he tells me. "She recognizes me, she knows who she is, and that she's in the hospital.

"Her pulse rate is normal and a cardiologist will be coming in to check on her."

"Why a cardiologist? Is something wrong with her heart?" I ask.

"They want to rule out damage because she used cocaine."

"Is she still on Parnate?" I push further.

"You can't just stop that drug, it has to be tapered off," he responds.

I repeat to him what my psychiatrist friend told me about risk vs. benefit of continuing Parnate, and Dr. Vasily assures me a UCLA psychiatrist will be called in to do a full work up on all of Pamela's medications within the next few days. He also says he plans to visit her again tomorrow.

Then I ask what I've been anxious to ask all day: "Can I speak to my daughter?"

"I thought about that," Dr. Vasily says hesitating. "She's still confused. It's hard to describe to a parent. I think it would be best if you speak to her tomorrow when the drug is out of her system. I will sleep a lot more comfortably tonight than I did last night, and so should you," he tells me, reassuringly.

But I desperately want to talk to my child. I need to hear her voice. It's the only way I'll know if she's okay.

"Shouldn't I be there?" I press on. "If she can't communicate, she may need me, especially when the drug interaction wears off."

"Mrs. Tusiani, it's not necessary right now," he responds, "but if you want to come out and help in her recuperation, when she comes out of the hospital, it wouldn't hurt."

I've heard enough. Something is still not right, if Pamela is not responsive and they're not letting me talk to her.

I turn to Mike, who's in bed beside me listening to the conversation, and ask him to get me a ticket to fly out to California the next day.

As it turns out, I do fly to California on April 19th, but not according to plan.

The next morning, I'm eating my usual diet fare of two rice-cakes with peanut butter and a cup of coffee, when Mike walks back in the house after already having gone to work. I look at the clock, it's 8 a.m. What is he doing home? Did he forget something?

I'm holding my rice-cake in midair when he comes into the kitchen. He's taking baby steps toward me, with his arms and hands extended. His eyes are red, and I can tell from his strange behavior that something terrible has happened.

I drop my food, and run to him, grabbing both of his arms.

"What's wrong? What is it?"

"I called UCLA when I got to the office this morning," he says shakily, "and the staff told me there was a problem, and I had to call a Dr. Lee. Once I was finally able to get through to him, he said Pamela's blood pressure shot up during the night."

While he's holding me, Mike is also trying to push me away, as if he can't bear to tell me what he has to say next. He tries to compose himself before continuing, but his hands are trembling.

"Pamela had a massive seizure overnight," he says, his voice cracking. "A cerebral hemorrhage left her brain-dead . . ." His face turns red, and his eyes well up with tears, as he delivers the rest of the news. "She is being kept alive on a respirator. They're waiting for us to get there before removing her from life-support."

I collapse. "My daughter, my daughter, my poor daughter," I scream and wail, smacking my bare fists into the hard, cold tile on the kitchen floor, pounding it as if it was the devil's heart. This cannot be happening to us. This cannot be happening to Pamela. She's only 23 years old. After everything we've been through to keep her healthy and alive, it's not fair to end this way.

Mike tries to lift me from the floor, but it's not possible.

My neighbors downstairs hear the commotion and call to find out what's going on. Mike tells them, and then turns back to me.

"Bea, I know this is hard, but you've got to get up and pack a bag. I booked us on a 10:30 am flight to LA."

"What about Michael and Paula? Do they know?"

"I already called them and told them. They're booked on a flight that leaves an hour after ours. They'll meet us at the hospital."

All my subsequent actions take place in slow motion. I feel paralyzed and numb, in total shock, as if my brain is disconnected from my body. I can't talk – not even to my own children. I should be concerned about how they're handling this tragedy, but can't even muster the strength to console them when they call.

I'm dazed. Mike pulls out an overnight bag for me to pack, but when I look in my closet, I don't know where to start. I feel as though I'm peering into a fun-house mirror where everything is distorted. My daughter-in-law, Cathy, runs over to help because I'm unable to make any decisions.

I have no idea how we get to the airport. Everything is a blur. All I keep thinking is, how can we possibly go on without Pamela?

The five and a half hour flight is unbearable. Through our sobs and tears, Mike and I rehash the events of the past 36 hours.

"I knew it! I knew it! We should have gone there right away when Penny called Tuesday night," I whine. "Why did we listen to them?"

"Bea, they told us she would come out of it," Mike says. "We thought they knew what they were doing. But you're right, this never would have happened if we had been there."

I'm full of rage, and take it out on the flight attendants who offer us champagne and earphones for the long flight.

"We don't want anything," I say, waving them off with a cold sweep of my hand. Can't they see by the tortured looks on our faces and the pile of wadded tissues growing between us, that we don't want to be bothered? It's insensitive for them to be so cheerful in light of our painful situation.

Even fellow passengers notice the thick tension in the air as they turn around every so often to glance curiously in our direction. The emotion of being a mother whose child is dying, is pouring out of me, and I can't stop crying. I know I'm making a scene.

To avoid eye-to-eye contact with those around me, I cover myself with a blanket and hide under it to muffle my sobs. Mike seems more in control than me, but I can see out of the corner of my eye that tears are dripping down the side of his cheek.

When the plane finally lands, the only thing that matters is seeing our daughter – still alive. Mike and I hit the ground running, but our feet don't actually touch it. In one sweep of perpetual motion we hail a taxi, break through the hospital doors, find the ICU, and fling our adrenaline-fueled bodies into an elevator.

When we get out, Pamela's boyfriend, Matt, and some of her friends from RR are huddled in the hall. They look at us with big sorrowful eyes, but we fly past them, craning our necks into each room looking for Pamela.

We finally find her with a monitor stationed outside her door. Mike and I bypass this stranger, who is momentarily stunned by our agitated presence, drop our bags and tearfully collapse onto Pamela's white-sheeted body.

"Pamela! Pamela! It's Mom! It's Dad," we shout, as we slide our hands over her arms and legs and brush our fingers through her hair. But only the whirr of machinery answers.

"Pamela, say something!" I repeat, frantically, over and over again.

"Pamela, if you can hear me, squeeze my hand," Mike says. He pinches her foot and asks her to blink her eyes. Both of us search for a twitch or eye movement in response, but there are none.

I step back from the bed and look at the breathing tube taped to her mouth, forcing rhythmic blasts of oxygen into her lungs, and all at once realize this is what's keeping her alive.

Reality starts to sink in. This is our daughter, but she's not here any-more. Her eyes are dilated and her hands are cold.

A doctor walks into the room and introduces himself as a neurolo-gist.

"It's necessary for us to remove the breathing tube from this patient because her brain is flooded with blood," he tells us.

But I don't want to believe she's brain dead. How can this vibrant mind that produced so many beautiful poems and paintings be forever gone?

Another doctor comes in.

"I'm Dr. Sharif," he says. "I'm so sorry."

Surely he notices I don't acknowledge him at all.

I'm a madwoman now, spewing my venom to anyone who gets in the way of me protecting my poor, forsaken daughter. She doesn't de-serve such a fate.

"Don't stop the oxygen!" I bellow from some deep place within my maternal womb. "How can I trust what you tell me when nothing any of you has said over the past 48 hours has been right?"

Emboldened by the awful truth of this statement, I decide to take charge and order them around. "I want another neurologist in here to confirm what you're telling me . . . that there is no hope."

They leave and Matt comes into the room. His eyes are rimmed in red.

"I'm so, so sorry. It's so sad," he says meekly. "I love Pamela and can't believe what happened to her. He pulls something out of his jacket pocket. "I found these in my apartment. They're Pamela's journals. He hands them to me. "I'm sure she would want you to have them."

I put them in my handbag and give Matt a hug. But when he lingers in the room and begins to move his hand up and down Pamela's leg, it unnerves me. I want to tell him to get his hands off my daughter, but can't bring myself to do it. Instead, I try to ignore him and call to my precious child.

"Pamela, Pamela, Pamela! It's me, Mom, I'm here, Pamela! Squeeze my hand, Pamela, if you hear me."

Standing on either side of our daughter's bed, Mike and I try with all of our might, to arouse her. We kiss her face – fold her hands in ours, rub her feet. . . . . despite what the doctors say, we're not about to give up on our baby girl.

The effort is doubled when Paula and Michael arrive, crying and upset, just as we were an hour before. The room becomes even more crowded when a hospital chaplain shows up to console us. Angrily, I shoo her away. After all, where has God been for the past three years? Lord knows, I've said mountains of prayers, and where has it gotten my daughter?

I stop obsessing about this when a nurse comes into the room.

"I was on duty in the ICU last night when this patient was brought in at 4:45 a.m. It was already too late. She suffered a massive seizure at 3 a.m., and that's when they sent her for a CAT-Scan.

"All the nurses agree, this never should have happened. It's a tragedy," she says, shaking her head.

We remain stunned.

Mike and I both look at her name tag at the same time. It reads Irene Murphy.

"She should have been brought up to the ICU immediately from the emergency room, because of her confused symptoms, and had a CT Scan taken then," she continues.

Finally, someone is not giving us the run-around. Finally, someone is telling us the truth.

They treated my daughter like a crazy drug-addicted psycho, instead of a regular medical patient whose garbled speech would have required immediate brain testing.

This compassionate woman went on to tell us she asked her mother, who's a psychiatric nurse, about Parnate, and her mother said a reaction usually takes place 24 to 48 hours after an incident occurs.

"A good lawyer would have a field day with this case," says Murphy, who by now, in our eyes, seems to have dropped out of heaven as an angel of mercy.

"May I have your contact information?" Mike asks her.

"Sure," she says, jotting down her phone number.

I see Mike's jaw lock as she walks out of the room. Now he's angry. Both of us have the same questions.

Why wasn't a CT Scan done before Pamela had this massive seizure? Did they even think of checking to see what was going on inside her brain? If she had been moved to the ICU, rather than a regular room with a "sitter" on suicide-watch, would it have saved her life? Where the hell were the doctors from RR to advocate on her behalf?

Both of us are wracked with guilt because, had we been here, as we should have been, we would have pushed the doctors to pay attention to Pamela's case. How did two very smart people turn into such dumb fools brainwashed by stupid doctors?

Paula hears us blaming ourselves and provides some keen insight.

"Pamela's condition was far more serious than we were led to believe. From 3,000 miles away, we were getting reports that she was stable," she says. "RR probably didn't want to alarm us because they were scrambling to cover their tracks."

As if on cue, the second neurologist breaks into our conversation to tell us that he concurs with the opinion of the first: there are no signs of activity in Pamela's brain. Before we can even comprehend the monumental significance of this, we are faced with still another shock.

A procurement coordinator from "One Legacy" quietly slips into the hospital room, in a manner that seems well-rehearsed, and asks if we will consider donating Pamela's organs for transplantation.

"Once the patient is unhooked from life-support, her organs will shut down within 24 hours. Before this happens, there is a window of opportunity to harvest her heart, liver, kidneys – whatever organs are usable – before she dies naturally," she explains.

I feel like I'm suffocating. Aren't we distraught enough? We haven't even accepted that our daughter is gone, and they want her organs? This is going to put me over the edge.

We're escorted into a small room to discuss this crucial decision among ourselves. Matt comes in with us and Mac, Pamela's therapist from RR shows up, pleading innocence because he was on vacation when this happened. I'm out for bear and frankly, not in the mood to absolve him of anything.

Mike, Paula, Michael and Matt all agree that Pamela is a giving person and would want to help others live by donating a part of herself. I totally shut them out.

"Hasn't my daughter been through enough?" I wail.

Mac suddenly sits up straighter and crosses one leg over the other.

"Pamela always said you were the one who protected her," he mentions, as if this was a therapy session.

I'm not having any of it. I'm offended by his presence. . . Matt's, too. How long have they known Pamela? Eleven months? I'm her mother, she came out of my body twenty-three years ago, and I'm not about to give her boyfriend or therapist an inch in deciding what should become of her.

"Our family needs to talk privately," I tell both of them.

I'm not being nice and for the first time in my life, I don't care.

When they have left the room, the neurologist and the nurse coordinator come back with still more upsetting news. The medical examiner's office just informed them an autopsy will have to be performed on Pamela.

"There's no way I will agree to that," I sob, banging my fists against my thighs.

They say we don't have a choice. The cause of death is unknown, and according to the State of California, the coroner will not issue a death certificate without an autopsy.

I am tormented over this, but try for a moment to think clearly. If the coroner is going to cut Pamela open, remove her organs and stuff them back into her despite my objection, I can no longer protect her from that. Under the circumstances, donating her organs would at least allow vital parts of my dear child to live on in others.

Hanging my head in defeat, I bite my lip and sign the consent form.

Then the four of us rise and shuffle back in to see Pamela. We try one last time to rouse her with our salty-teared kisses but her body just lies there, unresponsive. We nuzzle her feet, her hands, her hair while taking in long, deep breaths of her familiar scent.

We hold hands with her in a circle and Paula says a prayer. It's the last time our family of five will be together. Forever. . . in this world.

Each of us says our individual goodbyes. Michael and Paula go first. But Mike and I linger for an extra moment. I hold Pamela's head in my two hands, kiss her cheeks, and tell her, "I'll love you forever, my sweet Pammy, until we're together again." Mike nuzzles his face into her neck and whispers something I can't hear.

He then takes my hand and says, "C'mon, Bea, it's time we leave her." We're sobbing as we head into the hallway and bump into Dr. Vasily who is waiting for us.

"I'm so sorry how this all came about," he mumbles. We sweep past him with heads down and arms locked. There's no way I want to talk to the person who caused this.

We stop at a diner. It's late afternoon, and none of us has eaten all day. I have no appetite, but Michael and Paula insist I order something. To mollify them I get scrambled eggs . . . because I don't have the strength to chew anything of substance.

Putting the first forkful to my mouth, all I can think of is what they're doing to my child, who at this very moment is being ripped apart on an operating table. She always worried about how she looked, and now it doesn't even matter. She's just a warm body on a cold metal table, being gutted like an animal for the only things worth saving . . . her organs.

Mike brings me back to the moment.

"We have to discuss what to do next," he says. "I need to call RR to tell them we're coming there tomorrow to talk to Dr. Shiraz. Then we have to go to her apartment to pick up her belongings."

"She has a lot of stuff. How are we going to bring it all back?" Michael says, adding, "what will we do with her car?

"The car's not a problem. We can arrange to have it shipped back," Mike says.

"I can come back in a few weeks, after my classes are over," Paula offers," to pack up whatever we can't bring back with us."

That's a big relief, because I know I won't be able to do it.

When we return to the hotel, Mike receives a phone call from the hospital informing him that Pamela was declared legally dead at 5:31 pm, on April 19th, 2001. It is a Thursday.

The hotel room is claustrophobic. There is no way I can sleep and no place to escape to. I can't predict what I will do from one minute to the next; jumping out the window is one of many thoughts that cross my mind.

As dawn breaks, Mike and I start making lists of people we need to contact. We talk about making funeral arrangements but everything depends on when Pamela's body is released from the LA County Coroner's Office. In my wildest dreams, I never would have predicted my daughter would wind up in such a place, so far away from home. This happens on TV, not in real life. . . not in our lives.

A booklet given to us by the County Coroner's Office explains that our loved one will remain there for two to three days before a death certificate is issued. No viewing of the body is permitted, and it advises us to contact a funeral home and make arrangements with its director to collect the body when it's ready to be shipped.

I never before felt as though I was abandoning Pamela until now . . . leaving her in a strange place with strange people who will be invading her body. It's excruciatingly painful for me that she has to go through this by herself, I want to hold and comfort her throughout the ordeal the way a mommy would, because I know how much she feared being alone.

"Just my luck!" she would have said, had she known what was happening to her. She always felt the tide went against her, and not without good reason. She had an illness that caused her brain to think that way. In the past, I always helped her through one crisis after another. But this time, she is on her own, facing her final destiny.

We return to the hospital the following morning to pick up Pamela's belongings. A brown paper bag is handed over to us. It holds her clothes, underwear, a watch and a single hair barrette. Clutching it to my chest, I ride with Mike and the twins in eerie silence to RR.

We go directly to the main building, and no one is there to greet us. Today, it's Mike's turn to be angry.

'Why isn't Dr. Shiraz here?" he asks Rachel, when she finally appears in the foyer. "I told him we would be here at nine o'clock."

Some of the residents eating breakfast in the dining room, hear this confrontation and look up.

"He'll be here shortly, Mr. Tusiani," she says, sounding protective of the doctor.

"This is unacceptable, my daughter is dead, and I want answers. What exactly happened to her?" Mike asks in a booming voice.

The commotion prompts some of the patients to come over to us and mumble their condolences. As a crowd begins to gather around us, Rachel tries to prevent an emotional scene by coaxing us out the front door and toward the building where Pamela last stayed.

She leaves us on our own, like a ship without a compass, and Mike is fuming at her coldness.

We climb the steps to Pamela's second floor dormitory-style room and start stuffing all of her belongings in large black plastic garbage bags. We grab everything: underwear, shoes, sweaters, handbags, wallet, keys, make-up and a yellow legal pad with the last entries of Pamela's diary. It strikes me these very ordinary things are all that's left of my beloved child.

Before we leave, we notice that some of the residents have placed artwork and crayon messages on Pamela's bed. One resting against her pillow depicts an angel. We carefully fold them up and load them into the rental car with everything else.

When we return to the main building, Dr. Shiraz has finally arrived. Matt is there too sitting at a table. His face is bright red.

In a serenely calm manner, I break the ice, trying to defuse Mike's mounting fury.

"Thank you for coming to see us," I tell Dr. Shiraz. "We still can't believe what happened to Pamela." He nods, unable to say anything.

Then, sensing his pain, I turn to Matt and touch his shoulder. "I appreciate how much joy you gave my daughter over these last few months." Dr. Shiraz tears-up at this, but Mike is not feeling his pain.

I know my husband is just about to blow, when his large, 6-foot frame moves within inches of Dr. Shiraz's face.

"I want a written account from everyone involved with Pamela's care at RR," he yells, pointing his index finger repeatedly at the cowering doctor. "I mean everyone – Kathy, Penny, Dr. Vasily, Dr. Stedman, Assam, Mac, Rachel and Amber – to determine exactly what took place over the past four days," he says, taking charge as the businessman he is. "I want it faxed to me in writing immediately, and I expect to find it waiting for me when I return to New York."

Mike looks like he is about to punch Dr. Shiraz.

"It will be forthcoming," the doctor says timidly. He looks petrified, and he should be. For once we're not listening to the doctors, we're making the doctors listen to us.

With our daughter's belongings in tow, we make our way through winding canyons to Pamela's apartment in Calabasas. Along the way, I think how many times Pamela made this trip herself . . . remarkably . . . even as recently as four days ago.

Amber lets us in. It's awkward being in her presence, because she's the reason Pamela had to stay at RR over Easter. And she's also the cook who made the pizza Pamela ate. I want to be angry at her the way I'm angry at the doctors, but I can't because I know my daughter cared about her.

Besides, I'm aware she's connected to RR because of her own fragile mental state, and it's clear from her sadness that she is terribly distraught over Pamela's death too. So I try to be as compassionate as I can under the strained circumstances.

Sifting through Pamela's possessions, we come upon her sketches and drawings, and most painful of all, we must decide what to do with Angelina. Much as I have grown to love that cat, I don't think I could bear living with her, as her presence would be a constant reminder of

Pamela's absence. And the logistics of taking the cat back to New York with us on that evening's flight seem overwhelming, so I make a rash decision.

"Amber, do you want Angelina?" I ask, without consulting anyone else. "I'm just afraid she's going to remind me of Pamela, and I don't know if I can handle it."

"I would be honored if you would leave Pamela's cat with me," she says.

My family does not interfere. They give me a wide berth in making this and other decisions because they wisely sense I'm on the verge of emotional collapse.

"I will come back some time after the funeral," Paula tells Amber, "and pack up all of Pamela's remaining things to bring them home."

"I'll help with the rent for another month until Paula can clear out her room," Mike says. "And I'll send someone to pick up the Subaru and drive it back to New York. We'll be in touch."

On the flight home, the four of us sit in adjacent seats across a single row of a jumbo jet. Michael, Paula and I are all focused on our own internal sorrow, while Mike restlessly combs through Pamela's diaries, searching for some tidbit of information that might shed new light on what actually happened.

An hour after take-off, Mike suddenly lurches forward and let's out a deep-throated gasp, "Oh, God!" He drops his face into his hands and starts bawling. Michael and Paula unbuckle their seat belts and run over to him.

"Thank you, thank you Pamela!" he says over and over again, rocking back and forth.

"Mike, what is it?" I ask, frightened he's having a heart attack.

He hands me one of the diaries. I look down and see the entry he's pointing to, written in Pamela's own words: "I lied. My father never raped me."

"This is Pamela's gift to me," says Mike, hugging the journal to his chest. None of us have realized just how much he's been suffering over this accusation since it was made last summer. He's been carrying it around with a heavy heart because he never had the opportunity to clear himself of it, and it remained unresolved . . . until now.

I've never really believed in "signs" in a spiritual way, but Pamela did. I wonder whether coming upon this entry in her diary while we're flying high up in the clouds, near heaven, might be Pamela's way of apologizing to her father.

After reading the diary, Mike stares into space.

"It wasn't Pamela, but the illness that caused her to tell such a hurtful lie," he says.

A calmness that settles on all of us for the rest of the trip is soon shattered when we arrive at JFK.

Dragging our listless bodies through the airport's maze of walkways, we're startled to see familiar faces waiting for us at the terminal. My niece and nephews, Mike's friend and business partner and his wife, my brother-in-law, Cathy and Roger are all there huddled together.

I stop short and drop my bag.

"What are you doing here?" I ask in disbelief, trying hard to control myself from creating a scene.

But when I see the tears in their eyes, it makes the tragedy we suffered among our tight foursome so palpably real, and I can't hold back any longer.

"My daughter, my daughter, my daughter," I cry, burying myself in their outstretched arms. "She's gone."

"How did this happen?" they start to ask one by one.

The four of us eye each other, not knowing how to answer. We've kept so much of Pamela's struggle, and the details of her illness, to ourselves over the past three years, how do we explain it now? Where do we begin?

CHAPTER 11

New York

MR. DAVIS TO MRS. BEATRICE TUSIANI (WITNESS)

Q: *How did the subject of Parnate first come up in discussion about your daughter's care?*

A: *At that point she was very frustrated that she wasn't getting help with the depression. They were making a change in her medication so the subject came up.*

I sent her a sheet from the medical book that had a listing of all the meds that she was on and all the meds that she had not taken yet. Because I was afraid that given all of her problems, she would forget that she was on Ritalin or Risperdal or Neurontin.

Q: *So do you know who it was who first came up with the idea she should try Parnate?*

A: *It was between her and her doctor.*

Q: *As between her and her doctor, do you have any idea whether it was something she came up with or her doctor came up with?*

A: *As far as I know it was something they were discussing in their sessions.*

Q: *I understand that. I'm trying to find out if this was something she had independently researched, found for herself and suggested to her doctor, or if her doctor came up with it?*

A: *I wasn't there. I don't know.*

Q: *Did you do any research on your own to learn about Parnate?*

A: *Yes.*

Q: *What did you learn from your research about that medication?*

A: *That it's a very old drug, that it's food sensitive and that you could die from it if you ate the wrong combination of foods with it; that it had the ability to affect blood pressure in a crisis situation; and that there was a drug called Procardia that could be used in the event there was such a crisis. That's what I learned.*

Q: Was this all information you learned at the time she started taking it or after the incident?

A: I think it was an ongoing effort to find information about it.

Q: So it wouldn't be possible for you to find specifically what part you learned before or after the incident?

A: No. Because I went on some psychiatric web sites and chat rooms and I looked to see what people were taking Parnate, and what it was all about. I was very concerned about her being on it.

Q: Did you ever have any conversations with her before April 17th about what the risks were of taking Parnate?

A: Yes.

Q: Do you know if she was aware from conversations you had with her that if she ate cheese while being on Parnate that she could die?

A: I had a conversation with her that if she ate certain food products like chocolate, avocados, red wine, cheese, if she imbibed any alcohol it could have very serious effects.

Q: When you had this conversation with her, did it appear to you she already knew this?

A: She told me they gave her sheets of paper with this information on it.

Q: From your conversation with her, did you form an opinion that she was aware that if she took some of the restricted foods with Parnate that she could die?

A: Well, I was aware of it based on the research I did.

Q: I understand. I'm trying to find out if you understood she was aware of it based on your conversation with her?

A: I could never understand what she was aware of because I'm not in her head.

Q: You might if she said something.

MR. TAYLOR: Did she say anything about hey, mom, if I take Parnate and mix it with certain things I could die? Did she say those things to you?

A: No.

Back at home, we speak in hushed tones to the long line of mourners who snake in and out of our living room, as we wait for Pamela's body to arrive.

"I'm so sorry," people say repeatedly. They can't believe that eating pizza could kill someone. Neither can we.

"It was an accident. Pamela was on a medication that had special food restrictions," we explain, hoping to satisfy their curiosity. "The facility was supposed to be monitoring her, we're still trying to find out exactly what took place."

In the back of their minds, they must be wondering, "Was it suicide?" We've asked that question ourselves, too. With Pamela's history of overdoses and the low state of her mood during Easter, it's a logical conclusion.

"There's no way Pamela ever thought she'd die over a piece of pizza," Michael adamantly believes. "She probably thought, how much cheese can there be in it?"

We all agree, but in these long days of waiting, it's easy to let this possibility consume us. At night when everyone leaves, Mike places calls to California. He still hasn't received the fax he demanded from RR.

While he's on the phone, I hole myself up in our bedroom and delve into books on grief, searching for some kind of solace. My attention is caught by Harold S. Kushner's book *When Bad Things Happen to Good People*, in which he explains why two people with the same illness have completely different outcomes as "random acts of nature." I latch onto this thought because it helps to explain Pamela's death as one of many that are unexplained, and it leaves me with some degree of comfort.

Mike and I are in limbo. Every minute is excruciating because we can't mourn our child properly until the L.A. Coroner's Office releases her body. All we can do is make tentative funeral plans – contacting the church, choosing a coffin and arranging for a cemetery plot. Michael and Paula keep themselves busy organizing their sister's artwork and childhood mementos for display at the wake.

Pamela finally arrives in New York five days after her death at exactly 6:30 a.m. on April 24th, 2001. Although we think we're prepared, one task we have yet to face is getting her something to wear.

I always enjoyed shopping for Pamela because she had a unique sense of style. It was easy to find something that she liked, and almost anything looked good on her. But now it's impossible for me to think clearly, so I reach out to Paula and Cathy for help.

The three of us go from one small boutique to another along Third Avenue.

"I'd like it to be casual, her favorite color – purple – if possible, and something that will keep her warm," I tell the girls. "The last thing Pamela would want is to be seen in something fancy."

"What occasion are you looking for?" the shopkeepers ask when we walk through the door. Not wanting to reveal the delicate nature of our mission, we ignore their advances and talk among ourselves in riddles that leave them stumped.

"Which one of you is it for?" one persistent saleswoman asks. Our response is a triangular glance into each other's eyes.

"It's for our sister," says Paula, the strongest one of us. Cathy and I are about to cry. This is the most difficult shopping trip of our lives.

After an agonizing few hours, we settle upon a sweater, long skirt and whimsical pair of striped socks . . . an inside joke, just between the three of us because they'll be hidden under the bottom half of the casket. The irony is, after all this angst, the sweater and skirt won't be seen either.

"She doesn't look like herself," Paula tells me, after she and her father go to the funeral home to view Pamela's body. "Even with make-up, her face looks different. It droops," she says sadly.

I'm relieved that I followed my instincts not to go with them, because I knew if she looked bad it would haunt me for the rest of my life.

Given the low self-image Pamela suffered from, I'm not about to let mourners view her in a state that would have made her uncomfortable. It would be the last indignity. As it is, people are buzzing about the strange circumstances surrounding her death.

So to protect her from further scrutiny, we decide to have a closed casket. Everyone will have to remember Pamela the way she looked while she was alive.

The wake is packed with hundreds of people, a blur of faces from the past and present. But those most meaningful to me are Pamela's friends. There are two sets of them, the old ones she grew up with in Manhasset, and the most recent group she met during her last three years in treatment.

I'm struck by the dichotomy between the two. The old group hadn't seen Pamela for some time. While she was sick, they were off at college and busy building careers. They knew her the way she used to be, before the breakdown. The recollections they share with me of her early years seem like a distant memory.

But her new friends, some of whom Mike flies in from Malibu or has driven down from Stockbridge for the funeral, talk about the Pamela who struggled with mental illness for three long years. They recognize the pain she endured and are attuned to her deepest feelings. When they offer their condolences, I feel closer to them because they're broken, like my daughter.

When the funeral ends, all these young people say their goodbyes and move on. It's a sobering moment for me, because I realize all of them have the rest of their lives to live. They can look forward to getting married and having children and settling down. Why, I keep thinking, isn't my daughter with them?

Family and friends encourage us to get back to our daily routines in the ensuing days. Mike and Michael go back to work and Paula goes back to her graduate studies. But while the other three are able to escape to different environments, I'm trapped in the house, unable to write a thing, and everywhere I turn there's a reminder of the child I lost.

Her baby pictures hang up and down the hall. A bottle of her favorite shampoo startles me in the shower and the ceramic mug she made her father jumps out, when I open the kitchen cabinet. Even though I throw the still-fresh funeral flowers away and store the hundreds of sympathy cards in boxes, Pamela's presence remains in my nostrils and under my skin. I can't find any solace and the disturbing phone calls that start coming in, are making it worse.

"Ma, I have something very important to tell you," Paula says, her voice sounding strained. It's three days after the funeral.

"Is Dad there?"

"Yes, he just got home," I say. "What's wrong?"

"Put him on the speaker phone."

I call Mike into the kitchen and press the button. We're used to crises, but what can it possibly be now that Pamela's not involved?

"I just got an anonymous call from someone in California who seems to know the inner workings at RR. You're not going to believe what she told me," Paula says.

"Who was it?" Mike asks, "A staff member or a patient?"

"It was a woman, but she wouldn't reveal her identity. She said she found me by searching the telephone listings for Tusiani, and I am the only one in the phone book.

"We spoke for 25 minutes. She said she knew Pamela, and felt compelled to give us information about the illegal actions and unethical staff at RR. She said Dr. Shiraz deserves prison time, and she believes Pamela's was a wrongful death."

Mike and I tense-up and put our faces closer to the phone.

"What she told me is, they're shredding papers in the daybook that said not to call 911 when Pamela had the seizures last summer. Dr. Shiraz said he would fire someone if they did so, and that's the reason why the medical doctor who was overseeing her care at the time resigned."

"My God, can that be true?" I ask.

"The caller said RR is not licensed for psychiatric care, but only for drug and alcohol treatment by the California Alcohol and Drug Division. And Dr. Shiraz is licensed as a marriage counselor. Did you know that Dad?"

"No," Mike says, nervously pressing his thumb into his cheek.

"Well, apparently, the place is only licensed for six people, and right now they've got twenty psychiatric patients living there, and many of them can't get insurance coverage because it's essentially a rehab," Paula continues. "The woman gave me a list of phone numbers for California government agencies to follow through with and said they will verify everything she told me."

"Sounds like she's a staffer," Mike says. "Did you write all of this down?"

276

"Yes, I started writing as soon as she told me about shredding the daybook. But wait, there's more. She said many of the staff at RR are recovering addicts, and some of the therapists and even the nursing staff dispensing medications are not properly licensed for the positions they hold. That would explain why they screwed up with Pamela."

I feel like I'm in the middle of a TV drama, not my life. It's all so unreal. How could we have trusted these people with our child?

"Those bastards!" Mike roars. "I hope they don't think they're going to get away with this. We have to find out who the caller is."

"She must have been there when Pamela got the headache, Dad," Paula says, "because she knew specific details about Pamela's being nauseous and throwing up after eating the pizza and how she was put to bed by staff and basically ignored."

Hearing this, I wonder if they thought Pamela might have induced her own vomiting, but then realize she would never have told them if she did.

"Did the caller leave you any way to get back in contact with her?" Mike says.

"I asked if she would be willing to testify, if we ever pursued a legal case against RR, and she said although she's torn about it, she probably would and said she'd call back in a week."

I'm heartsick, and Mike is angry. He wants to call RR on the spot, but has to sit tight because the office doesn't open until 7:00 a.m., which is 10:00 a.m. our time.

All we can do is mull this startling news over as we toss and turn all night.

When Mike finally does get through to RR, a staffer he doesn't know takes his call.

"I'm sorry, Mr. Tusiani, but Dr. Shiraz is in a staff meeting and Rachel is interviewing new clients."

All hell breaks loose.

"I lost my daughter," he screams, "and that should be a priority. I don't give a shit about any new clients, and if they don't send me the information I requested, I'll come out and get it myself."

That gets their attention. The administrator calls back within minutes.

"We're still gathering our reports, there are many people involved," says Rachel, "I'm trying my best."

"Yeah, right," Mike says sarcastically, "you'd better or you'll hear from my attorney."

The next day, Mike receives a one-page summary of what happened on April 17th. It's incomplete and already contradicts some of what we've been told, causing us to doubt we'll ever be able to trust what RR says about Pamela's death. They're giving us the run-around, and it seems like they're hiding something.

This is confirmed by another jarring phone call tipping Mike off that renegade flyers about RR are being scattered along the Pacific Coast Highway.

"They say, 'Road to Ruin – How Many More People Will Have to Die in Your Neighborhood?'" the caller tells Mike, adding, "The administrators are very nervous that clients will see the flyers, and it will cause an uproar."

We're stunned. "Road to Ruin"?

Sensing this is insider information that we wouldn't ordinarily be privy to, Mike starts taking copious notes. Since we still have to wait another 8 to 10 weeks for the final pathology report from the L.A. Coroner's Office, all we can do is hang on to any piece of information that comes our way.

And to our horror, it continues to fall right into our laps.

A tender note from a fellow patient named Bob arrives in the mail. He writes that he was one of the last people to speak with Pamela on the morning of the tragedy. It shakes me up as I realize there are other people out there who can tell us more about what happened to Pamela that fateful day. I am grateful that Bob's phone number is written under his name.

"I spent half an hour with Pamela, in the morning, before she ate lunch," Bob tells me when I am finally able to reach him. "She seemed very depressed." He goes on to tell me that he is a 60-year-old former drug and alcohol user who lives in the building where Pamela was housed for the holiday weekend.

"What did she say?" I prompt him, anxious to know what was on my daughter's mind.

"Well, I asked her if she was suicidal, and she said no."

"Thank you," I sob. "I'm so relieved to hear that because we're being told she tried to take her own life."

"She said she was having a hard time sleeping," Bob continues. "She wasn't happy with her relationship in a fulfilling way, and was upset she didn't go home for Easter."

"So you think she was just feeling a bit down?" I ask, to confirm what I'm hearing.

"Yes. It's so tragic. Everyone here is wrecked over it," Bob says. "She called me Dad. I loved that because I told her, if I had a daughter, I would want her to be just like you."

I hang up in a flood of tears.

I'm on delicate ground these first few weeks without my daughter. I feel like I can fall apart at any moment, so I run, like a madwoman, from doctors to social workers to support groups – trying to survive – trying to find peace. Nothing works. The circumstances surrounding Pamela's death are becoming more complicated as time passes. How can I seek closure when there are more questions than answers?

Mike is handling it differently. Outwardly, he seems stronger and in control of his emotions, but underneath it all, he's seething with anger.

"They're all crooks, Bea," he says sourly. "They're frustrated because they can't make big money like cardiologists and surgeons."

"Mike, I need you. I can't do this alone," I beg, trying to convince him to come with me for counseling.

"Everyone grieves differently," he says softly, enfolding me in his arms. "Just because I'm not crying doesn't mean I'm not hurting."

Both of us know getting through this difficult time will test our marriage. We're very much aware that many parents who lose children end up divorced. It's not something we talk about, but we know it's a possibility, so we gently accept that we need to give each other space, and try to mourn in our own separate ways.

It's Paula who manages to be the courageous one right now. She flies back to Malibu to pick up her sister's belongings and attends a memorial service for Pamela organized by her friends at AA.

The ceremony takes place on the Bluffs, at the corner of the Pacific

Coast Highway and Malibu Canyon, just across from Pepperdine University. The date, May 14th, 2001, is significant because it would have been Pamela's one year anniversary of sobriety. In honor of this milestone, the group presents Paula with a One-Year Chip, embedded in a piece of wood, hand-carved with a beautiful image of Pamela's face.

Numerous attendees take turns speaking about Pamela, and how fond they were of her. Many tears are shed, but the private conversations that take place afterwards are even more upsetting for Paula.

"Someone came up to me and said he was so sorry to hear Pamela had a brain aneurysm," Paula tells me when she returns.

"I told him, Pamela didn't have a brain aneurysm. Where'd you hear that? He said that's what people are being told. It's just not right, Mom. It sounds like rumors are being created to hide the truth."

"Listen to this," I say. "While you were gone another caller from a confidential source told Dad those involved in 'the Pamela incident' – which is what RR is now calling Pamela's death – are not being allowed to discuss it with others at the facility."

Forbid people to talk about Pamela in a place where "talk" is a vital part of therapy? There is definitely a conspiracy taking place.

So I push forward to find out more. There's still one person I'm anxious to talk to, Pamela's AA sponsor, Teri, who wasn't at the memorial service. She visited Pamela in the hospital and was probably the last person to see her before she went on life-support.

I find her phone number in Pamela's address book, but can't seem to reach her, until one day she calls me.

"I'd just returned from Dallas when I heard Pamela was in the hospital," she explains, "but I didn't know why. I didn't know if she took pills or drank, so I went to visit her."

"I arrived at about 10 p.m. and found her in a regular room with the TV on. A 'sitter,' assigned to watch her, was engrossed in an episode of *Law & Order*."

"How was she?" I ask, hanging on to every word.

"She wasn't lucid at all. Her hands were shaking, and she was fidgeting," says Teri. "I couldn't believe she didn't recognize me, I said 'Pamela, are you in there?' and she said, 'I'm right here,' but that was it."

"She spoke to you?" I say, my heart quickening. "That means she had brain activity."

"I thought she was acting very strange, so when the sitter left to put coins in the meter for her car, I went to the nurses' station to ask what happened. Since I wasn't a family member, they wouldn't tell me. It was so unsettling. I dialed up Amber right from the hospital. She told me Pamela ordered a pizza and ate it at their apartment."

"That's not true! Pamela ate the pizza at RR," I cry out, stung by this latest bit of deceptiveness. Is Amber covering up because she was the cook the day Pamela ate the pizza?

What Mike and I are hearing starts buzzing in our heads.

All these new details and inconsistencies, popping up in mysterious ways, leave us no choice but to take action. We owe it to our daughter to find out if she received the care she was entitled to at RR, at UCLA Medical Center, and by the psychiatrists and doctors overseeing her care.

Mike and I work together but take different paths. He seeks legal advice, and I focus on government agencies.

The first thing I do is contact the Joint Commission on Accreditation of Healthcare Organizations (JCAHO) to alert them to Pamela's death. I fill out a "Quality Incident Report Form," and at their request, fax it to them immediately.

When I call to follow up, a representative informs me, "I have your incident report, Mrs. Tusiani, but can't act on it. RR in Malibu is not affiliated with JCAHO."

I'm confused. "What do you mean, they're not affiliated? It says right here in their literature, RR Malibu is JCAHO accredited," I respond.

"Their Northridge facility is accredited, but the Malibu location is not, and you can't blanket over accreditation from one facility to the other," the spokesperson explains.

Now I'm getting angry. This is the worst thing I've heard about RR so far. Lying about medical credentials to people who are desperate for psychiatric help is disgraceful.

I press further, seeking to convince JCAHO that it should reprimand RR for this misrepresentation.

"Being JCAHO-accredited was a determining factor in sending our daughter there, and now she's dead. Isn't there anything you can do to hold them accountable?" I plead.

"Please accept our condolences, Mrs. Tusiani, but since JCAHO does not currently accredit this facility, we are unable to take further action regarding your concern."

For a moment I'm speechless . . . then I collect my thoughts.

"So anyone can say they're JCAHO-affiliated and not be penalized if it turns out they're not?" I ask. The response is dead silence.

The next step I take is to file a complaint with RR's licensing unit, the California State Bureau of Alcohol and Drugs. According to its records, the Bureau was notified of this case by RR on May 5th, more than two weeks after Pamela's death. A follow-up report of the investigation found no deficiency in the way RR handled Pamela's care.

I call and ask if they inspected RR's "day book" to determine if it was tampered with and am told nothing was found amiss that their regulations apply to. I then bring up RR's false claim of JCAHO affiliation and am told, the Bureau does not have power over a facility's misrepresentation of services.

"But you give them their license, if you don't have power over their making false claims, who does?" I ask.

Again, no response.

"Even if a death is involved?" I push on.

"The powers of this agency are limited," the official says, a bit too dispassionately for my blood.

Does he think I'm a fool?

Here is a facility that is operating under a license as a drug rehab, yet treats psychiatric patients. Who is overseeing the "psychiatric" part of this equation? How could RR advertise as a dual-diagnosis facility, when they're properly licensed for only half of that?

This is unacceptable.

I write to the California Attorney General, explaining that JCAHO and the California Bureau of Drugs and Alcohol profess no authority over facilities that misrepresent their affiliation with them. In a letter he tells me his office is only able to represent cases on behalf of the collective legal interests of the people in California. Pamela was a New Yorker who died in California.

He suggests we get a lawyer.

But that's not so easy to do in California, because malpractice suits have a legal cap of $250,000 for recovery.

For us, it's never been about making money but that justice be served.

One prestigious firm that doesn't think it's worth it to represent us, refers us to a nice young lawyer in Newport Beach who is willing to take our case. The catch is, if this young lawyer wins, the referring firm is entitled to a percentage of the award. What then, would that leave the young lawyer? What would that leave us to give to charity in Pamela's memory? Why is my daughter's life so suddenly all about money?

While we bombard our newfound attorney, Henry Taylor, with mountains of our collective notes – by fax, courier, e-mail and phone – we're also trying to get on with our lives. But it's not easy.

Five months have passed and I look at the calendar. It's September and Pamela's birthday is not penciled in on the 14th.

Instead, what's written is, mass: 9 a.m. St. Thomas More, 89th St. off Madison Ave.; 11 a.m. order flowers, Mercer Greenhouse; 1 p.m. meet Mike, go to cemetery, St. Charles, Farmingdale, L.I.

I know it will be hard to get out of bed on that date and face Pamela's 24th birthday without her. But what I don't expect, is the cataclysmic tragedy of September 11. The epicenter of destruction is right here in New York, where I see the sadness on the faces of hundreds of people who lost loved ones. Most of the victims are young adults, like Pamela, and their parents are suffering too, like me. My own personal grief is swept up in the city's massive outpouring of mourning, and I realize I am one of many.

As time passes, Mike encourages me to move out of my semi-imposed exile.

"Bea, I have a dinner tonight, wives are invited, do you want to come?" He waits for a response and I stare back.

"You go along without me," I say, not at all in a mood to socialize. It feels fake, to go through the motions of making small talk and laughing simply because I'm expected to.

"Bea, you can't coop yourself up in the house forever. It's not healthy, and Pamela wouldn't want you to be doing this," Mike says.

"I don't want to be the elephant in the room and have people tip-toe around me," I say.

I set up roadblocks and hide behind them every time Mike pushes me to move on. With more and more frequency, he's asking me to join him for dinners and social events or even trips. Although his intentions are good, many times I come up with an excuse not to go.

It's not nice to act this way, I know, but the loss of my daughter is still so painfully raw. It's easier for me to talk to complete strangers, than to people I've known for 30 years. I can't bear to be in the company of my closest friends because most of them have children Pamela's age, and it brings back too many memories of happier times.

The truth is, I feel guilty having fun. Even on a trip, far away from home, I dive into the sea but don't feel refreshed, because I know it's just a temporary escape from the harsh reality – Pamela is dead. It smacks me in the face like cold water, wherever I go and whatever I do.

The only way I can protect myself from the hurt and pain is to take baby steps back into the real world on my own terms, not Mike's.

Although he is relentlessly persistent, to his credit, he is also supportive, and allows me full command to pursue accountability for those who were negligent in Pamela's care.

In that effort I find enormous strength and resolve.

Moving on to the Department of Health Services, which licenses the UCLA Medical Center, I call and report that a wrongful death occurred on the hospital's premises.

"Sorry, Ma'am, nothing in our records indicates UCLA is responsible for your daughter's death," the official there tells me. "If you want to pursue it, you can file a complaint with the California Medical Board against the doctor who wrote the orders in the Emergency Room."

"But my daughter was brought to UCLA Medical Center by ambulance, and the hospital assigned the doctor in charge of her care. Shouldn't the hospital be responsible for that?" I ask.

"Look," the hospital spokesperson says, "I'll keep your file open in case you come up with something more specific against the staff, but the incident that led to your daughter's death occurred before she came here."

When will this ridiculous game of passing the buck end? I'm driven to find out.

I do what she says and file complaints with the Medical Board of California, which is overseen by the State Department of Consumer Affairs, against the two doctors whose questionable actions ultimately determined my daughter's fate: Dr. Vasily, her medicating doctor at RR, and Dr. Sharif, the Emergency Room doctor at UCLA.

A young investigator from the Medical Board follows up with a phone call. He sounds enthusiastic about helping me, but doesn't seem to know what he's doing. Naively, he confides he's new on the job – so new that he has to check with his supervisor to answer every question I ask.

This makes me seethe.

Swallowing hard, I nevertheless follow his instructions to send him the release forms for Pamela's medical history and attach her death certificate – which forces me to read it over and over again:

"The cause of death is attributed to intra-cerebral hemorrhage due to acute hypertension. The acute hypertensive crisis appears to be from a drug interaction (Parnate, an MAOI inhibitor) with food (history of cheese pizza consumption). The manner of death is accident."

The response I receive by mail informs me that each of these investigations could take up to two years. Are they trying to discourage me from seeking the truth? There's no guarantee I'm even going to live that long. It seems there's a hands-off, hand-off policy in every government agency.

I'm just about to throw in the towel when I get a call from a friend who made a donation in Pamela's memory to a self-injury program in Illinois. She tells me she has spoken at length with its director about what happened to Pamela.

"The director," my friend says, "feels strongly that when fault is suspected, it should be vigorously pursued, because untold numbers of cases like Pamela's get brushed under the rug by insurance companies, the medical community and legal systems. Most young people are vulnerable, and often can't afford to take legal action."

This is exactly what I need to hear. It makes me realize that my ongoing effort to discover what happened to Pamela is not only for my child's sake, but for other lost youths whose parents lack the time, skills, money, or tenacity to seek the true circumstances surrounding their deaths. Now I feel a sense of responsibility to take all of them under my wing.

While I am immersed in state and medical agency investigations, our lawyer, Henry Taylor, is busy filing four separate wrongful death suits against the two doctors, UCLA and RR. The statute of limitations for filing formal complaints is one year from the time of death, and we are just getting them in under the wire in March 2002.

This doesn't provide the relief we expected, however, because we quickly learn that time is not on our side when it comes to witnesses.

"It's a full year later, and most of the 'tipsters' who called right after Pamela's death seem to have gotten on with their lives," Taylor explains.

The anonymous caller who promised to get back to Paula never did. And some of the others are nearly impossible to find, Taylor tells me, because they either moved to new apartments, or left the facility, or found jobs outside the area and didn't forward their addresses.

This is a terrible letdown. We need the testimony of these people because Mike and I weren't there when the incident occurred. We only know what we were told, and those accounts are conflicting.

Was a vegetable pizza served, or was it a white pizza topped with mozzarella cheese? Did Pamela order a pizza and eat it in her apartment or at RR? Was she left alone in her room in a delirious state or was someone monitoring her the whole time?

"The few who are available to testify," Taylor adds, "are psych patients or AA members, and that diminishes their credibility. Judges and juries are likely to factor in their dysfunctional backgrounds."

"You mean to tell me these people – who are eye-witnesses to wrongdoing – are not given equal status under the law?" I ask, implying the justice system is not as "just" as it purports to be. I already watched a Grand Jury discredit my daughter because she was a psych patient, after she was raped in Massachusetts, and I don't want to see others victimized for the same reason.

286

Our family doesn't have a choice but to proceed with these cases and hope fairness will prevail. In the meantime, I try to come up with a credible witness.

In one last-ditch effort, I pour my heart out in a letter to the doctor who, Paula was told by the anonymous caller, left RR in the middle of Pamela's care.

His attorney tells Taylor that the doctor left because of the heavy-handed way RR's director, Dr. Shiraz, dealt with patients. He was more interested in keeping them around for their money than treating them. But when Taylor asks if the doctor would be willing to testify, the attorney replies that the doctor does not want to go on record.

Another opportunity lost. Pamela would not have been surprised. Why would anyone want to come to her defense? After all, she saw herself as worthless, and this parade of "retreating" witnesses would have validated that in her mind.

But there are two people who are still committed to telling everything they know: Mike and I. We get a notice that the defendants are ready to take our depositions. They want us to fly out to California, but Mike wants them held on his own turf, right here in New York.

CHAPTER 12

New York

MR. DAVIS TO MRS. BEATRICE TUSIANI (WITNESS):

Q: Did anyone tell you they saw Pamela eat the pizza?

A: No.

Q: Did anyone tell you that Pamela had expressed any potentially suicidal ideation at a discussion prior to the lunch?

A: No, I was not privy to the group conversation.

Q: Did you ever hear at any time prior to filing a lawsuit that Pamela
had been moved to the main house because she had expressed some
suicidal ideation but didn't have any specific plans that day?

A: No. She was in the main house I thought because it was Easter Sunday and she couldn't sleep. The last I spoke with her she was upbeat.
When I got off the phone with her on the 16th, she said I'm glad I
talked to you Mom.

Q: Has anyone told you anything that would lead you to believe that
Pamela may have eaten the pizza in a suicide attempt?

A: No.

BEA

It's early fall, 2002 – a year and a half after Pamela's death – when
Mike and I give our depositions in the conference room of his New
York City office.

After months of combing through the timeline of events that span
from Pamela's mental collapse, to the questionable circumstances surrounding her death, I feel as prepared as any witness can ever be.

In a lot of ways, I've moved on with my life. I'm working on my mem-
oirs, traveling and keeping up with family and social commitments. But
despite my busy calendar, this legal case is the first thing I think about
when I wake up in the morning and the last when I go to sleep at night.
I know something very wrong happened between April 17 and April 19,
2001, and I can't rest until whoever caused it to happen is held accountable.

When Mike and I walk into the conference room, Henry Taylor introduces us to the attorneys who have flown in from California representing RR and Drs. Stedman and Sharif. We shake hands and try to be polite. They don't crack a smile. It's intimidating.

They begin by asking me soft questions about Pamela's childhood to break the ice, which I answer quite comfortably. But as their interrogation continues, the atmosphere in the room turns from warm to frigid. It's suddenly as if I'm the one on trial, being blamed for my daughter's mental illness, and the hidden cause of her depression and borderline personality.

"How much time did you spend with Pamela in her school activities? Did you have a nanny? How many hours did you work? Did you spend more time with your older children than with Pamela?"

Through his line of questioning, I can tell that Davis is trying to paint me as a mother who put pressure on her daughter to succeed at school; someone who meddled in her care and didn't recognize her drug use because I had a career of my own. How can I possibly defend myself?

It's very hurtful to have an outsider make such insinuations about me and my relationship with my daughter, but I try hard to maintain my composure. I've shed enough tears over the past 18 months, now I want to be alert and clear-headed for Pamela's sake, and let the facts speak for themselves.

They interrogate me for four hours, about each of Pamela's admissions: to Johns Hopkins, Lenox Hill, and Austen Riggs. I answer the questions calmly and factually. But when they finally ask about my impression of Road to Recovery, and what happened on the day Pamela ate the pizza, I become impassioned.

"We were asked to pay seven thousand dollars for Pamela to stay there for a week. So we were paying a thousand dollars a day for her to be safe, in a safe place. I feel that Pamela was not safe there. She could have been in my house and she would have been safer because I would not have put pizza on the table. I feel that they had food monitors there for bulimics and anorexics. They could have easily, with only seven people in the house that weekend, had a food monitor watching Pamela.

"I don't know the qualification of the people that handled her afterwards. I'm not sure if they are former junkies or if they are licensed, but I have the feeling that they were not qualified to take the measures that they took with Pamela. I feel that waiting for more than forty-five minutes to call an ambulance compromised her safety. And by not having an anti-hypertensive drug in their medical cabinet to save her, I feel like they were negligent. They put her in an ambulance with a bunch of papers they pulled off the Internet about Parnate, and RR wasn't her advocate at the hospital.

"If I had followed my instincts from the beginning I would have been there and seen that my daughter was not acting normally, and I might have advocated on her behalf and gotten help."

I am on fire, but in a good way. My rage and anger at what happened to Pamela at RR, comes out unfiltered, strong, and intelligent. After all these months of people trying to console me by diverting my attention and changing the subject whenever I want to talk about Pamela's tragic death, I am finally being listened to. I have a forum to express what I've been holding in for so long, and no one is ignoring or stopping me.

Empowered by this newfound confidence, I continue in the same vein when the attorneys ask about UCLA Medical Center.

"I had no choice where my daughter was going to be taken to. They took her to UCLA. They brought her in and treated her like a mental patient and not a physical patient. If they treated her like a patient that came in with a severe headache, like they did with Sharon Stone, they would have found she had a bleed in her head. They would have done something to correct it like they did with Sharon Stone. And she's walking around and my daughter's not.

"Dr. Sharif never heard of Parnate. How could you go to medical school and not know what it is? He didn't know what the drug was. How could he know what a hypertensive crisis was? Why didn't he know that a classic crisis is a bleed in the brain? Why didn't they take an MRI or CAT scan? Why didn't he have her vital signs monitored? Why was Pamela fidgeting and jumping and staring at the ceiling? Why didn't they put her in intensive care the way they said they were going to? Why didn't somebody from the hospital call us? Why didn't somebody advocate for my daughter? It seems sloppy from every angle. And it's my daughter and it's my blood, and I'm not accepting that sloppiness."

I held it together, articulating every point I wanted to make, and I could swear Pamela had something to do with it. I felt her presence during the questioning. It was as if she was sitting next to me saying, "C'mon Mom, I know you can do it," spurring me on to speak for her and be her voice, just as I did throughout her life. I can only hope this testimony is a final act of love for my daughter, because her story is finally being told.

The next day it's Mike's turn. Although I didn't cry during my own interrogation, I go through a whole box of tissues during his. The emotions that I controlled so well a day before can no longer be held in check, because these people are trying to demonize my husband far worse than they did me.

"How many hours were you traveling and working away from home while Pamela was in grammar school? High school? College? Why did you choose to send your daughter to California for treatment? Was the cost of her care ever a concern to you?"

I can't believe how evil they are making Mike out to be, trying to portray him as a workaholic who wasn't involved in his daughter's life – someone who sent her clear across the country and just wrote checks to make her problems go away.

I know this is a complete misrepresentation of my husband's character, but do they? Will a jury?

The testimony hardest to listen to is Mike defending himself against accusations of sexual abuse, right here in his own office, where people on the other side of the conference room walls revere him for his honesty, compassion and generosity.

This cuts to the bone. My instinct is to protect him, but I can't because it's not my turn to speak. Even though Pamela exonerated him in her diaries, the lawyers are focusing on this issue, and circling in for the kill.

I can see by the sad expression on Mike's face, he's torn up. They're going after his fatherhood and character, the things that matter most. I fear this is going to destroy him. But underneath it all, I know he's as strong as they come.

I'm grateful to get past this difficult part of his deposition and onto the events surrounding Pamela's death, hoping it will shift the momentum back in our favor. But I lose my composure again, when Mike reveals his version of what occurred on April 19, 2001.

"I called [UCLA] on the 19th. It was 6:45 in the morning, New York time. I had to find out how Pamela was doing. A nurse said, 'Who are you?' I said, 'I'm the father.' 'Hold on, we have a problem. You've got to talk to Dr. Lee.' So Dr. Lee, who was a resident, got on the phone. I said, 'What is going on?'

"'Well, there's been some seizure activity. Elevated blood pressure caused a bleed in the brain.' I dropped my pen and started crying.

"I said to myself, what do I do? The first thing that came to my mind is how am I going to tell her mother? I called the kids. I told them what happened. They immediately said they needed to go to California with me.

"Then I took a taxi to go home. I was sitting in that taxi, it was probably the most difficult ten minutes I spent in my life because I didn't know what I was going to tell my wife. In business, you do a lot of things. You lose a deal, you make one, but I didn't know how to tell my wife we just lost our daughter.

"I got home, and I just told her. It was very, very difficult. Of course, she started screaming."

As I hear Mike's moving account of what happened, I shrink back into my chair. Since Pamela died, I've resented him because he's reluctant to talk about her or the legal case. It's put a wedge between us. I didn't think he cared as much as I do, but hearing his testimony, I realize he does care. In fact, he cares so much, he was trying to protect me at a time when he was full of emotion himself. I misjudged him, and wish I could let him know how sorry I am. But there's no time for reconciliation now, as the questions continue at a rapid-fire pace.

When the 10 hours of depositions finally end, the both of us are wiped out. We've done our best trying to justify every detail of our lives. But it was brutal to be ripped apart like that.

Taylor reassuringly whispers out of earshot of others, "The attorneys for the defendants are impressed with the consistency between your written and verbal accounts. This makes you credible witnesses."

I'm puzzled, all we're doing is telling the truth. Why wouldn't we be credible? But after reading some of the conflicting testimonies of those being deposed in California, I understand what he means.

When Dr. Shiraz, RR's director, is questioned, he claims there was no reason to conduct an internal investigation of what happened to the daybook immediately after Pamela's death, because that was the Program Director's job.

But when Taylor asks the Program Director, Rachel, why she shredded the daybook, she tells him the Department of Drug and Alcohol Programs didn't require RR to keep it.

Unsatisfied with her response, he presses on.

"Well, then tell me why you waited 23 days to file an incident report to that agency about Pamela's death, instead of 24 hours, which is required?"

Rachel explains, "Everyone was so grief stricken, I didn't think to do it."

When Taylor requests a copy of that report to enter into the official record, RR's attorney tells him they can't find one.

It makes me sick to my stomach that they've shredded and are missing important documents that could reveal the truth. No wonder they took so long to respond to Mike when he asked for a written account of what exactly happened. They were too busy scrambling to cover their tracks.

Another startling contradiction that emerges during the California depositions is RR's hiring of its medical personnel as independent contractors. According to Dr. Shiraz's testimony, doctors at RR are not employed as staff. They work as "consultant clinicians" on a rotating basis, at other facilities as well as RR, and don't necessarily communicate about each other's patients. It allows RR to cut corners and avoid expensive insurance costs.

In fact, we learn that the only full-time medical person employed by RR is a Licensed Psychiatric Technician named Kathy, who has two years of nursing school experience. When Taylor questions Kathy about who was responsible for Pamela's care after her shift ended on April 17, she responds that she taught the staff how to monitor Pamela's vital signs. Upon further questioning, we discover that many of these staff counselors are in recovery themselves and have no medical training beyond first-aid and CPR.

So, after my daughter had a food reaction with Parnate, Kathy consulted the independent medical contractor on site, who was not familiar with Pamela's case, and then left her in the care of staffers unqualified to take blood pressure.

Taylor assures us that our testimony is strong, and their depositions are filled with holes and inconsistencies. His upbeat tone makes us feel hopeful that we have a chance of exposing RR's errors, and our case will move forward to trial.

We are optimistic too, because Taylor wisely discovers that Pamela signed a contract when she was admitted to RR, which states:

"RR is not liable for the services rendered by physicians, as they are independent contractors. We do not provide nursing services or administer medications."

Taylor argues to the California Court of Appeals that RR should not be covered by MICRA (Medical Injury Compensation and Reform Act), the law which places the $250,000 cap on malpractice suits in California because it doesn't employ or insure full-time medical staff.

RR can't have it both ways: not insure doctors and then expect them to be legally protected from malpractice suits. The Court recognizes this shill game and rules in our favor, allowing us to seek damages beyond the $250,000 cap.

It's our first victory, though Mike and I are hesitant to celebrate because it reveals how slippery the legal system can be.

At the same time this is happening in our lives, controversy over malpractice caps is all over the news. President George W. Bush is urging the U.S. Senate to pass a national malpractice law that would cap awards for pain and suffering at $250,000.

I'm especially incensed when *60 Minutes* does a segment on the issue focusing on doctors who can't afford the high malpractice insurance rates. I send a letter off to Mike Wallace telling him the other side of the story.

Out of the thousands of letters he gets a week, I'm not surprised mine stood out because of its passionate delivery. He calls and tells me a story is in the can about my side of the issue, then confides to me that he lost a son, and both of us find ourselves on common ground as grieving parents.

Still, speaking to this high profile investigative reporter doesn't do anything for our case. I receive word from the Department of Alcohol and Drug Programs in California that it has concluded its investigation of my complaint against RR and did not find any identifiable deficiencies based on its Department guidelines.

I'm very disappointed but not surprised, since I know that agency deals primarily with substance abuse violations, not psychiatric cases. It's unbelievable that the only regulatory agency overseeing RR, doesn't even give it so much as a slap on the wrist when someone dies under suspicious circumstances in one of its facilities. To them, my daughter is just another faceless psych patient.

As if this does not sting enough, the Medical Board of California, a state agency that licenses medical doctors, investigates complaints and disciplines those who violate the law, deals us another blow.

After reviewing our complaints against Dr. Stedman, the independent medical clinician on call at RR when Pamela ate the pizza, and Dr. Sharif, the ER doctor at UCLA, it absolves them of any wrongdoing, citing insufficient evidence for disciplinary action.

I feel like I'm on a roller coaster. At first, during the depositions, we were on a steady upward climb, and it felt like we could conquer the world. But it seems now we're spiraling downward with increasing speed.

Taylor's suggestion that we reconsider our legal strategy doesn't help.

"After taking the depositions and consulting with the experts, it's my opinion that the largest proportion of liability is going to rest with RR. If we go to trial, the crux of the argument will be that RR was negligent. As to the remaining defendants, the liability picture is still unfolding, but the best strategy is to go against the primary wrongdoer."

I'm not stupid and can sense through all his legal jargon where he's headed. Our attorney is asking us to cave in, by trying to convince us to drop or settle our cases against the hospital and doctors.

"But Henry, they made mistakes," I blurt out. "How can we absolve them of wrongdoing? UCLA put Pamela on suicide watch when they should have been testing her brain."

"It's very sad, I agree," he says trying to calm me down. "But unfortunately, the law states that negligence must 'cause' injury to the victim, and that injury occurred at RR."

"Well, I hope you never have to use that emergency room for one of your loved ones," I reply in disgust.

Mike and I have no alternative but to follow his advice. It might be different if the legal proceedings were in New York, where Mike knows people who could help us. But from a distance, all we can do is trust that Taylor has a strong grasp of California law, and is acting in our best interest.

The trial date is set for May 5, 2003. Mike and I are both anxious. It's been two years since Pamela's death and during that time we've been talking to lawyers and government agencies and filing reports in an effort to prove our daughter's death could have been prevented. Now the time has finally come to go before a jury in a court of law, and have them judge the facts.

While we wait for the trial to begin, Taylor unexpectedly flip-flops again.

"Anything can happen in a jury trial, it's unpredictable. I always believe a settlement is better than a verdict. Then the case is over, the stresses and expenses of trial are avoided, and you don't have to pin everything on the trust of twelve jurors you do not know," he says, and quickly adds, "but of course, I respect your choice to move forward."

Why is Taylor switching tactics now? This whole time we've been mentally preparing ourselves for a trial. We whittled all our lawsuits down to RR because he told us it was our best option, and now he's even trying to talk us out of that?

He may be proceeding in a way that is common in the legal world, but I don't know how the game is played, and I find it disturbing.

Feeling let down, I call Mike.

"Everything we've worked so hard for is falling apart, and I am not sure if Taylor really wants to see this through," I tell him.

"Bea, you've got to understand, this is how business is conducted.

He's trying to negotiate a deal. What I can do is have him put his recommendations in writing so we know what our options are."

"Maybe one of those options is finding another lawyer," I persist. I ask him if our friend Arthur can get us through to Johnnie Cochran, the lawyer from the O.J. Simpson case, who is his partner.

"Okay, Bea. I'll call Art," Mike says wearily, "but I can't promise miracles."

I know I'm pushing, but am not willing to give up . . . not yet . . . without a fight.

Taylor overnights us a thick packet explaining, in objective detail, his arguments for settling.

"RR will likely claim this was a suicide attempt; Pamela was fully informed of what not to eat and chose to ignore the warnings," he explains.

I'm not worried. Taylor can prove it wasn't suicide. But as I read on, I see just how attorneys can twist the facts.

"RR will argue that Pamela's death was caused by a brain bleed brought on by past cocaine use," Taylor continues, "because she was a former drug user, intimating she wasn't a 'good' person. And I can assure you, RR will try to present evidence that the relationship between her and the two of you was not very close.

"I'm also sure they will try to make these West L.A. jurors look at you like slick New Yorkers. There will be evidence which suggests that you are affluent, being able to afford $22,000 per month for RR's treatment, leading them to believe you don't need the money, and the verdict could reflect that," Taylor adds.

This really pisses me off. I'm from Brooklyn. Mike's from the Bronx. We may be wealthy now because of his hard work, but our roots are firmly planted in the middle-class values we grew up with. Having money shouldn't affect our right to a fair trial. We spent whatever it took for what we thought was the best medical care for our daughter, but all the thousands of dollars we paid for Pamela did not save her. Shouldn't that mean something to the jurors?

And besides, being wealthy actually worked against us, because we relied on private mental healthcare providers, which in our country are improperly regulated. That is why they were able to take advantage of us, lie about their credentials, and not keep Pamela safe.

When I explain this to Taylor on the phone the next day, he tries to placate me.

"Look, Mrs. Tusiani, I know this is tough to face but the bottom line is, even if we go to court and obtain a good verdict, RR has the right to appeal, and that process could take another one to two years. You have to decide if that's what you want."

Taylor also tells Mike that if we want Cochran to assist or take over the case, he has to know by the end of the week. Mike and I are being squeezed into a tight deadline.

As we turn this obstacle over in our minds, we learn that a court-appointed mediator has been assigned to our case. Her objective is to move both parties toward settlement.

Mike makes a trip to Los Angeles in early summer of '03 to meet with the mediator. I can't bear to go with him. I'm not ready to face those places where we last saw Pamela alive.

But instead of a mediator, Mike finds himself before a judge who tries to dissuade him from going to trial by citing cases similar to ours, in which the monetary awards were meager.

The mother of a 19-year-old part-time trucker who was killed by a tractor-trailer backing up, received $200,000. The family of a 75-year-old woman, who died when an asthma breathing-machine was mishandled by an airline, was awarded $226,000. The mother of a 32-year-old mentally ill inmate who committed suicide at a county detention facility settled at $400,000. The wife of a 52-year-old man who died during elective surgery after having his breathing tube removed was given $272,154.

When Mike shares these stories with me, I can't believe it. "Are you telling me that in all these cases, everything boils down to dollars and cents? Is that what a life is worth? All these people have died, but I wonder: has that trucking company gone out of business? Has the airline shut down? No. Life goes on. Just like at RR which is operating as if nothing ever happened. . . .as if no one ever died under their care."

"Bea, the judge said there's a possibility we might not win the case at all, and you can't be blind to that. What is it you want? What would satisfy you?"

"You know it's not about the money. We'll give it away anyway," I say. "We want to hold them accountable for their actions. No one else is, for God's sake, shouldn't we?"

I've always imagined this case would have the same impact as Erin Brockovich's fight against pollutants, or Karen Silkwood's exposing the effects of nuclear radiation in small industrial towns. A legal victory for us would, I thought, somehow impact the system and change the laws the way theirs did. But it seems that mental health is not as important as cancer. Nobody cares.

As if Mike is reading my thoughts, he says, "Look Bea, I don't want to see RR get away with this either. They're scoundrels. But you're acting on your emotions. These judges, lawyers, mediators – they see cases like Pamela's every day. Surely they know what they're talking about. We may invest years in a trial but actually get more by settling.

"Taylor tells me that the judge has put our case on the legal docket for September. We have three weeks to either accept RR's final settlement offer or go to trial. We don't have to decide today, but we need to figure it out soon."

Despite my strong convictions that Pamela was mistreated in so many ways, I am beginning to lose my resolve. Mainly, it's because of Mike, Paula and Michael. I have been dragging them on my coattails through this whole process.

Taylor encourages me to consider the impact on them of a trial. "You will have to come out to California," he says, "and stay for at least two or three weeks. It could be very taxing and tough on the surviving family members."

I'm torn. Michael and Paula insist they will not let Mike and me go through this alone. They want to come out to California to support us if there's a trial. The idea of uprooting everyone from their daily routines is beginning to weigh heavily on me. It might be an emotional upheaval of extreme proportions for them to leave their spouses, homes and jobs.

They're also beginning to express their own concerns.

"The lawyers will make Pamela look like a bad person, Ma," Michael says, clearly in pain over this. He is and always was extremely protective of his little sister.

"They're going to say she was raped and was a drug user and was out of control. It's going to be hard to sit there and listen to them drag her through the mud."

While he worries about Pamela's reputation, Paula focuses on her father's.

"It'll be very hurtful to hear them accuse Daddy of abusing Pamela," she says. "Even though she admitted it's not true, and we know it's not true, RR's lawyers will create reasonable doubt in front of twelve strangers who will be judging him, and I don't want to see Daddy go through that."

The two of them are also concerned about me and how I will handle the pressure of being on the stand. They don't want to see me fall apart when I've already been through so much.

Mike, ever the realist, voices what I never want to hear. "You know, Bea, we could lose. A jury could decide against us," he says.

All three leave the decision about whether to go to trial or settle, up to me.

I do not want to abandon my fight for Pamela. She was a victim of negligence. As a mother, it's still up to me to protect whatever is left of her, even if it's only her reputation. But unexpected circumstances have come up.

Not only am I worrying about my two other children and my husband, who are all hurting, but we just received news that Michael's wife Cathy is having a baby. We are expecting our first grandchild around the holidays. I doubt whether it's such a good idea for Michael to be separated from his wife during a lengthy trial, when it should be a happy time for the two of them.

Two and a half years have already gone by since Pamela's death, and even if we do win the trial, an appeal by the defense could take another two. Is this what I want for my family?

I begin to redirect my thinking in terms of protecting the living instead of the dead. There are lives – very precious ones – yet to be lived right now, and I recognize that I'm the one to salvage them.

I reluctantly bow to those around me. With a heavy heart, I tell Mike to settle.

Once that decision is made, Taylor quickly faces off against RR's legal team in an out-and-out numerical tug of war. What we get from RR's insurance company is quite a bit lower than where we started. But it is still more than the $250,000 cap, and that, in itself, is a small victory.

Of course, RR is still operating. Pamela would have predicted that.

EPILOGUE

My son lives in the City, a few blocks away from our apartment. Occasionally, his wife calls and asks me to babysit my 18-month-old granddaughter.

I rarely refuse because, although I thought I'd never smile again, this little angel has given me reason to.

She's napping in her stroller when Cathy brings her over. Normally, I would take her to the park, but on this day, the skies are overcast and rain is predicted, so I try to think of ways to amuse her at home when she wakes up.

Walking down the hall, past Pamela's bedroom – a door Mike and I pass daily, but hardly acknowledge – I stop short. I remember her stuffed animals.

She loved elephants, and kept a collection of them in all sizes on the floor in a basket under her window.

I hesitate before turning the doorknob, not wanting to face the flood of memories that I'm sure will resurface when I enter what was once Pamela's domain; but hearing a loud crack of thunder I decide, for my granddaughter's sake, to do it.

Once inside, I freeze. There is everything we shut out of our lives. The room is filled with piles of paper, stacked high from the bed to the window. A dozen diaries are scattered on Pamela's desk. Boxes are filled with hundreds of pages of medical records and hospital reports related to her care.

Artwork from sketchbooks and portfolios leans haphazardly against the walls. There are newspaper clippings, mounds of books about BPD, and thick manila envelopes stuffed with legal affidavits spread across the floor. It's hard to walk by it all without becoming emotional.

Bending down to reach for some elephants, I see a pile of Mike's neatly written notes – they chronicle every conversation he had with Pamela's doctors and care-givers throughout her three-year ordeal. Right next to it is a similar stack of my own notes.

Seeing my handwriting from a distance startles me.

It takes me back to a time and place I've been avoiding for over a year. Instinctively, I start to thumb through what I jotted down – "Don't be co-dependent, set boundaries, treat Pamela like an adult, not a child." Reading my own words describing in detail how I tried, but failed, to help my daughter, I'm overcome with guilt.

As much as I'll always blame myself, the truth is, I'm not the only one who failed my daughter – mental health professionals, the protective legal system and government agencies failed her too.

Looking around the room, surrounded by all these remnants of Pamela's life on paper, it suddenly becomes clear that these papers aren't meant to collect dust. They're meant to be read. They've been sitting here all these years waiting for someone to pick them up and tell the story of a girl who struggled just to be normal – and never made it.

I know now that someone has to be me. I'm Pamela's mother, the one she trusted the most, the one who she knew would find meaning in her existence. And I'm a writer. What greater story could I tackle than to piece together the tragic circumstances surrounding my daughter's life and death.

The baby cries. Jolted back to reality, I grab some elephants and run to her.

But after she goes home, I'm drawn back into Pamela's room. I pick up her first diary, dated March 22, 1998.

"This is the second full day I have been on Meyer 4, at Johns Hopkins University in Baltimore, Maryland . . ."

Captivated by her long-forgotten voice, I turn on my computer and start to write.

POSTSCRIPT

In the years following Pamela's death, Mike and I both turned to charitable efforts to help us through the grieving process. I became president of the Italian Welfare League in New York City, which helps children of Italian descent who are sick or disabled. Mike was asked to serve on the board of a major hospital. With his acceptance of this position, we started a dialog with doctors and mental health professionals about Pamela's struggle with Borderline Personality Disorder.

What we learned, coupled with our own experience, is that only a handful of doctors recognize BPD's symptoms and diagnose them properly. Few short- and long-term facilities exist to treat BPD. There's a lack of information and support for families suddenly faced with it, as we were.

To fill this void, we founded The Borderline Personality Disorder Resource Center at the White Plains campus of New York Presbyterian Hospital. Since its inception in February 2004, it has fielded an average of 850 phone calls and 80,000 website visits a year from those seeking information about doctors, programs, hospitals and residential facilities.

The callers are patients themselves, or their parents, spouses, children, relatives, doctors, social workers, medical students, lawyers or friends. They have called from all fifty states and from France, Greece, Mexico, Denmark, Canada, New Zealand, Kuwait, Australia and Puerto Rico.

If you, or anyone dear to you, is struggling with the signs of BPD and you wish to know more about this condition, we invite you to refer to the information below.

Writing this book hasn't been easy. It's forced us to go back and open chapters of our lives that are painful, and at times has tested our resolve as we continue to question how we could have done things differently. But what makes it worthwhile is the realization that Pamela's story, and our family's story, might prove helpful to others faced with this mental illness. This book represents the role in her future Pamela "never lived to see."

For more information about *Remnants of a Life on Paper: A Mother and Daughter's Struggle with Borderline Personality Disorder*, visit:

www.remnantsofalife.com

or

www.facebook.com/Remnantsofalifeonpaper

For clinicians, Dr. Frank Yeomans has written a Teaching Guide to accompany the book which can be downloaded, free of charge, on the book's website:

www.remnantsofalife.com/clinical-teaching-guide

ACKNOWLEDGEMENTS

Since its inception this book has been a family affair. First and foremost, it could never have been written without the explicit blessing of Pamela's father, Michael, who believed in the effort and was willing to expose his utmost vulnerability in the telling. Her brother, Michael, and his wife Catherine, were equally supportive, and her brother-in-law Roger was masterful in graphically transitioning her artwork into the manuscript. Uncle Joseph, who Pamela revered as a brilliant poet and scholar, has been the guiding spirit for this project.

Pamela's art was photographed by Doug Behar who was sensitive to the nature of the emotional undertaking; and the illuminating photo in black and white at the end of the book – one of a series of photos of Pamela when she was beginning to thrive again – was taken by her close friend, Sheryl Freedland. Many thanks are extended to readers whose input we depended on: Catherine White, Laura DeAngelis, Jim and Maxine Frank, Drs. Frank Yeomans and Philip Wilner. In particular, feedback from Eve Feldman, Jennifer Huntley and Christine Antoneck had a major impact on what direction the manuscript would take.

Thanks to the staff at Regus Executive Office Suites and The Garden City Hotel, both located on Long Island, New York, for accommodating our privacy while Paula and I met to work on the manuscript over a period of two years. In addition, Paula's trustworthy babysitter, Melanie Goetz, and countless friends and neighbors who helped with the children, earned our gratitude for giving us peace of mind during that time.

Lastly, we thank Baroque Press, especially Melody Lawrence, the book's editor, and Emilia Fazzalari, its publisher. Both women believed in this story and were determined to see it through to publication.

SELECTED RESOURCES FOR BPD

Symptoms

Individuals with this disorder typically have five or more of the following traits:

- fears of abandonment
- extreme mood swings
- difficulty in relationships
- unstable self-image
- difficulty managing emotions
- impulsive behavior
- self-injuring acts
- suicidal ideation
- transient psychotic episodes

Statistics

- BPD affects 6 to 18 million Americans
- it represents 2% – 6% of the population
- at least 10% of mental health outpatients are treated for BPD
- an average 20% of psychiatric inpatients are treated for the disorder

General Resources

For assistance in locating resources for treatment in all levels of care of BPD, contact New York-Presbyterian Hospital's BPD Resource Center at 888-694-2273. The informational website address is http://bpdresourcecenter.org

For Individuals and Families

1. Family Connections 12-week manualized family programs are offered around the country. For information, e-mail neabpd@aol.com

2. Family Tele-Connections, a weekly teleconference group of Family Connections. To participate, e-mail neabpd@aol.com

3. TARA – Treatment and Research Advancements, National Association for Personality Disorder – provides workshops, referrals, information. Call 1-888-4-TARA APD or go to www.TARA4BPD.org

4. NAMI – National Alliance on Mental Illness – Offers resources, information, local support groups for families of persons with mental disorders including BPD. The website is located at http://www.nami.org/.

BEA TUSIANI is a freelance writer published in The New York Times and Newsday, among many other magazines and newspapers. She has written a memoir, Con Amore, and a children's book, The Fig Cake Family, both strongly rooted in her Italian heritage.

Bea founded the Writer's Network of Long Island, the Frances Hodgson Burnett Collection at the Manhasset Public Library, and the Italian Welfare League's charitable I Nostri Bambini Program. Most recently, together with her family she established the Borderline Personality Disorder Resource Center at New York-Presbyterian Hospital.

PAULA TUSIANI-ENG worked as a labor and community organizer before receiving her Master's in Divinity from Union Theological Seminary in 2001. She served as a pastoral associate for youth in a congregation on Long Island from 2000–2004, and as campus minister at Fordham University in the Bronx, New York from 2004 to 2006. Married, with four children, Paula is pursuing a career in social work.

Set in Aldus type. Designed by Jerry Kelly.